Corey Laine Hilton's
Take It Off

Take It Off

Revelations
Of A
Male Exotic Dancer

Corey Laine Hilton
Introspective Influencer

 Daring to Share Global

Published by Corey Laine Hilton
January 2022 ISBN: 9781778014703

Editor: Diana Reyers
Typeset: Greg Salisbury
Book Cover Design: Olli Vidal
Cover Photo: Austin Isagawa

For Jamie...
I wish you were here for this ride
Forever young

Testimonials

The art of storytelling can be developed over time and with careful forethought to the flow and execution of the message you are trying to get across. In other words, if you work hard enough, you can master it.

My feelings as I read this book, though, is that the masterful art of storytelling was born inside Corey. In his book "Take It Off", he manages to draw you in with every word. The "blocks" that are revealed to him are ones most anyone can identify with. However his unabashed approach to forgiveness and acceptance gives the reader their own courage to do the same.

This is much more than a story of a male stripper. This is a story of a man who owns his stuff and believes so strongly in the power of choice. This is a story of accepting oneself through the imperfections and authentically, using the life lessons handed or inherited as jumping-off points. This is a story most won't expect in a life most can't imagine, being told in a way that will make you think through the blushes.

This story has it all, and everyone should read it.

~Candace Chisholm
Author, CEO and Co-Founder of He Changed It

Corey's raw, unfiltered account of his career as a male dancer gives us a glimpse into a life many of us will never experience—yet it feels so relatable. Take It Off is a wild ride; a long and crazy journey to a meaningful and purpose-driven life.

~Jeff Felten
Marketing Strategist, Content Remedy

A rare insight into the world behind the scenes of male exotic dancers. Corey tells his story in an easy-to-read autobiography that anyone can relate to. TAKE IT OFF was a joy to read and knowing Corey personally, I can say it was written from his heart.

~Darren Ewert
Marketing Mentor and Founder
of one of the world's largest online business communities

Corey's book Take It Off, is an authentic read sharing the life of a man shedding his old masculine ways stepping into his authentic skin. An interesting and inspiring book to see through the lens of an ex exotic dancer. A definite must read.

~Velva Dawn Silver,
Author.

Acknowledgements

To every person I met face to face in my past, or will in my future, I appreciate you. My desire is to never look up or down at you but to look you in the eyes. Whether our experience was good or bad, I'm grateful to have had it. Like forming clay, my relationships form me into a better person. Everything is temporary, but while we are here, I hope to impact and inspire.

The characters in my story impacted and inspired me to share my struggles, values, and truth. Because of them, great memories were created, and lessons were learned. Whether you helped me discover my authenticity or understand my accountability, I thank you.

To my family—those I see and those I don't—you don't have to say it back, but I want you to know that I love you because life is short, and again, everything is temporary. Without your support, this book would never have been written, and my story would never have been told.

Lastly, for the finger that I lost, but still feel... I miss you so very badly, but I'm still hanging in there.

Foreword

A few years ago, the stylistic and polarizing director, Michael Bay, released a film on the big screen starring Mark Wahlberg and Dwayne *The Rock* Johnson called *Pain and Gain*. The movie, based on a true story, is a dramatic—albeit loose—retelling of the exploits of *The Sun Gym Gang* in Florida in the 1990s. That particular gang was a group of body builders, who went down a path of outrageousness, barely believable hijinks, mischief, and activities outside of the law. Their actions did little to contradict the stereotypes Florida has regarding the behaviours of its residents. After reading *Take It Off*, the first thing that comes to my mind is that *Pain and Gain* hit closer to home for more people than we might realize; Corey Hilton's life could place itself right in with those characters like a perfectly fit bow tie.

I have known Corey for more than a decade, and I must begin by telling you that no matter what thoughts might come into your mind while reading this nearly unbelievable autobiographical tale of Corey's colorful life, this is a true story that is not embellished. But please don't get me wrong, I am not just talking about the scandalous, delicious moments that Corey experienced in the years he spent—beginning well before he was legal—in the exotic entertainment field. The other true story in this volume is about a man who ultimately wants to help people, impact their lives, and desperately, almost obsessively, desires to lift others to personal clarity, causing them to take action and make decisions to improve their lives.

Corey's past vocation came up the very first day I met him. Not being exposed—no pun intended—to such things, I instantly had MANY questions, intriguing questions I think most people would have, encountering someone with such an exotic past. By the way, every single one of those questions gets answered in this book. As we got to know each other, Corey gradually revealed some of the adventures he had been on. After he regaled a couple of these tales, my reaction was much like the ones many others have said to him for years—Corey, you should write a book! Obviously not his first rodeo—again, no pun intended—he calmly and confidently told me that he has indeed been cataloging all his exploits and would definitely be releasing a book—he even had the title, *Take It Off*. Yet year after year, no book was ever released. I believe I know the reason: Corey wasn't finished collecting the material needed yet. How could that be? After all, Corey was no longer associated with that business—or the other *businesses* he talks about in this book—at all. So, why not just get the story out there to entertain us mere mortals?

The truth is, Corey has been on a personal development journey since the day I met him. Not only that, but he has also always wanted to impact people in a big way with every new discovery or insight he learned for himself. As he dissected the granular details of what makes him tick, he studiously noted each one, constructing a unique collection of pillars that provide massive food for thought and ingredients for action that can be used to improve one's life. Considering all the aspects of what he saw during that part of his existence, both in Canada and in the US, that is a lot to unpack. As he writes this fantastical book you are about to read—*I will never forget some of those times, but I also wish I could forget some of them*—Corey shows us how his past not only affects his future, but if he has his way, will also affect the future of thousands, tens of thousands of people who take up the call to apply the wisdom he amassed during his life.

Sometimes, after seeing a movie or reading a book about *sex, drugs, and rock and roll*, I feel kinda slimy, like I need a shower. Going in, the intrigue of the story gets my blood pumping, but when the details impact my head and heart, it's not so much fun anymore. I think that extreme decadence causes such feelings for many. This book does the exact opposite. It's guilt-free salaciousness because Corey took the extra decade to write it. For every wild experience we get to vicariously live through, there is also a lesson and a grounding that Corey has received and deduced the universal truth from it, and then given to us, the reader. This is every bit of a personal development book as it is a fascinating true story. And at the end of the day, Corey Hilton's crazy experiences, along with his ups and downs, triumphs, and successes, and yes, his pain, are our gain.

Mike Chisholm
Co-Author, She Changed Me: One Ordeal; Two Perspectives
Host of He Cast, the Official Podcast of He Changed It
HeChangedIt.com

December 2021

Introduction

I was blessed with a stable support structure within a family that used tools handed down to them, which in turn, provided me with a roadmap for the journey I am about to present to you—my reader who is seeking the raw, unscripted truth of pivotal moments in a foregone industry. I am about to share the truth about the people who impacted my life, both positively and negatively, and how they brought me to the seat I am sitting in today.

Through the lens of my revelations, I have painted this picture without any filter of political correctness or ideology. Take It Off is a metaphor, providing stories of my past, which will entertain and also possibly disturb at times. The Naked Truths installed at the end of each chapter represent my current view of myself and the world, both past and present. They were written after many layers of my past limiting beliefs were removed, and I came to an understanding that my worth is not represented by my status—void of the haze of addiction, regret, and blame blurring my vision. For so many years, I used that blame to point my finger when I should have been using my thumb in most cases.

I was admired for the alter-ego status that I portrayed on stage for 25 years, literally *Taking It Off* for thousands from as far north as Yellowknife in the Northwest Territories to as far south as Orlando, Florida. To have this *dream* lifestyle, I made many sacrifices and endured struggles that many cannot comprehend. Some of these struggles may be relatable and some may not, so my hope is that you take what resonates and simply be entertained by the rest.

After retiring, I entertained curious friends and strangers by sharing stories of my past. Most could never imagine being in the position I was in, being stimulated on stage by the same kind of emotional reaction I witnessed when I told these stories. However, after taking the time to write them all down on paper, I realized that I have far more to provide than just the outrageous accounts developed from my former career. My struggles and victories created the very revelations you are about to experience as you absorb each chapter of my evolution—my hope is that it inspires the emergence of yours.

From the age of 17 when I started this journey, I leaned on status, refusing to address subconscious blocks by not connecting to my authentic self. Once the lights went down and the crowds were gone, I struggled for many years with a blurred vision of the person I truly was, stricken with the limiting belief that I was unworthy. With a self-perception of mediocrity, I was never happy with the person I saw in the mirror. It took many years to battle my inner saboteur to be clear about who I am and obtain confidence in my self-worth. The saboteur made me believe that I could not provide enough value to the world, and from a very early age, I chose a destructive path of comparing myself to others with a lesser-than mentality by putting them on a pedestal. It took putting my clothes on to discover my truth in my quest to find inner peace many years later. Exposing this different kind of vulnerability was far more intimidating than anything I had experienced in my career as I exposed the *real me*, rather than the persona I dedicated a quarter century creating.

I experienced relatable lessons that I knew could dramatically impact other men who struggle with emotional disconnection, addiction, and unworthiness. I realized that

I was not alone anymore. So, after three and a half years of putting pen to paper, I chose to detach and put everything on hold to focus on the most important mission of my lifetime— sharing my story to support those enveloped in their struggle. During this process, I teamed up with Diana Reyers of Daring to Share™ Global, who opened the door, inspiring authenticity and emotional feelings into my writing—this was something I had not experienced in well over a decade. The excitement of this creativity, which is one of my most prioritized core values, makes me feel alive again. This process healed wounds I believed would never be healed. It also proved to me that regardless of the damage from my past, by working on the struggles associated with the value pillars in this book, I could be the best version of myself without leaning on my alter-ego anymore.

Each chapter heading includes one or more of my core values along with the struggle I endured. This provides some foreshadowing to be mindful of while reading the story. Each chapter shares my honest perspective of the relationships I formed from my childhood through to the ironic ending of my male exotic dance career at the age of 43. My perspective is unique for more than one reason. Being adopted at an early age by my grandparents injected in me an old-fashioned outlook of certain core values such as morality and integrity. Keeping these values in mind, I sustained a career in a relatively unknown industry, working by certain rules in Canada and others in the U.S. I saw a side to both sexes that most never see, yet still held faith in the opposite sex realizing that one does not represent both. Through introspection, I came to the realization that although I was a male exotic dancer, I also did not represent all. I am unique, I have value, and I am worthy.

Corey Laine Hilton

Take It Off

Perspective & Truth

I

Goodbye Caterpillar;
Hello Butterfly

I opened my eyes to the world around me, seeing butterflies everywhere I went—It was the spring of 2021, and I was finally creating a new life after being in a cocoon for what seemed like forever. There were two occasions early in my childhood when I experienced trauma. No psychiatrist would consider either to be massively dramatic. Still, through the lens of my young soul's perspective, they formed a great inner sense of abandonment that I didn't understand until much later in life.

The first incident was when my aunt and uncle took me to the fair. Putting me on a Ferris wheel by myself, they watched me go around and around until I got stuck up at the top. I sat there way up high, crying my eyes out. All I could hear was the creak of the seat as it swayed gently back and forth; I was scared to death about what might happen if it somehow fell to the ground. Once a grown adult, I asked my aunt why on earth they put me on a huge Ferris wheel at the fair all by myself! She started laughing, and I was very confused at first, but then, her answer both shocked me and provided me with some relief.

3

She told me that we were not at the fair and I was not on a massive Ferris wheel. It was a little Ferris wheel that only stood seven feet tall at the mall—the one you plug a quarter into. For most of my life, my perception was completely different, and as a result, I developed a fear of heights. This mistaken belief became my reality created from a brief scary experience that wasn't really that traumatic.

On another occasion, I was with my mother in a department store. While she was clothes shopping, I wandered around playing in the coat racks, not paying any attention to where she was. The racks were bigger than me, and I remember moving in and out of the coats with the sleeves brushing across my face and head. I became very disoriented and wandered so far off that I couldn't find her. Eventually, a store clerk found me lost and frightened. She went back to her desk and called for my mother over the loudspeaker. Everything ended well with my mother coming to get me, but this minute trauma stayed burned in my memory for a very long time.

I recognize that I established an addiction to emotional reaction from a very early age. I chuckle to myself now, thinking about what I did to get an emotional *rise* out of people as a young boy. My folks had company drop by from time to time, and while they sat around the kitchen table playing cribbage and chatting about the weather, I stripped down naked in my bedroom and ran to the bathroom back and forth in front of them to make them all laugh. Of course, they thought it was hilarious that this reserved little kid streaked by them with no care in the world other than to see how he could make them react. But I can only imagine what they must have really thought. What I know is that this was when I began feeding my addiction to experiencing emotion—the emotion I was rarely able to express and that was rarely expressed to me.

I was blessed to be raised by my grandparents, who I refer to as my mother and father. They adopted me when their 17-year-old daughter, Gayle, gave birth to me way back in 1970. I painted them as what the perfect picture of a family was supposed to be through my eyes. My father had a long career in the construction industry that supported him to raise three kids long before I arrived. He was a dedicated worker who earned every penny he made, working harder but not necessarily smarter at times. As a child, I admired him so much, and when he arrived home at five o'clock every evening, I ran to the back door to hug his legs as he smiled and hugged me in return. He was not one to show emotion and was even awkward when trying to verbally express how he felt, so this display of connection from him was special. He did everything in his power to support his family, and in my young, innocent eyes, I saw him as a superhero. He was not a friend, but a father, who gave me every tool he had available to show me right from wrong, but there were certain tools he just didn't have. However, he was a kind man who would give the shirt off his back to help someone in need.

Born into a depression-era family that endured hardship most cannot comprehend, he dealt with an ingrained mentality of lack. His mother committed suicide by drowning herself in a river when he and his brother were just young boys. They struggled to earn what they could to survive. As a young adult, he joined the navy and fought in the North Atlantic during World War II. Unfortunately, the military embedded the mentality that sharing emotion was a sign of weakness, so instead of opening up when he was upset about something, he learned to bottle it up and say nothing. There were times when frustration built up from not expressing himself, and his words finally came out the wrong way, saying something extremely painful to his loved ones. His intention was never to hurt anyone, but he avoided conflict at all costs, which resulted in a ticking time bomb in many cases. He later apologized for what he said, realizing the damage he had done.

He had a very tough time letting love into his life, which I believe was simply due to his deep sense of loss at such an early age. He only had a tenth-grade education but did the best with what little knowledge he had—I am proud of the man who chose to make the sacrifice of taking on another child when he and my mother were almost empty nesters. However, much later in life, I discovered that this was not his initial suggestion when he found out his daughter was pregnant with me; he wanted her to have an abortion to avoid dealing with the reality of the situation.

On the other hand, my mother was not about to entertain the thoughts running through my father's head at that time. She often spoke her mind to him when she felt it counted and stood up for what she believed was right. In her early years, she worked as a nurse in a mental health facility, but as time went on, she eventually settled for being a housewife as it was a more realistic option in that era based on my father's occupation. When I say she *settled*, it's because I think her goals and dreams were left behind when the decision to leave her career was made. In a way, I am grateful she did because I was blessed to be raised by two parents when so many of us do not have this luxury.

However, I later realized that she didn't have much choice in the matter. When she and my father met, she was already pregnant with another man's child in a time when single parenting was beyond unacceptable. That child, my Aunt Linda, was adopted and raised by my great grandmother, however, was not truly accepted by my father like the other three children they raised. I can't imagine how rejected my mother must have felt in more than one way because she truly loved Linda's biological father who chose to move on without her. I also cannot imagine the psychological effect this must have had on Linda who was and is a family member who never truly gained acceptance like the other children. From what I understand, the only time my mother opened up about it was when she was drinking, but that was a side I never saw throughout my childhood. To me, she was Mom. She did everything from washing my hair in the kitchen sink to tucking me in at night. She did the best she could but followed my father's lack of expressing himself and didn't open up in most cases.

It was almost like saying the words I love you were taboo.

When I was a young boy and especially as a teenager, there were times when we argued every single day. I later discovered that she was just trying to help me avoid falling on my face— that was how she expressed her love for me.

Being raised by parents who grew up in the depression had advantages and disadvantages. Yes, I always had family around, and I knew they loved me, but they also planted words into my head that lasted a lifetime. Words that caused barriers and blocks carried and passed along to their children and then to me. Through my young eyes, I saw them as perfect. Moving into adulthood, I saw that I was trying to mirror the perfect image I painted, even as imperfect as it actually was. It took many years to understand I was dealing with what I call *generational lack*, and for most of my adult life, I fought the battle to defeat this lack, believing I had an invisible block I was always trying to pinpoint, but could never figure out.

Gayle, my biological mom, dealt with similar blocks. One

similarity we both have is that we chose to live our lives and jump at certain opportunities that other family members would not. This was a good and bad thing. She was a bit of a wild child and had many friends in the Vancouver rock music industry. During my childhood, the moments we shared were like gold because we only had so many. She was out there living her life, and some may look down on a few of the choices she made, but I am proud of her in more ways than one. Back then, she didn't let anyone hold her back from doing what she wanted, even if a few of those choices could have killed her. She made memories, had experiences, and formed relationships with people who performed in front of thousands of screaming fans and were admired for all the wrong reasons. But even though that's all she had to offer them and vice versa, their friendships were, nonetheless, true. Through the good and the bad, I admire her for being the person she was and the person she currently is because she is real.

My journey of pinpointing the invisible block in the back of my head started a few years ago when I took a good hard look at myself. I determined that I had so many things handed to me over the course of my life that I could have used to achieve success and fulfillment, but I pushed them away instead. I chose the comfortable path instead of the uncomfortable one, self-sabotaging by not finishing a job or project. Worse yet, I avoided developing into a leader and settled for being a follower. I came out of the gate on fire in most cases but sputtered out just before the finish line, taking the majority of the weight on my shoulders.

Why was this?
Why would a person who was given so much in so many ways have such dramatic self-doubt?

Why did I see myself as so low and put others on such a high pedestal?
Why did I have such high expectations for others but not for myself?
Why could I never be truly be at peace with the person I saw in the mirror?
Why was acceptance so important to me, but I never truly accepted myself?

One word—Unworthiness. It took me decades to determine that two of my most important values in life include developing memories and relationships that create true fulfillment, not only based on what they provide me, but also on what I can provide them. However, I didn't always feel this way. Due to perfectionistic tendencies and an egotistical mindset, I had a very long road to travel to find what true fulfillment means to me. I knew I had the potential to be fulfilled, but I always seemed to search for it with the wrong goal in mind. I placed people who came in and out of my life at such high standards that my expectations were never enough no matter what they did. I became critical of them at times, and even though I did not address my own issues, I expected them to manage theirs. It was unfair, and in many cases, I left a trail of sadness behind me after starting with the best intentions—in some ways, kind of like my father.

Going back to my first day of grade eight after leaving elementary school to start middle school, I see myself sitting at my desk in homeroom. This was a scary time for me. I heard all sorts of stories—nightmares about being initiated by having my head flushed down the toilet, which never even happened. There were so many kids like me trying to be accepted in one group or another, and even though I never felt like I really belonged in any group in particular, I did form a few great friendships and still maintain a few of them to this

9

day. However, throughout it all, I definitely lacked one thing: Confidence. I was socially uncomfortable, to say the least.

When I looked in the mirror, I didn't like the person in front of me. This is the way I saw myself during my most awkward time. When I was about 12 or 13, I carried a couple of extra pounds. It wasn't a big deal, but I was a tad self-conscious about it. I was entering my teens, so I guess in a weird way, my priorities were one-dimensional—being accepted by my peers seemed so very important. I wanted to achieve any chance of fitting in, and I believed my physical appearance was something I could control to gain that acceptance. On top of everything, hormones kicked in without me knowing what to do about it. I didn't really belong anywhere, but I hoped I would if I could somehow change that person I was looking at in the mirror.

I didn't know many of the kids in my homeroom that day. Feeling nervous, I looked over to my left and saw this one girl sitting in the last row at the back of the class. She had no idea that I even existed, and she was dating someone about three or four years older than her. She was part of the *cool crowd*, so to speak, and she had that typical 80s feathered hair, along with wearing too much makeup. But I instantly felt I had to know her. Her name was Jessica, and I genuinely believe she was the first girl I ever had a serious crush on. I lived roughly a mile and a half from her place, and her family lived a few blocks away from my middle school. Later when I got to know her better, she told me that a car with a bunch of guys in it drove by her once while she was waiting at a bus stop. They all turned their heads to check her out and got into an accident. This didn't surprise me because she was strikingly beautiful.

I had butterflies every time I saw her, but initially, she never saw me. It sounds a little bit creepy, but I used Jessica for motivation. She motivated me to get into better shape and push out that next repetition when I was a bodybuilder. I guess at that time, she became the extra push I needed to focus on my goals, and I pushed myself beyond my limits with the scattered belief that if I changed my outside appearance, someday I might stand a chance. The caveat was that I was young and didn't understand yet that I needed to be better inside, not just outside.

When I was trying to get in shape, I did little things like give up the bowl of ice cream that my father gladly made for us. I then jogged from our place all the way to Jessica's. Upon arrival, I always looked across the street and thought to myself: One day. Then, I jogged back home. I carried this motivation into the gym when I wanted to squeeze out one more rep. And when the weight felt too heavy, I pictured the end goal of having a chance with Jessica—just one chance with the beautiful girl in my homeroom class. Almost every single time, this dream motivated me to get through my struggle.

In middle school, I was desperately trying to fit in. I would watch some of the more *popular* kids stealing from the corner store across the street from my school called *Steve and Dots*. It seemed like every day those kids would come out of that store with something they stole, and they would share what they had stolen with the others who gathered outside. I chose to follow their lead and attempted to be a little thief myself. As I walked up to the cooler, I opened it up and started shoving ice cream sandwiches into the front of my zipped-up jacket. I kept one out to pay for and stood in line nervously waiting for the people in front of me to finish up. As I stood there, I heard the man in front of me say to Dot, the cashier: *You want to see something interesting?* He then turned around and unzipped my jacket. As the ice cream sandwiches hit the floor one by one, I felt the fear and embarrassment hit me all at the same time.

She walked around the counter and took me upstairs to the main office. She angrily told me to give her my parents phone number. We sat there in silence for ten minutes until my father showed up to deal with the situation. He apologized to her and offered to pay for what I had stolen, but she declined. He again apologized and once we got into his truck, my father handled it in his own unique way. He sat there for a few seconds, again in silence and then asked me to explain what had happened. Of course, I lied. I explained that I was only putting them in my jacket to soften them up before I gave them to my friends because they were frozen solid. He accepted my lame excuse and told me that he believed that I was telling the truth because I knew how important telling the truth truly was. He didn't punish me, but my guilt was so strong that the mental punishment lasted far longer than anything else he could have done. I never stole again because although he knew I was guilty, he supported me—reverse psychology at its finest.

I spent the next couple of years at that school and saw many kids simply trying to find their way. One of my childhood friends, Steve, was also trying to do exactly that. He wanted to be in a particular crowd that I did not fit into. Kids are driven by different things at that age, and even though we were very close childhood friends, he decided to start bullying me for some reason. I was minding my own business one day while standing at my locker when he came up with a couple of his buddies. He wanted to fight me for what seemed like no other reason than to make himself look good in his own way. It was the first time I ever had someone step on me to get ahead—to get what they wanted by damaging others.

Having low self-esteem, I reluctantly backed down. I was embarrassed and held my head in shame—the little pride I had was shattered. Barely having any friends at the time and feeling like a victim, I was shocked that he would do this to me. Fortunately, this motivated me even further to better myself, or at the very least, to become bulletproof within these types of situations.

At this time, I still had no communication with Jessica whatsoever. Frankly, I didn't have the guts. When I went to tenth grade, I had the choice to stay in middle school or transfer to another school with an older demographic. Princess Margaret Senior Secondary had kids between Grade ten and twelve: the rockers, the jocks, the nerds, the punks, the new wavers, and the mediocre with no label like me. I wanted to go there to start a new beginning—an opportunity to start over. I wanted to surround myself with new people and do whatever it took to transform myself into someone more appealing, from the caterpillar I was to the butterfly I could be. I wanted to level up instead of staying in a stagnant pool of kids trying to be something they weren't. My grades suffered because my focus was on being accepted rather than on becoming educated.

Back in those days, we all went to these places called arcades. I usually played alone, and I don't want to know how many quarters I put into those video games. Then one day, I saw a kid in there who lived on my street, and he was a regular customer. He was a couple of years older than me and known locally as a bit of a badass and a tad crazy. His name was Cody, and he was a good person, but he had issues and could get very angry at times. For some strange reason, we gravitated towards one another, and that was the beginning of my transformation. I was 15 years old, and I started working out with him in his parents' carport. There were two benches, a mirror, and a boombox. He kept me accountable and showed me what I needed to know. I think my parents must have cringed knowing I was associated with him, but they trusted I had enough common sense not to get into trouble. I give Cody credit because, at that young age, he taught me discipline and consistency. Something about him motivated me to stay dedicated to my goal. I worked out with him for roughly a year, and then out of the blue, my dad offered to get me a membership at Golds Gym. He saw how committed I was and figured a gym membership would keep me off of the streets; he was right, and I made sure that his money didn't go to waste. So, while many other kids back in high school were partying or getting into trouble, I was in the gym. When I started working out that year, I weighed 165 pounds. At the end of the year, my weight had not changed, but I looked and felt completely different.

The next two years were very interesting. My old friend, Steve, who bullied me in middle school, moved up to high school. I had formed this friendship with Cody, along with one of his other big, badass buddies. His friend, Malcolm, was rumoured to have bitten a guy's nose off in a football game, which I still don't know if that was true or not. He was actually a pretty good guy who was simply misunderstood. I still have no idea why I gravitated toward these people, but they came into my life for a reason. I did build some self-confidence, but I still had insecurities mixed with anger due to the bullying I experienced at my previous school. I could not forgive Steve for his actions, and I manifested that negativity instead of working through it. For the next few months, I made his life hell as a result. When I saw him walking down the hall, I intentionally bumped into him, seeking revenge by constantly harassing him. Finally, one day, we fought it out in the hallway, and after I slammed him into a wall, we were told to take it outside.

After the school day, when most kids had already gone home, my big buddy, Malcolm, and I stood at the end of the hall and waited for Steve to go to his locker. When he arrived,

Malcolm approached him and explained that I wanted to kick his ass and would meet him outside with no one else around. He declined the invitation, and looking back, I can't blame him. He was staring into the face of a huge, scary-looking juice monkey—I probably wouldn't have gone outside if the tables were turned. We waited for him to go out the doors and proceeded to chase him off the school property as he ran home with his tail between his legs. The next day, his father showed up at my house. He was a good man, and I always got along with him, so when he asked me to leave his son alone because I was affecting his grades, I did just that. I wonder what it must have been like for Steve's father to have to deal with us at that time. The point is that he did, and my battle with Steve was over. We were just kids, and I suppose we were trying to belong in all the wrong ways. Years later, we had a conversation, and we were very civil to one another. I am thankful for that because we were both able to forgive one another for our actions. Besides, we were just a couple of screwed-up kids from Surrey, a place known for badass, criminal little punks trying to fit in any way we could.

Twelfth grade came along, and I took uncomfortable action on day one. I had still not talked to Jessica, and well, that changed immediately.

**This showed me that accepting discomfort
and being bold is the only way to truly get results.**

I knew almost every guy in that school would consider asking her to graduation, so I took the initiative to finally approach her, nervously asking her to go with me—shockingly, she actually said: YES! Based on a couple of the guys she dated in high school, I thought maybe her decision wasn't that much

15

of a stretch. And then, it all made sense: once I got to know her, I realized she didn't look at what people seemed to represent on the outside as much as who they were on the inside. That is the part I came to love about her—how she viewed the world around her. She always took the time to appreciate the little things that most people passed by without recognizing the beauty standing right in front of them. Years later, we were walking down the street, and she stopped and grabbed my hand: *Look at that tree. It's just so beautiful!* She took the time to live in the moment and appreciate everything, including nature, for what it was. While in school, she dealt with disfunction at home, but I had no idea she was experiencing so much inner pain. There were days when she looked into empty cupboards because there was no food on top of dealing with the sexual trauma inflicted by an older ex-boyfriend. I didn't understand because I only focused on what she presented on the outside, never showing how much she hurt on the inside. Through to the end of high school and beyond, she and I remained nothing more than distant friends, eventually going our separate ways and living worlds apart.

As my final school year went on, I formed a friendship with a guy by the name of Wayne, who also trained at Gold's Gym and went to my high school. Like many of my friends at that time, he was a little older than me. He was a bouncer at a local nightclub called Casablanca's. Some of my high school friends used to get into the club even though they were underage, and Jessica was one of them. One day, Wayne invited me out to the bar and told me he would let me through the door. He said to wear a university or college shirt so I wouldn't set off any alarms. I showed up at the nightclub just as it was opening, around seven o'clock, and the only ones there were David, the manager, myself, and Wayne. David asked me if I was in school, and I said: *Yes.* The next question was if I needed extra income. Once again, the answer was: *Yes.* He asked me to take my shirt off, and since there was no one else in the club, I did. He immediately told me I was hired if I wanted the job, and I would be working on Tuesday and Thursday evenings for ladies' night. The job entailed serving drinks and shooters to the ladies who came to the show while the male dancers performed. Talk about a good time for a 17-year-old kid! I had no right to make the amount of money I was about to at that club because I had no idea what the value of earning a dollar was in the first place. I worked there as a male waiter for a couple of years. Initially, I was so unfamiliar with the reality of the bar scene, but it was a good introduction to working in that industry.

> *Yes, I met many women—some older, some younger,*
> *and I realized after many years that*
> *there was no love to be found there.*

On one of my very first nights, I experienced one of my most awkward moments. The male and female dancers all used the same change room, which doubled as the office. After ladies' night ended, I went inside to get changed. As I walked in, I saw two beautiful girls doing a show together just outside the door. It was a duo act, and it was hot. Naked, they busted through the door once they finished. They both smiled, seeing me with my pants down around my ankles. I felt so embarrassed at that moment, but it didn't faze them one bit. This wasn't the first rodeo for them, but it was for me. I never experienced anything like it; there I was, chatting with these two tanned, sweaty, beautiful blondes, acting as if we were out on the street fully clothed. I was beyond nervous for many years, having nightmares about being exposed to the world with no clothes on and being mocked for it. I started in this industry as a naive kid, but that most definitely changed as the years went on.

Back in the 80s, Casablanca's had the most original, popular ladies' night in British Columbia, Canada. As you walked to the top of a massive flight of stairs, the smoke-filled bar was separated into two different sections high above street level overlooking the downtown core of New Westminster. One side was for the ladies with a good-sized dance floor, and then, a velvet rope separated them from the other side, with female dancers doing random acts providing entertainment for the men with a very small dance floor just outside the main office. Ladies' night usually started at eight o'clock and ended around eleven when the entire club opened up with the most popular dance tracks of that era blasting through the speakers. The atmosphere was amazing most nights and I quickly realized why it was one of the most popular clubs of the era. One of the more original DJs I met was Richie Rich—he even looked like the cartoon character. Richie used to go behind the bar and steal Heineken beer; he put them in a mini fridge in his DJ booth and sold them for a lower price to certain people. He had a cable strung over the dance floor connected to his booth, and when he really wanted to get the crowd going, he wound up a siren and swung a rubber chicken across the dance floor. The crowd always went absolutely insane.

Ladies' night was top-notch. Tuesday nights had a Hawaiian theme, and our outfits consisted of Hawaiian shorts and leis, which we put around the necks of the girls as they entered the club. On Thursday's, we were more upscale with bowties, cuffs, collars, and black dress pants. I was hired as a male waiter, which not only consisted of serving drinks but also required doing a choreographed dance routine at the end of the night alongside the other male waiters. After the show was finished, we gave away a free bottle of champagne to the loudest group of ladies in the house. It was always a hit. Some nights, the roof felt like it was going to blow off, all for a ten-dollar bottle of champagne.

I built a relationship with one of the other male waiters at the club. His name was Darren. One night, he was hooking up with one of the girls at the bar, and she had a cute friend with her. He came over and asked me to be his wingman, and I gladly accepted. We ended up going back to Darren's place with the two girls. He went into his bedroom with his girl, and the action began. Meanwhile, the other girl and I were out in the living room. This was the beginning of my sleazy phase to a certain extent. At only 17 years old, I, admittedly, loved meeting the older women at the club. I did my best to put on a more mature face for fear of being exposed because if my age was revealed, the house of cards was sure to fall.

This girl was the second person I had sex with, and she was 23. Somehow or another, she figured out that I was underage; it might have been from something I said, or maybe she noticed my lack of stamina. Well, I somehow let the cat out of the bag, and she was so shocked that she loudly said: *You're only 17-years-old?!* Darren overheard this from the bedroom, and my secret was out. However, he never revealed this to anyone at the bar. In fact, when I turned 19, we pretended it was my 21st birthday. That night in Darren's beautiful apartment, it felt like my virginity was broken for the first time. Of course, that wasn't the truth because I lost it a couple of years before on a bad one-night stand, but being with this woman, it felt like the first time all over again. It only lasted one night, but it was spectacular.

There is one Casablanca's story that sticks in my head as a moment of reality when I opened my eyes to how others perceive relationships. I had a couple of regular clients who used to come to see me and only purchased drinks. One lady often came to the bar and bought 130-dollar bottles of Dom and would tip me 50 dollars at the end of the night. On top of that, I made 15 percent commission on all the drinks that I sold, so she was a very valued client. Every week or two, she showed up and left right after ladies' night. She watched the male dancers and enjoyed our interactions. One night, she introduced me to her husband. I shook his hand, and after a couple of minutes of conversation, she asked me to give her a kiss. I kissed her cheek, but she wanted more. Even though her husband was perfectly fine with it, I was not. I refused to give her what she was looking for because I was uncomfortable in the situation. It was about my morality, not theirs. Unfortunately, this ended the money train because she was upset and never showed up at the bar again.

I was still going to school through all of this mayhem, and as the year went on, I saw Jessica from time to time, including one night when she showed up at the bar while I was working—she was blown away to see me there because in her eyes, I was not some charismatic entertainer, but a somewhat distant school friend with a reserved personality. By the time we hit graduation, she was dating a guy on and off for roughly six months, but she remained true to her word and went to the grad ceremony with me. The high school year ended, and as friends got together to sign yearbooks, I prepared to go to my graduation with the girl of my dreams. A group of roughly ten of us went together, and it was an experience with people who I had tried to fit in with at times, but never truly connected with until that night. It proved to be the end of many friendships, but the beginning of my adulthood. Before the official ceremony, we had a small get-together at a friend's house. Jessica looked stunning, wearing a frilly, peach dress which at the time made her beauty stand out even more than it already did. I wore a grey rented tuxedo trying to be cooler than I was, but for me, graduation was not only the time to celebrate, but to level up and bring you're A-Game. I awkwardly tried to pin her corsage to her dress, but she could tell I was struggling, so she grabbed it and pinned it on herself. She then showed me the leg garter she had made, and I had no idea if it was a sign or if she just wanted to show it to me, but it was hot—really hot. I never did get to take that garter off her leg; she just handed it to me after the ceremony. Lack of confidence, along with fear and self-doubt, defeated me, but the ceremony was fun, and the after-party was even better, lasting until sunrise. Unfortunately, Jessica's boyfriend showed up at the party, and that pretty much ended my night. I was depressed, but what did I really expect? I was Corey—the person she knew but didn't really see.

My work at Casablanca's merged from waitering on Tuesdays and Thursdays to including working the door as a bouncer on Monday, Friday, and Saturday nights. This was where the fun really started. I think I got myself in more shit doing that job with the guys at the door than I ever have in my life. Jason, Gill, and Joe were the main bouncers, along with another guy named Aaron. He was huge. I think he had more steroids rolling through him than anyone I had met at that point...and he was a total slut. In fact, he was quite proud of it. It almost seemed like a game to him. He took girls from the club down the street to have sex with them in the church parking lot while working—definitely a class act.

Along with many black folks from the US who crossed the border into Canada, I dealt with some crazy characters who came to experience Monday night Funk Night, including pimps, hos, and gang members who frequented the bar. I was the bouncer who checked the IDs, and I worked out a sweet deal with Shannon, a girl I formed a great friendship and business partnership with. She was the coat-check girl and the person who took the cover charge. We had a good thing going because we made a deal with each other working the door together. We had to do this because I was only getting paid 50 dollars a night for putting my ass on the line, and she wasn't making enough to live on. Here's how it went: Pimps showed up in line with 20 girls behind them on some nights, and once they got to me to pay their cover charge, I asked them how many underage girls they had with them. I told them not to lie, or I would check every girl's ID. They paid me 20 dollars for each underage girl I agreed to let in. Shannon and I split the profit, and yes, this made us some extra money. Hell, I was a guy who had developed a passion for becoming a pro bodybuilder, and what I was getting paid wasn't cutting the mustard for the amount of food I was eating.

That nightclub had some interesting characters walking through the door! One of the pimps who frequented the club was Charles, otherwise known as Snake. He was an older guy who had been in the industry for quite some time. He did something that might be considered very out of the ordinary for someone in his *career*. There was a lost girl from Vancouver featured on America's Most Wanted. Her parents had no idea where she was but thought she may have been on the streets. Snake tracked her down, found her, and was able to get her off the streets and back to her parents.

I guess there's a little bit of good in everyone—even a pimp.

But life at the bar wasn't just about the pimps and hos as the gang members made their mark as well. There was one

22

guy who stood out, and his name was Ruggy. He was an East Indian fellow who thought he was invincible. The reason being that he was somehow caught up in a gang fight at one point and took six bullets. One of the bullets went right through his Adam's apple, and crazily enough, the guy survived, but he was left with a raspy voice and at times was hard to understand. He and his brother thought they owned the place most nights, and in fact, his brother, Noah, was a prick who never followed the club's rules, one being no hats or jackets—they had to be checked.

One night, Noah was asked multiple times to take his jacket and a hat off. The manager asked me to chat with him about it and make sure that the rules were enforced. Instead of walking up to the guy and being the usual bouncer, I chose to let him save face and had a one-on-one with him. I told him I had a job to do, but I understood his position. He wasn't about to be pushed around by some bouncer, and I wasn't about to be pushed around by some gang member. But even though I had never talked to him before, he respected me. I reciprocated and asked him one last time to abide by the rules, which he did—I never really had a problem with him after that. That night after the bar closed, Ruggy and I talked. He said he had something to show me outside, so I walked out with him. It was roughly three in the morning when he opened the trunk to his car. He had more illegal guns in the trunk of his car than I had ever seen in my life. In his own way, he was making a statement to me. It was a show of force without having to use force. After that night, I never had a problem with either one of them. I guess there's something to be said for helping someone save face.

On another occasion, I was at the bar on my night off. Somehow or another, a fight broke out. While helping my fellow bouncers, I ended up in the middle of it, and the fight was wild. While being tossed around all over the place, I was slammed into a mirrored pillar that smashed. We all ended up in a big dog pile on the floor. My adrenaline was pumping so hard that I didn't even realize I had a piece of the mirror sticking into the back of my arm. The fight continued, and we were pushed outside. When everything settled down and the drunken assholes left, one of the waitresses came up to me to tell me I was bleeding. I responded: *Not my blood!* She looked at my arm and asked me to rethink that. I walked back inside the nightclub, and low and behold, I had a nice little shard of mirror sticking out of the back of my arm. Getting sick to my stomach, I went around to the back of the bar and grabbed a bar rag to help stop the bleeding and yanked that piece of mirror out. I still have that scar to this day.

I remember another altercation in the bar, and the guys were thrown out immediately. Usually, the bouncers hung out after the club closed and had a couple of drinks with the rest of the staff. On this night, I was waiting for the bar to close, and as usual, it was packed. While people were being let out, the guys involved in the fight were at the top of the hill, waiting for all the bouncers to come outside. They wanted to get their revenge, and as I walked out with my fellow bouncers, the blast of a sawed-off shotgun rang out along with the sound of the shrapnel hitting the telephone pole above our heads. I have never seen so many people in pure hysteria.

I went back inside, and the shooters jumped into a red Jeep and took off. While all this happened, I waited inside the club and watched the street below from the office window. As I safely stood there, I saw four or five police cars surrounding the red Jeep with their guns drawn, protecting themselves behind their cars. I believe the police were acting accordingly in the situation based on the lead that they had as they prompted a tall, skinny black man to get out of the Jeep. He got out and knelt on the ground with his hands behind his head. Then I saw another person in the passenger seat and two people in the backseat. The poor guy on the ground was scared shitless and in tears. The police had the wrong person kneeling in the middle of that street, and the assholes who were shooting at us were on their way out of town in a different red Jeep. From what I understood, they were caught, but to this day, I still have no idea what happened to them, or the poor people caught in the crossfire.

During another Monday night experience, a naval officer from the US military and his girlfriend were on the dance floor. We heard them arguing over the music and gave them two warnings, but they weren't listening. There was a three-strike rule, and they were on their third strike. I went up to them and said: *It's time to leave, folks. Your coats are in the coat check. Have a good night.* I then escorted them to get their stuff and directed them out of the club. When someone was booted out of the club, they were gone for the night. But things took a turn when roughly one hour later, the girl came limping back up the stairs. I reminded her that she was booted out and not allowed back in. She looked up at me with tears flowing down her face and told me she had been stabbed. I looked down at her leg, and the gash must've been six inches long. She was bleeding everywhere—I determined the argument had obviously turned physical. The paramedics showed up after we did everything we could to control the bleeding. She was taken to the hospital, and we all assumed she was fine. I never saw either of them for months but assumed they had gone their separate ways. Then, six months later, they showed up back at the club together as if nothing had ever happened. I guess love comes in all shapes and sizes, but all I know is that if somebody decided to shove a knife into me, it would be over for good. However, who am I to judge? What I felt was acceptable in my relationships may not have been the same as someone else.

Working in the bar made me realize that people can go to extremes to find satisfaction, either sexually or just generally in life overall. However, that kind of gratification is usually short-lived. As much as I enjoyed working in an adult environment as a young man, I never found true satisfaction from any woman I met in that club. I will never forget some of those times, but I also wish I could forget some of them. I saw everything from dicks swinging in women's faces to a pimp cutting another pimp's ear off and throwing it on the floor. I could write an entire book called: The Stories of Casablanca's, but I only included the ones that impacted me most during the beginning of my career. As I was serving drinks, I used to look at the guys who stripped on ladies' night and thought: *I could never do that!*

Well, I did, and with little regret. However, I did see some dancers who simply shouldn't have been on stage anymore. In a way, I found it to be kind of sad because they were past their prime and didn't know anything else. I never wanted to be that guy—the one out there trying to get the same the response from the crowd as he heard in his prime. When I saw him, I made a promise to myself I would never be *That Guy.*

The Naked Truth

The inner voice tried to control my actions based on past situations that presented a false reality. As much as I desired something more with Jessica, I never thought the person I saw in the mirror was good enough to have her in my life. I viewed her as flawless—a deceptive story I created in my mind. Also, the gang members and the pimps were perceived to be horrible people, but in some cases, I was able to see past what they represented to find a positive in an otherwise negative situation.

Perception of the childhood trauma I experienced, as well as the adult I looked at in the mirror dramatically affected how I chose to live my life. Those little traumas of being bullied in my teen years could have held me back from many life experiences if they were never addressed, but I rose above them and found resilience to be a better person through self-acceptance and uncovering my truth.

Discipline & Acceptance

II

Put Down the Remote if you Want to be the G.O.A.T

I believe that having a dog-like focus on my abilities can create life-changing moments. Moments when I don't allow anyone or anything to get in my way and make something purposeful happen. It may be a time when I push myself to a limit that even I didn't think I could achieve. I always remember this when I'm going through a rough patch—a time when self-doubt creeps in, and I start using the word, *can't*. It's when I regress and believe I can't be the G.O.A.T—the Greatest Of All Time. In the end, I may not be the G.O.A.T, but I will be the best version of myself at that moment.

One of the key components I use to address self-worth is discipline. It is the best skill I learned for the ultimate chance at success in anything I do. Discipline gave me the ability to choose to put down the remote control of distraction—to get up off the couch and put one foot in front of the other. The remote control has a nice little easy red button that allows you to get off that comfortable couch. The successful bodybuilders I crossed paths with have no issue putting the remote down.

They fully realize that the person on stage next to them puts the remote down, providing the vital time necessary to compete at a level most are unwilling to commit to. They fully realize that the competition in this arena will use next-level discipline, so there can simply be no shortcuts.

I learned that pushing my internal remote-control button off is not that easy, especially during this era of distraction. There is no easy button that allows me to complete daily tasks and manage my smartphone, social media and work all at the same time. I have tapped into my strong will to determine the why behind achieving my goals and dreams. At that time, my discipline came from obsession, and instead of just trying—it became a non-negotiable with no grey area whatsoever. I started by asking myself: *Why is this dream so very important to me?* Once I had an answer, I asked again: *Why is that important to me?* I kept digging deeper, continuing to ask myself: *Why?* For example: To form the mindset I needed to succeed, I recently asked myself why my external image was so important to me and why I neglected to work on my internal-self most of my life. I found my answer on the eighth level of asking: *Why?* To be honest, I was surprised when I discovered that focusing on my exterior was the easy button to ignoring what was going on internally. Trying to perfect the exterior is far from easy, but addressing the interior was beyond hard.

I obsessed with the external to avoid managing the internal. It worked when it came to certain components of my life, but it held me back from being proud of the person I looked at in the mirror. It held me back from being responsible in my relationships. In my mind, it even gave me the option to self-sabotage, allowing me to settle for just using my exterior to get by instead of figuring out how to be a better person internally. At that time however, I didn't realize that settling for

30

who I was on the outside, diminished my self-worth; avoiding looking at who I was on the inside became my easy button. My defence mechanism was to build an outer façade to deflect confrontation with others or avoid working through my inner frustrations developed from my inability to consistently express emotion. I am grateful I had the self-discipline to put down that remote control and find the passion for bodybuilding because it showed me that I could perfect myself physically, regardless of what anyone did to me or thought about me. If I attained perfection, I could earn the respect of the people who mattered to me at the time. I would be accepted, respected, and appreciated for what people saw on the outside without switching off my inner lack.

One method I used to enhance my self-discipline was setting up the proper environment. I decided to flock with the birds who were disciplined at what they did, and better yet, at what I wanted to accomplish. I also made sure that my personal environment was clear of distraction. For example, if I was trying to drop a few pounds, I kept garbage food out of my house as a start. I realized that the way I did one thing transitioned into the way I did everything. When I want to accomplish something, discipline is my base, and I am always aware of any resistance. If I find myself about to push that easy button, I acknowledge it and do what is necessary to get up. I know that no one will do it for me.

It starts with asking myself: *Where do I need to show up, and where is my resistance?* Once I have the answer, I move towards it. It's not about waiting until I'm motivated to do it but rather pushing past the resistance, especially when I don't want to. I've tended to do more for others than I would for myself, and I learned to shift that way of being.

Activity Now Cures Captivity Later

~ Anton Gunn

When I lack self-discipline, I make a contract with myself and sign it. I put it up where I can see it every single day. If I break the contract, it's similar to not brushing my teeth, and that's nasty! To maintain motivation, I need a consequence for inaction and a reward for action. For instance, if I have to skip a day of cardio, I make sure to do something more the next day—maybe an extra 30 minutes. I also celebrate my actions by treating myself to something when I finish a goal, like incentivizing myself with small rewards when I get the house cleaned or hit a target in my job. It gives me something to look forward to within the journey and keeps the ball rolling. It's literally a game between my mind and body. No matter how big or small the accomplishment is, my self-worth improves due to staying disciplined. I didn't change my whole world in one day, but I avoided discouragement and possible paralysis by doing it in bite sized chunks.

Walking into Gold's Gym at the age of 18 was intimidating, to say the least. Heads turned, and the facial expressions said everything. In their eyes, I was just some long-haired kid who showed up for a week and would likely be gone by Sunday. Yes, the juice flowed strongly in this place. The owner, Lou, ran a very professional gym for bodybuilding and powerlifting. I received some education from him about the best ways to start off and then progress from there. What sticks in my mind is the first thing he taught me: *It's all just common sense; you just need someone to tell you how to do it.* And he did! I started off with a simple three-day per week schedule and eventually developed into a six-day per week obsession. I even exchanged two spare classes in my final semester of high school for time in the gym. I sacrificed my education to build my outside appearance—doing what was in my comfort zone and that I could control.

I had to start small and grow into my discipline. Otherwise, I would give up because I wouldn't enjoy the journey. There were many days when I didn't want to go to the gym and train, but instead of thinking about how hard it was, I kept laser-focused on my destination. I believe that to be truly self-disciplined in anything, the reason for committing to it must be substantial. I had to have enough drive inside of me to do whatever it took to get the job done—the reason behind doing it had to be strong enough. When bad days came, which they did, the vision of my final destination ensured that I didn't hit that red button on the remote control because it was just that important. I always looked at bodybuilding as the ultimate art form. Although genetics is a factor, dedicating oneself to sculpting their body is one of the hardest things a person can do, but also one of the most gratifying. I educated myself as I progressed with my training on the realities of what it would take to hit the big stage. The bodybuilder's cycle is everything: the cycle of how they sleep, eat, train, take their supplements, along with bulking and dieting phases. It's pure dedication, doing what the other guy won't in order to win. In some cases that is good and, in others, bad.

Simply said, discipline is training your mind to do the work that the body doesn't want to do.

In other words, be a freak to be a freak, and it entails striving for perfection, which can, unfortunately, be a double-edged sword. I always knew that nobody is perfect, but I still tried to be perfect far too many times and, in most cases, that ended in disappointment.

Only one percent of society carries the discipline journey from the first day through to the day they walk out on that stage. This reiterates what a rare breed the bodybuilder is—the type of person who goes all in. They leave absolutely nothing on the table. Nothing. However, many of them like myself have an overwhelming desire for acceptance and experience scarcity compared to what others have. What looks good on the outside isn't always what is happening on the inside. Before I became a bodybuilder, the word discipline had a negative connotation. It meant being disciplined by my parents for something I had done wrong. However, I discovered that it had a whole other meaning in the gym as the power of being disciplined became achieving *greatness* and pushing through a mediocre day. Suddenly, discipline meant finishing a daily, weekly, monthly, or yearly goal while pushing aside just being *good* for the chance to be *great*.

After five years of training, I no longer settled for being the kid who walked into the gym on that first day. I got my wings, and after being blessed enough to meet a few pro bodybuilders, I was hungry to become one myself, but this was an industry that required making another sacrifice to reach the top of that mountain: Steroids. This was in no way an easy ticket to reach the top of the mountain. It was simply a supplement to everything else I was doing inside and outside of the gym. At 23, my body was tuned in from years of natural dedication and was like a sponge, primed to receive this supplement. So, I took that first steroid shot, and that sponge absorbed the supplement—through massive action, I exploded.

There were two or three guys at the gym who sold steroids. I built a relationship with Cade, a dealer who had a reputation for providing quality product on the black market. I knew him, I liked him, and I trusted him. In fact, he was the person who gave me my first injection because I was too afraid to do it myself. When I pictured 40 pounds of hamburger meat, it was astonishing what gaining 40 pounds of muscle in ten weeks looked like. Previously, I was satisfied if I gained five pounds of muscle in a year, but this transformation was dramatic. Cade sold me a combination of anabolic and androgenic steroids from Spain that gave little to no side effects. People who I knew even asked me where I bought the build. I was very careful about what I was purchasing because at one point, I snapped open an ampule to give myself a shot, and it broke in my hand. I took what was left of it and threw it into my bathroom garbage can. I then, opened another one and gave myself the injection. The next day, while cleaning my house, I emptied the garbage and was shocked and disturbed by what I saw. What was left of the original ampule had burned through the plastic, and I suddenly realized that whatever I had taken the day before was beyond toxic. I will never know what I took, but whatever it was scared the hell out of me.

I also had to consider the fact that I have an auto-immune disorder commonly known as Psoriasis; it stems from the liver. The amount I took was far from abusive in comparison to what others I trained with took. However, I still kept my diet clean, had zero alcohol intake, and drank water as often as possible to flush out any toxins in my system. I knew it wasn't good for me, but in my eyes, it was kind of like drinking alcohol at a moderate level. There is a massive difference between having a beer or two now and then compared to drinking excessively on a daily basis. In steroid terms, I had the beer. However, it took me to the next level in more ways than one—to achieve greatness, I needed to grow. Not just in a physical sense but in technique, strategy, and mindset. I took it to the next level by surrounding myself with two of the most hardcore bodybuilders in the gym, Dan and Ronny, and we trained like animals.

There is no growth without failure, inside or outside of the gym. We pushed each other by incentivizing our squat routine. In our disciplined mindset, we made our weakest body part our favourite, and legs always seemed to be on the agenda. We loaded up 225 pounds on the squat rack, and the count was on, each taking turns while the other two were spotters. We started with eight squats, moved on to nine, and so on, and so on, and so on—no breaks between sets. Some days, the count hit anywhere between 20 to 25 before someone failed, and the one who failed bought lunch, and lunch wasn't cheap, especially since we didn't have much money to start with. We were three freaks who wanted to be freakier. Dan, in particular, was the freakiest. He had already competed at a pro-level, and his training proved it. If it was calf raises, we went until failure. If it was shoulder shrugs, same thing. Dan had a back like a pile of rocks, and he showed up all the time. He had been around a very long time and had discipline on an incomprehensible level. Dan saw my potential and fit in the time to support my journey the best he could. He held me accountable and shared what he knew.

Success leaves clues, and he gave me a few.

He was also quite the character, and I remember him telling me that when he came back across the border from Mexico into the US at one point, the border guard asked him if he was bringing anything across, and he replied: *Nothing externally.* There was a steroid market available, and he was shopping, even though the quality wasn't the same as other markets in the world.

During another memorable moment, Dan and I were doing pull-ups on this bar that attached high up on the top of one of the gym sets in the powerlifting room. It was right at the door entry that looked over the entire gym floor below. From that location, everyone could watch what you were doing. We strapped in our wrists for better leverage and repped out as many as we could. I was struggling to finish my last few reps when Dan pulled the bench out from underneath me and left me literally hanging with no way out. Then he proceeded to pull my sweatpants down to my ankles, exposing my bare ass to the entire bottom floor. Fortunately, he didn't leave me hanging there too long, but embarrassing doesn't even begin to describe it.

I had access to everything I needed to pursue my bodybuilding dream and hit the professional ranks, and in 1992, I dedicated myself to a competition put on by our gym called The Gator's Classic. It was a step up from the average entry-level competition and was open to all ranks below national level. Although my adversaries were fierce, I was up for the battle, and when game time finally arrived, the real discipline began. Lou was my trainer, and he asked me to write down everything I had eaten for a week previous to starting my diet. He then converted the calories from the food I was eating to the food I needed to eat. It was all portioned to ensure maximum energy, and it equated to putting rocket fuel in my engine while simultaneously giving me a tune-up.

I was six feet, two inches tall, and roughly 235 pounds when I started my diet, and I was perfectly positioned to go for my goal with absolutely no distraction. My roommate, John, was a football player in the Canadian Football League, and he spent his off-season at home. However, he was in Toronto playing for the Argonauts in the regular season. He was well over 300 pounds and played for many years, earning three Grey Cup rings from three different teams. I wanted to get to the next level, and I knew I needed to surround myself with people taking their own lives to that place—John was the next level. I was fortunate enough to stumble across many next-level people at this time in my life, and I learned as much as I could from them.

Living alone at this time allowed me to not only stay focused but also be organized and motivated. All of my days were scheduled the same from when I woke up to bedtime—same food, same schedule, same sleep pattern. Thinking back, my obsession with perfection at this point was borderline insane. I had my living room set up with my bike in front of the T.V., and I rode it for one hour before breakfast at a slow pace, barely breaking a sweat. I then did another one-hour session midday and another hour session in the early evening. I was burning calories without burning muscle mass. I even sprayed Niacin on my skin when I rode the bike to get my blood flowing. I ate six meals, did one and half hours of weight training, tanned for 30 minutes, took in a balanced amount of water and slept eight hours…every single day. I was making the minutes count.

The hardest part of dieting was not the decreased amount of food but the lack of flavour. I used mustard on almost everything. I even ate boiled chicken dipped in mustard—amazing. And knowing that I was even burning calories when I slept, I woke up some nights and blended up a can of tuna with half a cup of water and drank the nasty tuna shake to keep my protein levels up. It was next-level rigid discipline and dedication, but the experience was powerful. If I had low stamina one day, I added an extra potato to my diet and felt the energy hit me almost as soon as I ate it. This is the level where I was so in tune with my body that the slightest adjustment had an effect—it's a level at which water passed through me so fast that I needed to keep a bucket next to the bed to pee in. If I didn't, I wouldn't get enough sleep due to all the bathroom trips. There was no way that a girlfriend could be in the equation at that level. I found a deep connection with myself physically at that time, and I proved to myself that I could be a freak to be a freak. Regardless of everything else going on in the outside world, I had complete control, and nothing could stop me.

Some days Dan and I rode the bike together in the gym, and he motivated me with his words. At 9:55 p.m., with the gym closing at 10:00, he would break a long silence, look over at me with five minutes left on the bike and ask me one simple question: *You see anyone here? The reason why you don't see anyone here is because they aren't you. They don't want it enough. For true greatness, you have to have the drive and will to attempt what others are not willing to do. You have to show up until the bitter end, and that's exactly why you have a legitimate shot at winning this thing. Whatever it takes to win. Whatever it takes.*

One of my favourite moments with my father came the night before my show. I stopped by my parents' house to give them some tickets, and I took off my shirt to show him the results of dropping 40 pounds in ten weeks of isolation. The look on his face was priceless—admiration mixed with concern. My skin looked like cellophane, with every muscle striation and vein showing; he touched it and asked me if it hurt. He just couldn't comprehend what he was looking at. I still smile to this day when I think about that moment of emotion that he rarely provided. It took a lot to get it out of him, but he had it in him.

The next morning was pre-judging. It was the part that counted the most and where the judges usually solidified their choice. This is the point where some push themselves over the line, with many cases of bodybuilders using strong diuretics to drop the remaining bit of water out of their system. Dan suggested I take a mild diuretic, and I took it that morning before going on stage. Bodybuilders drop water intake by cutting it in half each of the last few days prior to competing. I had done everything right, but this scared me. I had not peed in almost 24 hours, and I suddenly had to go. Once I started, it didn't seem to want to stop. Thankfully, it did, and my moment of fear diminished, but only for a split second because now it was time to get on stage. I finally had my big shot, but when I hit a front ab and thigh pose, my quad instantly locked up due to low potassium. They gave me some water, and it almost instantly unlocked. When I went back out to do my first compulsory pose, it required that I place my hands on my hips and push on the side of my trunks which were a little loose because of my massive drop in weight. When I looked down, I saw that my trunks were wide open. Thankfully, it was a view only I could see, and I can only imagine how embarrassing it would have been if anything happened to fall out.

Dan was one of the judges, and he had been checking in on me through those final days. He was very supportive, and I appreciated him. My parents came to the night show, and the place was packed. There were so many people there who stared me down as an 18-year-old kid on his first day in the gym; they cheered me on, and that in itself created an overwhelming sense of accomplishment and acceptance. My father was so proud—it was a moment when I carried a mission through until the very end. It would be one of the only times in my life when I did this. The judges selected the winners, but I already realized that I wouldn't win my division because the competition was too strong. I was still hoping to place in the top three out of twelve because I would have qualified to move to the next level. But after the dust settled, I found out that the majority of judges had me placed in either second or third, and Dan placed me in fifth, knocking me out of the top three. At first, I was disappointed and a little shocked, but then I understood why. He was too close to me and was afraid of being considered as biased. It wasn't intentional, and I never mentioned it to him afterwards. He was the person who supported me more than anyone else at that time, and I could do nothing but express my gratitude for everything he taught me. Feeling on top of the world that day, I experienced an unforgettable wave of accomplishment.

When I think back to that memory so many years ago, I realize that I had the ability, and I just needed the passion.

There have been so many people who employed me who mentioned that if I put even half of the effort and discipline into my career as I did into bodybuilding, my success would be limitless. I agree, except that there's only one issue with that statement—passion comes from within. It can't just be created from someone else's perception. Unfortunately, my former employers simply didn't get it. It's ok, though, because they aren't in that space. I believe that some people are watchers, some are wishers, and some are workers. I worked extremely hard to climb this mountain, but it was because I was driven to see the breathtaking view at the top.

Seeing my parents after the show was the icing on that beautiful cake. My hunger for receiving my father's emotion was satisfied for a special moment—the moment when the way he looked at me expressed how worthy he felt I was. His pride overflowed about something that he never pictured himself doing. He looked at me and said: *You did it, son, and besides,*

41

between you and me, I think those guys that were in the top three took steroids to beat you. I replied: *Ya, Dad, I think you may be right.* I smiled as I walked back to the change room alone. He always gave me the benefit of the doubt, and even though he was limited in some ways, he had a way of teaching me things that impacted me immensely. Even if I only heard him share them a couple of times throughout my life, they counted.

To top everything off, my favourite bodybuilder was guest-posing at the show. Mike Matarrazzo was a beast of a man. He had twenty-three-inch arms, and his calves were close to the same size. Mike never held the realities of bodybuilding back. The drug use was extreme, and he was rumoured to have been blending small amounts of nine different types of steroids at one time. He would then do a cycle of growth hormone. Only a year before this event, he was Mr. USA. He came up to me after I exited the stage and told me that I wasn't necessarily the biggest guy on the stage, but I was by far the most ripped. He said that most guys don't get that leaned out for the Olympia. It was a compliment well received. I was like the kid in the Pepsi ad as I looked up and said: *Thanks, Mike.* We had a separate conversation in the change room just before it was his time to go on stage. The crowd outside was bursting with excitement to see this mammoth of a man make his entrance while he stretched out his calves on a staircase right in front of me. I watched him as I drank water and ate a bucket of Oreo ice cream with a spoon. The one thing I craved the most during those last few weeks was Oreo ice cream, and I had two buckets in a cooler ready to go.

Our conversation at that moment was unforgettable. He knew I had placed fourth out of twelve. He turned and asked me if he could have a drink of my water, and I gladly passed him my bottle. The overall winner of the competition stood within earshot of where we were, and during a moment of silence, he gave Mike a compliment about his insane calves. He then added that his calves were so impressive that he could never see himself achieving the same. Mike turned to him and said that he was right, that he could never have calves that size. The winner had admitted that it couldn't be done, and Mike solidified it even more. Then he turned back to me and told me that I had the potential because anyone who could do what I did can push themselves beyond that line—they push themselves beyond their own limitations in their head. For a moment, I felt bad for the winner, but in the end, it made me feel like I won that day. I may not have had the trophy to prove it, but I now had the memory. A memory that I will never forget as long as I live.

Sadly, Mike passed away in 2014 from a massive heart attack. In the end, he made a huge effort to warn others of the dangers of steroid abuse, but it was too late. The body can only take so much, and unfortunately, it became his demise. He taught me that if I still wanted to do whatever it took to win, I needed to know the line between the integrity of what was healthy and what wasn't, and that would influence what I was willing to do. Crossing that line could be fatal, and one of my bodybuilding heroes was gone because of it. At my current age of 51, I often wonder where some of those people are now: *Are they still alive, and what is their quality of life?* This was one of the questions I asked myself when I decided to give up on going pro. I also asked myself: *Did I want to sacrifice quality of life in later years to be a star in present day? Did I want to sleep, eat, and breathe bodybuilding for the rest of my life? How long would it be before I died or maybe ended up with thyroid issues like so many others?*

To cap off a fantastic night, we all went out for a feast at a local eating spot called Fresgos in my hometown of Surrey. The mushroom burger was massive, and yes, I ate the whole damn thing. The boys tried to get me to jump up on the table with my gut sticking out to do my routine again, which I declined, of course. The place was packed, and although it would have been a memorable moment, my night couldn't have been any better. The next day I stayed home and ate more crap food than I ever had in my life. I just laid on the couch and savoured every bite. The starvation of flavour, along with the exhaustion of intense training and stress, made me crash. I gained back almost 30 pounds over the next two days.

Then the unthinkable happened. I was standing at the door of Casablanca's chatting with my buddy, Jason, about the show, explaining how crappy I felt with all this garbage food in my system, and he reached down and squeezed my ankle. When he removed his hand, there was a clear indent in my skin. I had water on my ankles, along with stomach pressure so hard that I could not stand or sit comfortably. Outside of mood swings, I think I am one of the only males on this planet who sort of understand what women go through during pregnancy. Thankfully, I am pretty confident I will never understand the process of childbirth, but at the very least, I can relate to the uncomfortableness of the physical pressure of pregnancy.

I went for a doctor's visit the next day, and he told me that I could have killed myself. The amount of sugar and garbage I ingested over a short period of time was very dangerous. It's scary to think about what I put my body through from the beginning of this process to the end, but I will say that I felt better than ever when I was on my diet. I was at an unstoppable age, and there was no ceiling. As I got older, I have since discovered that the ceiling seemed to lower and as is typical with most people, I began limiting myself. Reality is reality—I cannot physically do what I was able to when I was 23. However, that doesn't mean I can't use the things I learned within other aspects of life in my fifties and beyond. Discipline can be applied to anything, and I interpret it as a very positive motivator. Without it, greatness cannot be achieved.

When I think about moments in my life when I was on top of the world, they usually include times when I followed through and finished something I doubted I could do. Sometimes, I received the acceptance of others because of the actions I chose, and other times, it allowed me to reward myself with that shiny object I worked hard to purchase. The ultimate is when I experience absolute value from within my heart and soul. These are the moments when I believe I am truly valuable, and not necessarily monetarily, but in a way that influences someone through my words or actions and has a positive lifetime impact on them. It is the kind of value that money cannot buy and smashes the sense of lack I subconsciously carried with me from an early age. It also provides clarity in a moment that allows me to truly enjoy it without fear or concern about what the future may bring. Even if I know it may only occur within that one moment, I think about how liberating it is to have experienced it as it provides true love for the person I see in the mirror and who looked different in the past.

I often reflect on these moments and appreciate
them for what they are
because they affirm my potential when
the current world around me
carries so much judgement.

Even the judges on one of the most significant days of my life got it wrong, or maybe they got it right—that isn't for me to decide. Only I can decide how much value I carry. I continuously check in with myself to see if I'm settling for the value of what I'm paid or the value of other's perception of me. Almost always, I am my own worst judge, and I discover that I settle and carry more value than I originally think. I now have the visual to compare what it was like on the other side of the velvet rope with my actual value on this side.

My obsession with perfectionism was evident. I have painted a picture of a time in my life that most never experience, but even though I committed to a job to the best of my ability, it was never enough. I still picked myself apart, seeing pictures of myself on stage with my mind going straight to criticism. It was all exterior, focusing on what I had or didn't have. I overcompensated for the things I lacked on the inside with what I could achieve on the outside, and my emotional struggle ate me alive. I didn't really understand these things when they were happening, and I thought I had it all under control. It's a lesson I had to learn the hard way more than once, and I know I am not alone. Others may never have stepped foot in a gym, but their struggle might be relatable as they strive to overcome the same self-doubt I did within whatever their scenario is. I had to drill down to realize that lack was taking over my life, affecting my self-worth, and I know it was also affecting those around me.

My struggle held me back from my true potential for many years. I took many roads to find this thing called purpose that everyone strives for. I even struggled writing this book and delayed finishing it for four years because I didn't think it would provide enough value to the world. However, I'm not here to share this with all eight billion people on this planet; from the bottom of my heart, I only want to inspire worthiness in those ready to receive it and whatever it may be for them.

One of my missions in life is to help bridge the gaps in people's lives by using my own experiences as examples. Being 100 percent real, I have never considered myself an expert in anything, but five of the letters in expert are in the word experience, and I can only share mine through the lens that I saw myself through so many years ago. If I can support anyone to manage those gaps or inspire them to become a master of their passion through sharing my story, it will be worth being vulnerable.

I have seen so many people starving to live through their passions and seek support from family members or friends they have known for years. Unfortunately, in many cases, this ends in disappointment because those closest to them may not show their support, given they don't think the same. For their own reasons, they don't think bigger or haven't started following their dreams. It might be because they don't believe in themselves yet, or don't think their support will be impactful enough to voice. Unfortunately, there are also times when their closest relations don't have as much faith in them as they thought.

I found that some people I had been around for a very long time could not see the greatness waiting to explode out of me and that I was excited to share with the world. However, the person I was meeting for the first time often saw my potential because they had no judgment about my past. They saw me for the person I was in that moment and the ability I had to utilize and make an impact on my future. Discipline became the bridge between my goals and accomplishments. It was and still is rewarding. It is the natural consequence of consistently applying basic fundamentals regardless of how small or large a step I take forward. I just keep showing up and growing within whatever I do. Using this skill and consistently applying it to one thing over and over again, it automatically transitions and blossoms into other areas of my life.

It's like a rubber band that stays stretched out. My discipline was extreme, and although I used it as a bodybuilder in my early twenties, I still carry the same degree of discipline into my passions today. Currently, one discipline I stay truly consistent with is yoga. I find this practice provides well-rounded benefits for mental, physical, and spiritual wellness. It gives me a sanctuary from the ups and downs of everyday life, and I look forward to the challenge because it keeps my momentum going. It helps me realize that I can still push myself out of my comfort zone towards resistance. The resistance is temporary and trains my mind to stay calm when things go sideways, which, in turn, reduces stress. Although I have only been practicing yoga for a couple of years, I truly wish I had started earlier in life. It was a game-changer for me as a progressive practice instead of striving for perfection.

The only negative side effect I had with practicing self-discipline was when I took it to an extreme by being too hard on myself. However, the positives are endless as it cultivates self-love by not breaking promises to myself. I also find that others benefit from my self-discipline as it naturally inspires them to be the best they can be. I meet many people who hold themselves back due to the lack of support from some of the closest people around them. It's important that complete strangers understand I am here to support them to move through their journey of finding greatness within themselves. I loved being an entertainer, and I believe I supported my audience in my own way at that time, but in this socially disconnected world, it is essential for me to show my support in a more genuine way—one that is shared from my inner being, rather than my outer. It's real, and it's honest because, although

I had people in my life supporting me during my most crucial moments, many had normalized me. Perfectionism drove my desire to be the G.O.A.T in the bodybuilding arena. However, currently, progression allows me to become the greatest version of myself.

The Naked Truth

Self-Discipline has an infectious way of motivating others to do the same. Through leading by example, I have motivated others by gently guiding them in the right direction for them without telling them what to do. It all depends on the passion and desire within them. My friend, Dan, was an accountability partner to a certain extent, but he simply showed me the way based on the walk he had already taken. In this realm, discipline was a derivative of acceptance because, due to my own efforts and consistency, I found acceptance from my friends and family I had never experienced before. Understanding that progression is far more practical, I still carry the same self-discipline in a more balanced manner, which allows me to accept my and others' imperfections in life—physically, mentally, and spiritually.

Regardless of what I was trying to achieve, in my eyes, it is important to only open one garage door at a time. Otherwise, dilution comes into the equation. Setting boundaries and having non-negotiables is essential to achieving the goal. Outside distractions can take me off course. If the goal is important enough, *I Just Say No!* Friends will understand, and if they don't, they may not truly be my friends. Regardless of how big or small the goal is, staying on schedule until the goal is complete is gratifying. When I encounter resistance, I push toward it with an understanding that some days will be a struggle. Telling myself that it can be done tomorrow diminishes my momentum, and days easily turn into weeks and possibly even months.

The best accountability partner is me. Lying to myself is counterproductive and destructive. Being true to myself is constructive and a form of self-acceptance and confidence, which in essence, is the definition of self-worth.

Morality & Exposure

III

Get Comfortable Being Uncomfortable;
Get Uncomfortable Being Comfortable

At this point, I had been working as a doorman and was beyond dedicated to my bodybuilding career. Most bodybuilders don't have expensive clothes and nice cars; they have baggy shirts and torn sweatpants. I invested everything I had into it, but my job at the club just didn't pay enough to sustain the cost, so I had to make some changes.

Having a steady rotation throughout the lower mainland of British Columbia, I met quite a few dancers who entertained for ladies' night over the years. Casablanca's booked four dancers a night, and some of the shows were just insane. I saw the usual cop, construction worker, fireman, and cowboy, but some were just plain funny with dancers coming out as the *Energizer Bunny*, a character in a puppet show or portraying a nerd. I had to admire the originality that some put into their performances. One of the rare dancers who always showed up as a true professional was Dylan. He dressed well and always treated people with respect. We became friends, and one night he asked me if I would consider working for the agency that managed all the male dancers. I was blessed as a naïve rookie to have such a positive male influence supporting me the way he did without the pressure of doing something that made me uncomfortable. I also knew that this was a way for me to make more money.

I stood from afar watching shows during ladies' night but never imagined myself going to the extent of exposing myself fully. Just the thought frightened me—it wasn't just the dread of stripping that intimidated me, but the fear of what others would think about me as a person. He reassured me, saying he would help me put an act together, and we could figure out a name, which didn't take long. He asked me what my favourite movie was, and I told him: *Roadhouse*. He asked me what the main character's name was, and I said: *Dalton*. He said I was big and would need to have a dominant name to represent my size. After a few minutes, we came up with Strong, and my stage name was created—Dalton Strong! This became my alter ego, who adapted to expressing emotion on stage, getting an instant reaction from the audience—good or bad. Adding this new element of creativity into my life was exciting, to say the least.

From there, we needed to put my first act together. We came up with the idea of *The Terminator* and recorded a voiceover with the soundtrack music in the background. It was a cheesy act, but it got the ladies' attention in a big way. I walked out through the stage fog, using my laser scope to draw attention. The dramatic entrance transitioned into a somewhat comedic performance, including me looking for *Sarah Connor* —the protagonist in the *Terminator*—in the audience. With a subliminal message built into my first song, I danced to *Bad to the Bone* by George Thorogood. I barely knew how to dance

54

and was far from fluid. Being a bodybuilder wasn't an asset for great range of motion, but I managed to pull it off. The pressure of going on stage that first time was massive, but the daunting task of Tying Off before the show was exponentially worse.

In Canada, I was required to go into the change room, do whatever it took to get an erection, and then tie an elastic band around the base of my cock to hold the blood inside to maintain the hard-on while I performed. This gave the illusion of being massive. We all had to do it, and on my first night as Dalton Strong, there was no exception. So, I went backstage, took out my can of Vaseline and started masturbating until I was rock hard—then, I tied it off. Dylan told me the right-sized elastic to use and instructed me to loop it three times around the base. I was beyond nervous. Over and above exposing myself to the public for the first time, I was just praying to have the ability to get it up in the first place. With sweat dripping off my forehead and voices with club music playing in the background, I got nervous and decided to loop the elastic around four times instead of three because I was so anxious to make sure my penis stayed hard. I believe that Dylan was more uneasy than I was that night because he checked in on me multiple times to see if I was alright. I didn't tell him about my extra precautionary tie-off and moved along to get my costume on, trying my best to stay calm and prepare for the show. My heart was pounding because my debut audition was in my hometown of Surrey in a club called *The Ozone*.

The music came on, and the DJ introduced me for the first time. The butterflies in my stomach were extreme as I made my way out from backstage through the fog to the dance floor. My red laser was beaming off my gun while I focused on doing my best *Terminator* impersonation. Then, on cue, I entered the stage and smoothly went into my voiceover. It was my voice

55

lip-syncing with the recording, and it sounded strange to me, but I did my best as my heart simultaneously beat a million miles an hour.

As the smoke cleared and I was about to segue into my first song, I looked at the ladies sitting in the first row and noticed a group of girls from my high school graduating class. I was embarrassed for a split second, however, there was no other choice but to carry on. I couldn't just walk offstage, so instead of focusing on the fear of the unknown, I moved toward my resistance and did the best I could. As uncomfortable as it was, I broke my fear of being seen nude in public, being self-conscious in front of people I knew, and the nightmare of being exposed to the world. Surprisingly, it wasn't as bad as some might think. When the big moment came to remove my G-String, I covered up with a towel, as I was only required to do one complete spin fully exposed. The ladies seemed to enjoy the show by the sound of their cheering and clapping while my agent, Marilyn, was in the crowd, who told me later that I passed the test, so I suppose I provided what everyone was looking for.

After everything wound down, I quickly went backstage to get changed and get that elastic off my cock. The pain was indescribable as I snipped it off, and my eyes rolled back into my forehead. That was when I realized I had roped it off one too many times—I should have heeded Dylan's strict instructions. Suddenly, the numbness set in, and it was extremely scary. Thankfully, within a short time, the blood flow returned, and I was fine. I was lucky, and looking back, the pay was alright, but the pain sure as hell wasn't.

As rough of a beginning as it was, my official dance career had begun. I had to get a photographer to put promotional material together, and I was being booked three times a week throughout the province of British Columbia. Every time I got on the stage, it was a new and exciting experience, and although I knew in my heart that the occupation could only take me so far, I enjoyed entertaining for the most part. And it just kept getting better with the gay bar shows coming next. I will admit that as a straight person, I didn't want to do them at first. I was already intimidated enough entertaining women, but I had never even stepped foot into a gay bar, let alone danced in one. It was a requirement by the agency to dance in these bars, so I was, once again, forced outside of my comfort zone. Although I am far from homophobic, the thought of exposing myself within that environment as a straight man was terrifying at the time. However, I came to realize that it was the same process in the gay bar, just a different audience than what I was used to—people are people, no matter what gender. Just like when I danced for the ladies, I had to tie off before going out, and I wanted to make sure that I was fully erect before going on stage, especially there. The pressure of having to tie off in this foreign environment was next level for me. Tying off was not easy to start with because I only had so much time to get an erection before the show began, but in the gay bar, there was added pressure with the distraction of male voices in the background. I sometimes heard conversations between the DJ and some of his friends talking about me while I was trying to concentrate in a small bathroom at best, and in some cases, behind a curtain.

My first gay bar show was at *The Shaggy Horse Saloon*, a very dark nightclub below street level in downtown Vancouver with black rubber matting for a dance floor. The bar was in the back, and there was a Harley Davidson parked beside it. As I nervously started to walk in, I saw a man come around the corner wearing bottomless leather chaps. He continued towards the back of the bar and sat down with his bare ass on the motorcycle. This was my introduction to working in the gay bar arena, and I was fortunate to be booked that night with my friend and mentor, Dylan. He was very well-respected in that territory, and I knew he would support me if I needed him. I watched him do shows in the past, but not in this scene. He was a stud, and he showed me how he took total control of his performances. He shared everything that worked for him, and although it bent my morality, I never broke. We each did two shows that night, and dancing before a legend like him was tough. It was hard to compare myself to someone who had not only been entertaining for years but was famous in the gay community. Along with his accent and chiselled body, Dylan could spin on a dime, and he was hung like a horse. He said that if I wanted to succeed in that environment, I needed to dominate.

When we went through my routine, Dylan told me to approach someone watching from the side of the dance floor and walk straight up to them. From there, I should grab them with both hands by the jacket or shirt, stare into their eyes, smile and pull them into me—rough sex style—he reiterated that I needed to be aggressive. If the audience was really into it, he told me to throw one lucky customer down on the floor and get on top of him, pin him down and do whatever it took to be the dominator. Well, I did what he said, and he was correct. By following his directions, the tips started flying. The reactions were hilarious most of the time, but occasionally, the odd person wouldn't react at all. As a straight young man, I found all this difficult, but it also made me realize that the show was just a show, and I had to push myself right up to the line of morality that I didn't want to cross.

Masturbation shows were part of this package as well,

which bent my integrity even further. Being on stage covered in baby oil, standing in front of a fire pan, pretending to be sexually turned on in a room full of horny gay men was not an easy task for me. I had to block out everything in my mind and remember that it was all just an act—it was all an illusion. And even the idea of being turned on in that environment was beyond comprehension, especially with an elastic tied around the base of my penis. Little did I realize at the time that while doing this, I was slowly chipping away at my self-worth. It wasn't so much about who I was dancing for in the crowd, but instead, about what I was doing to entertain that crowd. It was extremely degrading, but that's what I signed up for.

From dancing in the gay bar scene,
I realized that men respond the same
regardless of whether they are gay or straight.

They all clap at the end of the song, and, in general, they watch the rest of the time with the occasional random comment. When I first walked into the bar that night, I wondered if I would come out of there the same way I went in. And, of course, I did, but I saw another side of society I had never experienced before. They were all looking for their version of acceptance while dealing with their self-doubts—just for different reasons. Like most people, some lacked the approval of people near and dear to their hearts. Although there were a few comments inquiring whether I was gay or straight, or even a hand that ran up the side of my leg now and then, I was given instant respect. Part of that came along with Dylan introducing me as his little brother. He was an absolute rock star, so I, along with most others, admired him and anyone affiliated with him.

In fact, throughout my entire career, I was well respected

within the gay bar community. Over the years, I received offers to do gay porn or private parties, but I always declined. I left selling myself on the stage and gave a little back some nights by signing a promotional poster for a gay couple. I told them to hang it on the wall and fantasize about me while they had sex. No one got hurt, and I would never judge someone based on sexual orientation. They tipped me, and I took it as a compliment just like any other dancer would. As insane as it may seem to some people, it was a business.

I rarely saw Dylan make a mistake the entire time I knew him, either personally or professionally. He would hate to admit what happened, but I remember a funny incident that wasn't so funny for him. He had the picture-perfect image of a male dancer who could do no wrong on stage, and most dancers looked up to him based on his long career and unique personality. Most of the time, he carried himself with class in a somewhat classless industry. We were often booked together, especially when I was a rookie, and Dylan always had a tradition of making sure he had a cold beer waiting for him when he came offstage. One night, I had just finished my act, and when I went backstage, I saw Dylan standing there in his cop outfit, looking extremely uncomfortable. He was frustrated because the bathroom was located out in the bar, and he was already in costume. So, instead of changing, he resorted to using an empty beer bottle to pee in simply because he had no other choice, and it was the only option available. As usual, he rocked the crowd, did a couple of encores and left the audience begging for more. When he came bursting through the change room door, looking completely exhausted, he grabbed his beer as usual and took a huge pull off it. To his surprise, he grabbed the wrong bottle. I never saw him so upset, watching him spit it out onto the floor. Looking around for someone to blame, he suddenly realized he had done it to himself. As embarrassing as it was, in the end, we had a good laugh about it. Even the best of us make stupid mistakes sometimes, and that was one I will never forget, even if it was at the expense of one of my closest buddies.

I often worried about my nightmare of exposure when it came to my parents knowing what went on behind the scenes of my dancing. But I managed to conquer that hurdle without massive compromise. They would have had a hard time understanding this phase of my career. That is part of the reason why I took so long to finally release my story. My folks would have accepted it, but they would never have truly understood it. It was beyond foreign to them. Life is temporary, so out of respect for them, I waited until they passed before releasing it. I never wanted to tarnish the image they had of me as a child; that kid they thought the world of was still there in their hearts, and I'm glad I waited. I suppose some things are just better left unsaid until later.

I often think back to my father coming to my bodybuilding competition and how proud he was of me. If he had known what it took for me to get into that kind of shape, he might not have been as proud of me as he was. My desire to compete was not as strong as it was before that contest in 1992. I saw the reality of what it took to get to the pro level, and I was not willing to sacrifice my future with the common health concerns many bodybuilders experience. Steroids were still in my life, but in a whole different way. I partnered with my dealer, Cade, and his buddy, Jimmy, who had a massive client base of very satisfied customers. Multiple people were contacting me looking for quality product, so my move in that direction was motivated solely by money. Working as a doorman with the occasional ladies' night wasn't enough.

My partners had a connection named Juan who was the middleman located in a tourist haven called Torremolinos in Southern Spain. Cade made orders, and Juan shipped the product via airmail to Canada. This was long before 9/11, and security was not as tight as it is today. Therefore, the risk of being caught was minimal compared to the payoff, even including the large cut that Juan took. By eliminating him from the equation, the cut would have been substantial, but it was far too dangerous, and my partners were not willing to take the risk. However, I was willing to take it if or when the time was right.

My football roommate, John, had a career-ending injury that forced him to move out, so I, unfortunately, had to find a new place to live. To cut costs, my friend, Shannon, offered to share a little basement suite she was renting—it seemed to make sense since we had mutual respect for one another. We were still working at Casablanca's together, and we both worked similar hours when I wasn't running the road, doing shows. It was a tight squeeze in that little place, but the trade-off was that the rent was cheap. The only possessions I had were enough to fill my little bedroom. Not only was Shannon gracious enough to share that place with me, but she was also there for me when my heart truly broke for the first time.

Early in 1993, I was booked at a club where many American girls frequented just over the US border on the Canadian side. The legal age for drinking in Canada was only 19, so the girls from Washington State who had to wait until 21 migrated north in droves for ladies' night. My assumption was that this would just be another booking, but this night was different. My eyes caught the attention of a girl watching my every move, who was standing at the front of the stage with her friend. When I danced, I typically treated every customer the same, hustling the crowd for as many tips as I could. However, on this evening, I noticed this girl watching me with intent. Suddenly, I was enveloped with that whole *Love at first sight* thing. If I was to go by looks alone, she was an absolute knockout. As the two ladies watched my show, I tried my best to connect with them as much as I could, hoping they would stick around.

After the show, the friend approached me and introduced herself as Candace. Then she introduced me to Kaitlen, but I had difficulty hearing her name over the music. We made small talk for a while, and I'm sure it was obvious I was interested in Kaitlen because I had a hard time taking my eyes off her, and we carried the majority of the conversation. We left the club together, and while chatting outside, Candace called her Kate instead of Kaitlen. As the conversation continued, they started messing around with me about being a dancer and a player; they mentioned that I probably wouldn't remember their names after having my way with them. Kaitlen decided to test me on the spot and asked what their names were, and I replied: *Candace and Kate.* She put me in my place in her own way: *Candace is the only person on this planet who calls me Kate.* Although I was a little embarrassed, I was attracted to her confidence—I didn't get her name right, and that was important to her. I really liked her because she was straightforward and had massive sex appeal. We started dating shortly afterwards, and as a young man in my early 20s, I thought I had found the ultimate girlfriend. She had it going on, and she knew it, but I saw another side of her. I was hustling my clients, but she was also hustling, just in a different way...

Kaitlen worked in a shoe store at a mall in Bellingham, Washington, and I travelled across the border to see her and vice versa. We connected when we were together, but since our relationship spanned two countries, we could only take things so far at that time in our lives. We were also at an age when, in my opinion, we were each trying to find our own roads. Part of her path included Candace; they were like two peas in a pod, and it didn't take me long to realize they were a package deal. I had never opened myself up to romance as much as I attempted to with Kaitlen. I wanted to create a special relationship, and my heart was truly in the right place.

However, my expectations were high, and I was beyond excited to see her one night when we arranged to meet at my place. I wanted to make it a special night, so before she arrived, I went to the local florist and picked up as many rose petals as I could get. Then, I made that little bedroom I had into the perfect scene spreading the petals from the door entry all the way to the bed, which I also covered in petals. Finally, I lit white candles and prepared to give this incredible girl a night to remember. However, when she arrived, I was disappointed to see Candace with her—it was the ultimate third-wheel situation, but Candace wasn't the third wheel…I was.

Kaitlen gave me an excuse that they had something to do that night and couldn't stay. All my preparation went down the drain, but I wouldn't let her leave without her knowing what she was about to miss out on. We walked into the bedroom, and Bed of Roses was playing on my little boom box. I could tell she felt horrible because the look on her face said it all, but whatever they had planned to do that night, they went ahead and did it. I was confused, upset and probably expected too much from her. We broke up before she left that night, and poor Shannon was there to clean up the mess. I was devastated; I would say over the top devastated. I cried in her arms, and to this day, I am grateful she was there for me at that moment. My true friend picked up the pieces and let me know that I was going to be alright. She was there for me like a sister helping her brother. I'm sure she wanted to voice her opinion, but she didn't, allowing me to process everything without judgement.

Kaitlen and I had an on again, off again relationship, and the next time we got together was at a nightclub. That was when I saw the true player of the game show up. Right in front of me, she let other guys buy her drinks all night, and although some people may not have cared, I did. If the roles had been reversed, I don't think she would have cared as much. It was like she wanted to show me that she was in control by accepting those free drinks from other men. She wanted me to know that she was doing what she wanted to. As much as I wanted to be in control, I knew it wasn't going to get me anywhere. Once again, we walked away from one another because I didn't want to play those kinds of games with my partner. I refused to leave with her, regardless of how much I wanted everything to be right.

Months went by, and although I rarely considered going back to an ex, I was glad I did with Kaitlen. Although she and I didn't have a great track record, I took the chance because there was something about her that I couldn't resist. I was beyond ecstatic, having her back in my life. We got back together right around when I decided to move in with my dancing mentor, Dylan, and his roommate, Lance. Dylan was a man who had many opportunities when it came to choosing women, and there were usually more than one. We had a three-bedroom house together, and I often came home to some interesting situations. It was like rolling the dice sometimes because I never knew what I might see walking through that door. One night, it might be Lance just sitting on the couch watching T.V., while another had Dylan getting tag teamed by four women, and yet another, a crowd of male and female dancers partying their asses off. Although these situations were out of the ordinary for most, I had a very unexpected surprise when I came home one particular night. Dylan was on the couch with a couple of girls, and after introducing them to me, he told me that a package had arrived that day, and it was up in my room. I walked in, and there was Kaitlen, lying on my bed wrapped up like a gift. It came at the best possible moment and made up for the rose incident that previously broke my heart. In all my years on this earth, no other woman had the timing that Kaitlen did, whether she was doing something that destroyed me or made my heart sing. If life is about making memories, she provided many unforgettable ones. I started to fall for her in a big way, and I like to believe it was reciprocal. She was in my circle of dancer friends, and it seemed right—for a while anyway.

My agent booked me to do a show in Nanaimo on Vancouver Island, and timing was everything when going to the island. If I arrived at the dock and the ferry was full, I had to wait for the next sailing, so I couldn't be late because the show must go on. Kaitlen was coming with me, but she was delayed. Although I knew we would miss the ferry I wanted to catch, I decided to wait for her because I really wanted her to be there. However, I was pushing it because I had no idea if the next ferry would be empty or full of reserved spots. Of course, she showed up with her sidekick, Candace, and I was pissed. But I gritted my teeth and stressfully attempted to make it on time. When we arrived at the ferry terminal, the next ferry was full, and we had to wait for the following sailing. I made a call to the club and my agent to let them know I was delayed, but by the time I finally arrived, the show was over. Ladies' night was just finishing, and I messed up. Not only did I miss the show, but I also lost the income that came with the territory. My stomach sank because I take pride in being on time and getting a job done properly. Regrettably, I should have left them behind and met up with them later, but my mind was focused on Kaitlen instead of being responsible. However, the club had a paid hotel room waiting for me, so all things considered, I made the best of the situation. It was like dominoes falling on that trip with almost everything that could go sideways, going sideways.

I was just hoping to get some time alone with Kaitlen and make the best of the situation. Admittedly, I was in a depressed mood, but then everything changed when she walked through the door of my hotel room. Staring at one another, we stood there in silence, experiencing an extreme sexual connection. She slid her hand down my pants, unzipped my zipper, and pulled my cock out. If I didn't already have enough ego, she gave me a little more with what happened next. She looked down at my cock and said: I can't believe how perfect this is. It just doesn't get any better. Then, she started to go down on me. It was beyond hot, and this was a first for us. We had already slept together, but this was raw and real at a time when it seemed like everything was going wrong.

There's just something appealing about having sex in a dirty little stripper motel.

I was loving every single second of it, and then it happened. The knock on the door…Of course, it was Candace. If the roles were reversed in my eyes anyway, heaven and earth could have been crashing down outside, and I wouldn't have stopped, but Kaitlen did. She chose to answer the door—it left me beyond frustrated. It was a shitty trip already, but this made it even worse, and things like this seemed to be part of our destiny. Kaitlen and I went back and forth trying to make it work, but the stars just never seemed to align. We had a special love for one another and created some great memories, but as much as we tried, something always happened that pulled us apart. So, I went on my way, and she went on hers, but she stayed within my circle of dancer friends. I learned that being in that territory can bring a person to either good or bad places, whichever they allowed.

Even when apart, she found a way to stun me. While I worked at a popular local club, one of the other dancers in my agency announced that he had just got married, and his new bride was Kaitlen. I was shocked, and my heart sunk when I saw her being introduced to the crowd as his wife while he wrapped up his show. When I approached her about it, she explained that it was a business agreement. They only married because he wanted to move to Hawaii, and her American status could get him there. He paid her, and I wasn't surprised that Kaitlen took the money because she was a hustler through and through. During our discussion, I mentioned that I would have married her, but it wouldn't have been about the money. My heart sank even further when she told me that she would have said: *Yes.* She was looking me in the eyes and holding my hand at the time, and as she walked away, I felt it slowly leave mine. There was something about that moment as her hand lingered just a little longer before slipping away. In my heart, I knew I would see her again one day, but I had no idea when.

The touch of Kaitlen's hand was unlike any other woman I have met. I could be blind but still recognize her touch. Just because I chose a career as I did, doesn't mean I couldn't feel or love any less. As emotionally detached as I could be at times, when I was connected with someone, I held on with everything I could. It was difficult letting that hand slip away as she disappeared through a packed, smoke-filled nightclub. Our unique emotional connection was still there, but our priorities were vastly different. Once again, she took her road, and I took mine.

As time went by, she ended up with another dancer named Rob, who I knew from high school. It was a very strange dynamic when I initially saw her with him at yet another show on the circuit. She had dramatically changed her outside appearance, and at that moment, sadness enveloped me because I remembered her natural state as near perfection. She had her breasts done and had chosen to enter the dance industry herself. In conversation, they explained they were also doing porn together and claimed they only did shoots with one another. Whether I believed that or not was irrelevant in my mind. What was significant was that this new, made-up version of the woman I felt so deeply for wasn't as appealing to me as the one I initially met.

Rob proudly showed me his new arm tattoo flaunting her portrait—I wisely refrained from saying what I wanted to say. By showing me, I understood that he wanted me to know how committed they were to each other. They eventually had a kid together, and that truly solidified how permanent their relationship would be. They even appeared together on an episode of *Jerry Springer* and explained to me how staged it all was. I saw them from time to time, working the circuit and kept my thoughts to myself for the most part. I have zero judgement for the road that she took, but a part of me wished I could have changed her path somehow. Maybe I shouldn't have let her hand go that night, but I didn't have it in me. That's not how it works, though. Living in the past wasn't getting me anywhere, so I decided to let it go because I had a journey of my own to take. I was excited to hit the road with a new dance revue out of Vancouver. I had always worked solo, but I embraced the change, knowing it was sure to provide some great memories. Some may not comprehend living life flying by the seat of your pants with an unpredictable future, but I believe that's how some of the best stories are created—flying like the butterfly that I knew I could become.

As with almost every relationship I've had, being faithful to my partner was vital, regardless of the constant temptation surrounding me. For me, integrity is a non-negotiable and a key element to self-worth. During these struggles, the emotional discomfort I experienced contributed to my growth as a young man within a unique industry. Although it may be a dream for many men, I had multiple sexual opportunities with more than one woman at a time over my long career, but I turned them down every time. Although I still needed to acquire a more well-rounded perspective on relationships, the sexual connection I had with someone had to be one on one. It was more than just trying to get off in the moment for me, even if it was only a one-night stand. Having a sexual connection brought out satisfying emotions for both me and my partner, which meant something more. In my heart, I wanted that emotional connection so badly, and I could not split it between multiple people in my world.

I was beyond disappointed about Kaitlen because we had an extraordinary connection, and I couldn't help but paint a picture in my mind of where her road led her. Mine was far from perfect, and I say these words without judgement because I have made my fair share of mistakes. However, I meant what I said to her that night in the club—I would have married her. In saying that, I would not have married the woman who recreated herself to succeed in the industry. However, I would have committed my life to the woman who was so unbelievably and naturally beautiful and exuded confidence. She was the epitome of femininity, and during our time together when everything was aligned, I clearly saw us in my vision as the perfect fit for the future. I look back with a deeper understanding and appreciation for living in the now because I realize that everything is temporary in my life. Regardless of how this part of our story ended, I am grateful I met her and for the memories we created that were erratic and yet spectacular when we were together, just the two of us. The integrity I carried and used to make life-changing decisions back then were put to the test later and at the most unexpected time.

The Naked Truth

Although dancers are stereotypically perceived to lack morality and integrity, I took pride in being aligned with these values—they provided me with ease of mind, especially when it came to relationships. In a somewhat archaic mindset, I understood that males are the *spreaders of the seed*, but I saw chaos, guilt, and stress trying to juggle between one partner and another in a career that was unstable to begin with. Sexual satisfaction was a two-way street for me, creating a bond between my partner and myself because I genuinely wanted them to enjoy the experience as much or even more than I did. As erratic as my relationship was at times with Kaitlen, when we were together, one on one, it was fantastic. My stance on monogamy may have fed my hunger for control in our relationship to a certain extent, but as much as I may have bent my morality on stage, I held firm when it came to my personal life.

When I looked through my lens, I realized that monogamy was and is still essential to establishing inner and outer ease. Adding another element into the equation may be enjoyable for a short time, but in the end, someone is bound to get hurt, which tends to happen when there is a deep sexual connection. I make no judgement on others who choose to take a different road, but life can be hard enough without bringing unnecessary instability into my sanctuary. Creating this barrier of integrity gave me the confidence that I could put aside what my alter ego was required to do on stage without compromising my own inner-being, both personally and professionally.

Clarity & Perception

IV

Looks Can be Deceiving,
Regardless of What You May be Perceiving

Many things come to people's minds when they think about a male stripper. Some assume we are uneducated and taking the easy road. Others have the perception we are overly confident. And some believe there is no possible way to follow through on being faithful in a relationship. I agree that depending on the dancer, just like any other person with any other career, any one of us could have been any of these things; maybe I was, and maybe I wasn't. However, the most common perception I heard from those who didn't know me is that I must be living a dream life—one where money comes easy, and sex comes even easier. They assumed that because I presented myself as a *Macho Man*, I must be *Man Enough*. I mean, what woman wouldn't want to spend a night with a hot male stripper?

Well, not all of us are created equal. When I was on stage, I did exude massive charisma and confidence. However, before I walked on stage, I was nervous almost every single time. I literally had to flick a switch inside my brain to take the first step out there and present my alter-ego to the crowd. To this day, I still have difficulty approaching a beautiful woman to simply introduce myself as Corey as opposed to Dalton Strong. All that *Macho Man* perception is bullshit.

Over a 25-year career, I entertained thousands of women in this industry, but I am human just like everyone else. I made many mistakes, and I am sure I will make many more as life goes on. The life of a male exotic dancer can be solitary at times, and I spent many more nights in bed alone than with someone next to me, and that was by choice. The dancers who partied all the time did not last long, and, in many cases, the aftereffects showed long before they chose to finally hang up the G-String. Top-performing male dancers always focus on keeping in optimal shape, dressing well and not spending every dollar they make. My career was far from ordinary, but people's inflated perceptions of me were deceiving. It wasn't all it was cracked up to be, with the highs being really high and the lows really low.

For many years, I judged others without having a clue about their story or how they got to their destination of finding pleasure or satisfaction in places that are now so foreign to me. There may have been mental, physical, or sexual abuse that drove some of them to choose to take the actions they did. It's not my place to criticize them for what some may consider sins. If I were looking through the so-called sinner's lens, I am sure I would not consider their situation the same way. Some may wonder why I kept going back to Kaitlen, who kept throwing dirt on me. Or why I still remember some of those moments in pictures that either broke my heart or made it sing. The reason is that I didn't possess the tolerance to understand emotion the way I do now. It was a boulder in the middle of the road I just kept staring at without finding a way to get around it. I had to finally figure out that not everyone on this planet thinks as I do.

I received an assigned name when I was born, but a name is not as important as the impact I can leave on others. My legacy is not about popularity or acceptance, but about helping others avoid some of the struggles I dealt with in, what I like to call, my *former life*. As an entertainer, my desire was not to be considered a stripper god. My mission was to bring out emotion, even if I couldn't truly understand it at times—to make a person in the audience cry laughing at the insanity they were witnessing or cry tears at the story being presented. I would do whatever it took to bring out emotion in them, even at my own expense. In the end, it was the emotion my heart was starving for that I only unlocked for a short period of time and only for certain people in my life. However, I was consumed with my own lack of truly connecting when it counted the most.

My assigned name at birth was Corey, but Dalton was my alter ego created to satisfy the audience he served. Dalton was an entertainer, willing to be creative and take risks, but he was left on stage to a certain extent when the lights went down. The show was just a show, but I tried to find Corey for decades afterwards. I'm grateful I finally found him because he had unlocked potential far beyond what was left on the stage. I was my own worst critic most of my life but learning and growing came from failure and acknowledging the mistakes I had made. The world is filled with many people trying to present themselves as perfect, but again, that's bullshit because I'm not perfect, and neither is anyone else. As much as I tried to be perfect in my own way, others perceived it as fake because I wasn't being my authentic self. Likewise, Dalton wasn't perfect, regardless of whether he was a made-up character or not. I have learned not to be so hard on myself or others because we are all human.

I began truly realizing what some people are
willing to compromise for a good time.

I still have faith in women, but what happened next put it to the test. Paul was a veteran dancer in our agency who didn't have the best reputation with other dancers. He managed a group of quality entertainers with relatively good promotion, and they needed an extra man for their revue. He was Italian and had the stereotypical hot temperament. The group was brand new, with five solo dancers who had thrown some simple choreography together. It wasn't a far cry from what I was already doing, except they had an opening and a closing routine. I was offered a position with them, and I took it.

The group consisted of Paul, my lifelong friend Cole, Frank, James, and a dirty dog by the name of Mikey. Cole was my road warrior for most of my career. He stood up for me and vice versa because we both realized we had to look out for one another. He had an extensive background in martial arts but rarely used his physical ability simply due to his intimidating presence. If someone crossed either one of us, he put them in the ground with the words that came out of his mouth. When I was down, he was there to help me up, and I like to think that I supported him as much as he supported me. Our short-lived tour together started in Edmonton, Alberta, and I will never forget that first show. The bar circuit in Edmonton was popular for male dance revues, and it was exciting working in a place so far away from home. We were never seen before, and that drew large, enthusiastic crowds for ladies' night in every venue.

The first club we danced at was called *The Gas Pump* on a cold, snowy winter night. I assumed it would be a good show, but I had no idea what this night would bring. The other dancers in the group had worked in revues before, but I was a virgin to this scene because it was a totally different format. Being the rookie, they chose me to go on first. Nervously, I built up my confidence to do my first show with them. My act went over well, and a very cute blonde girl was anxiously holding up a ten-dollar bill on the side of the dance floor. She was out for her bachelorette party, and she had all the appropriate gear on, wearing some crazy hat and a T-shirt with little life savers candies sewn onto it so that the dancers had to bite the candies off her shirt to get the tip. In the industry, this was known as *the suck for a buck*. They seemed to be a wild bunch, and I approached her, bit off one of the candies, and accepted the tip. We smiled at one another, and I continued to hustle the crowd.

After the show, I blasted through the change room door with a huge smile on my face. I was so confident and excited that my first tip was from a cute girl, and it was a ten-dollar bill. Shortly afterwards, the rest of the dancers quickly injected their perceptions. I was still quite naïve, living the sheltered childhood I was brought up in. I tended to give people the benefit of the doubt, but they all referred to her as a dirty rat, later defined as a slut or a bar whore within the male dance community. I didn't believe them, and I assumed they were putting her down because I had complimented her. She was a good-looking woman, but I was more inspired by the ten-dollar bill. She was out with her crazy group of friends celebrating getting married, so why would she be into some random stripper from out of town anyway?

Relaxing after the show, I had a beer at the bar, and Mikey came up to me with a massive grin on his face. He asked me if I had seen the bachelorette girl around anywhere. When I replied: *No*, he asked: *You know why? She was around the back of the club giving me head!* I totally brushed it off and thought: *Why is he messing with me, and better yet, why would she be with him of all people?* My guard was up because I didn't want to be considered gullible, and at the same time, I was just getting to know some of these people, so I knew my inexperience might be taken advantage of. As the night went on, Frank came up to see how my first show went. He carried himself as a relaxed, down-to-earth person who unfortunately didn't have the best dance moves. After some small talk, he put me in a state of shock when he asked in his thick Jamaican accent: *Hey Dalton, you know that girl that was here for her bachelorette party? Well, she just took me around to the back of the bar and gave me a spectacular blowjob!* That confirmed that they were all fucking with me, so I just chuckled and said: *Whatever, dude.* He laughed and replied: *Believe me if you want to or don't. That's your choice, my friend.*

The waitress serving me was very attractive, and at first, I thought she was just hustling me for tips. She kept coming over to chat when she wasn't busy, so I boldly asked her if she wanted to meet up after work and she accepted with a little grin on her face. It was getting late, and the crowd was starting to thin out. I was already thinking about leaving, but then the bachelorette girl and her friend came up and introduced themselves. I asked them if they enjoyed the show, and of course, they said: *Yes.* We chatted for a few minutes and then she astonished me with what came out of her mouth: *My friend and I are here for my last night on the town before I get married, and we wanted to see if you are interested in going behind the club so that we can take turns going down on you.* I almost spit my drink out! The other dancers had been telling me the truth, but my naivety blinded me to the reality of the moment. My perception instantly changed.

I was not about to go around to the back of the nightclub. I remember saying to her: *See that beautiful waitress over there at the cash register? She is meeting me in my hotel room later, so thanks for the offer but I'll pass.* She replied with: *Your loss.* They walked away with a look of disappointment. As the night carried on, I hung out and waited for the waitress to get off at two in the morning. We agreed to leave before closing time, and she would come out to meet me in Leduc, a small town outside of Edmonton where we were staying. I couldn't stop thinking about the poor guy who was about to get married to the bachelorette girl.

Maybe they had an open relationship?
Then again, my perception was based on the lens
I saw my life through, not theirs.

Paul and I decided to go back to the hotel, but this night was far from over. I was relaxing in my room on the bed when the phone rang unexpectedly. I was hoping it was the waitress, but it was Mikey, and I could hear the enthusiasm in his voice with music playing in the background: *Dude! You have to come down to my room right now! I have 15 girls in here. There are two on me, two are on James, and there are 11 standing around watching! You have to see this!* I threw on my sweatpants and went down to the room, and he was correct. They were having a little after-party, and I found it so insane that all these women had followed them out to this hotel to be standing around drinking, waiting for a turn. Then Paul showed up and mentioned that the front desk had called with a noise complaint. He said: *Two girls to each dancer and the rest have to leave.* I kind of chuckled to myself when he said that because it was so far beyond anything I could comprehend. One by one, the girls exited the room, but the bachelorette girl was left in bed with Mikey, and her friend was with James. I suppose they wanted to go out with a bang...literally. I left to go back to my room and anxiously waited for the waitress to show. My room was located on the bottom floor of the hotel, so the parking lot was literally at eye level right outside my window. As I lay there, I was startled by a flash of high beams coming through the window from outside. I nervously peeked through the blind and saw two men sitting in a white Ford pickup truck staring me right in the eyes. However, I was fixated on the shotgun rack that was in plain view.

The first thing that came to mind was the fiancée. I called back to Mikey's room and had him ask her what kind of vehicle her man drove. *A White Ford F-150*, she said. As soon as I mentioned the pickup with the gun rack, they got the boot. I had to see what was going to happen next, so I crouched down on the floor and cracked the door to see down the hallway without being too obvious. They both came busting out of that room, still naked with clothes in hand. They walked down the hallway at three-thirty in the morning, high-fiving each other, ecstatic they got some action with the male strippers from Vancouver. Then, they went outside in the cold Alberta weather, ran across the parking lot, and jumped into the truck's rear cab, speeding away, never to be seen again. I sat there in a state of shock, and if I hadn't witnessed it personally, I might not have believed it. Unfortunately, the waitress stood me up, but we did get together a couple of times during our two-week tour. She was a nice girl, but looking back, I can't remember her name. It ended up being a memory of a woman who showed an interest in me, and we shared some sweet moments for a short time. I can still see her picture in my mind, but the impact just wasn't strong enough to remember her name.

This was my first night on the road dancing with a revue, but it wasn't my last. Through all the years I entertained, it was one of my most eye-opening moments. This short-lived tour had many ups and downs, but the icing on the cake happened when we flew back to Vancouver. As we exited the plane, the police were waiting for Paul to arrive. He had charges against him that he had avoided, and there was a warrant for his arrest. They put him in handcuffs and escorted him out of the airport. Not only was the tour over, but the group disbanded shortly after that. He had dirty little secrets, but I have no idea if he was innocent or guilty. It was no surprise to me because that world was full of shady people. I perceived him to be something that he was not, and I was too naive at the time to even recognize it. Shortly afterward, another opportunity dropped right in my lap.

Along with my wild adventure with Paul's group, I worked as a full nude male dancer for only a short time and was already considered one of the top five out of roughly 50 to 60 dancers in my agency. My agent arranged a meeting with another from Japan who saw my pictures along with a dancer named Antonio. We were both selected to work at a nightclub in Tokyo, which was one of the most popular clubs in the country at the time. Fortunately, my contract was canceled because roughly one week before we were set to leave, the nightclub was busted for drug use and prostitution. It was a blessing in disguise. Shortly after that, my agent asked me if I would be interested in working with three other dancers in a male revue by the name of *The West Coast Men*. She explained that she was going to book the group in Edmonton for roughly three weeks. The revue would be booked solid with a base pay of one hundred dollars each plus tips from the show. This was a low price compared to what I was making doing solo shows in Vancouver, but since we were from out of town and booked solid, we were destined to make a lot of money. Although my last experience was interesting to say the least, I was excited to go back on the road and try again. My *Road Warrior*, Cole, was part of this new group which solidified my decision.

We desperately needed to put something together as a group with minimal experience. I had only been in one dance revue previously with Cole, and the other two dancers had never practiced any choreography, so the crash course began. The group consisted of me, Cole, Rob, and Tyler, a good-looking young stud with a stocky build. We put together the revue from scratch in a matter of one week, and although we practiced, it was far from a perfect situation. We arrived in Edmonton and met up with the agent, Jordan, who put me in charge of managing the money. I have to admit Jordan was one of the more original people I have ever met. He said *buddy* after every second word: *What's up, buddy? Buddy, buddy...I don't know what to tell you, buddy!* Cole and I mocked Jordan for years about his *buddy* talk. Rumours also flew around that he was a pimp on the side. He had been in the business for many years, so I knew I had to be very straightforward with him. He immediately tried to screw us on our pay when he said we would get to get seventy-five dollars a show when we were promised one hundred. I explained to him that my agent in Vancouver had guaranteed us all one hundred a show, and if he lowballed us, we would get right back into our van and head home. He agreed to the original offer, so I guess in my own way, and to a certain extent, I earned his respect at that moment.

Our first night on stage was at a place called Club Malibu, which was one of three under that name in the city at the time. We were all beyond nervous going out for that first show. It was a Monday night, and the bar was wall-to-wall women. As we walked in, the group of girls all turned to look at us like we were fresh meat. Outside of my former group, I believe they had only seen one other male dance revue for quite some time. It was exciting and scary, but we went out there and did the best we could with the tools that we had. It was a huge success, and the crowd loved us, regardless of our mistakes. After the show, Cole came up to me and mentioned that some hottie just blew him. He said the coat-check girl had a friend taking care of customers while they did their deed behind the coat rack in a small space with a chair. We walked back to the coat-check, and Cole introduced me to her. I met her friend at the same time, and within a few minutes, I was back there behind the jackets getting a blowjob as well! As nasty as that may seem, to this day, it's a story that Cole and I still bring up occasionally and chuckle about. He was the ultimate wingman. Afterwards, I went up to the bar where Cole stood and ordered a beer—we tapped bottles and continued with the night. We just did the dirty deed right there in the bar, and it was, admittedly, risqué. The next day was my birthday, so I called it a night and went back to the hotel.

The next night, we danced at the second of the three Club Malibu's we worked on this tour. It was located in West Edmonton Mall, and once again, it was a packed house. It seemed like everything we touched turned to gold, and we had another fantastic show. Jordan came up to me afterwards and said: *Buddy, I heard it's your birthday!* After I confirmed, he said: *I'll make you a deal, buddy. I'm going to line up ten Sambuca shooters for you. If you finish them all in the next ten minutes, I will buy you another ten, buddy.* Of course, I agreed, and within ten minutes, I had finished them all. He came back and ordered another ten. Through my drunken haze, I could only remember so much, but the shooter girl stood out with her gun holsters fittingly holding the Sambuca bottles and her shot glasses strapped across her beautiful body. She knew she was hot, but she also knew it was my birthday, so she paid special attention to me. I drank the next ten shooters, and to the best of my memory, Jordan ordered yet another row. I believe I drank 25 to 30 shooters that night, and somehow, the whole group of us ended up on the bar performing the YMCA.

I was beyond hammered when the closing bell rang. It was all a bit of a blur, but I do remember making out with the shooter girl after the bar closed. She was lost in the shuffle when the other dancers found me, and I went back to the hotel without her. It was a bit disappointing, but I was so out of it that I wouldn't have remembered much, and my performance was bound to be sub-par. Looking back, it was unreal how much I could drink at the age of 24 while recovering for the next day with a minimal hangover. The next day, I picked myself up and tried to reset for the next show at the third club on the tour. It was called *Club Malibu The Morgue*, and it was an actual morgue at one time. It had a creepy yet cool vibe, and we had another packed house for the third night in a row. It was like a stripper's dream when the opening music came on, and the crowd began screaming at the top of their lungs. Although I was still dealing with the hangover from the night before, I did my best to follow along with our opening choreography. Midway through our routine, I locked eyes with a woman who made my head spin—the shooter girl suddenly became a distant memory. This was the third woman in three nights, and she stood near the front of the stage—an absolute stunner. She had piercing blue eyes, long blonde hair, and a body that didn't stop. But I did. This girl stopped me in my tracks on stage. And then, after skipping a beat or two, I joined back in.

I had this thing with blonde girls for some reason,
and if blonde was a flavour, I loved the taste of it.

One of the dancers came up to me in the changeroom after the show and told me that this blonde beauty was waiting for me right outside of the door. He said that if I wasn't going to go talk to her, he would. As I stepped out the door to introduce myself, she reached out her hand, looked me in the eye and said: *Jenny.* There was an instant attraction, and I smiled back at her and gave her my real name: *Corey.* After the club, the group went for pizza, and when she tagged along with us, they knew instantly—*that love at first sight* thing happened again. They all hoped I would continue my little slut fest, but my focus was on her for the rest of the tour. It started off dirty, which was thrilling, but I was locked in with her almost immediately. The next night, Jordan asked us who was willing to do a gay bar show, and Cole and I chose to take it on. The booking was at a club called Options, and we still chuckle about that to this day. The underlying question was: *Which option are you going to go with tonight? Man? Woman? Or both?*

The other dancers in our group came down to the show with us, and as we walked in, we heard a woman's voice on the mic. They were finishing up a drag show, and when we saw the emcee, we realized that *Twiggy* was a man. He wasn't the best-looking drag queen I had ever seen, and Twiggy wasn't just gay—he was flaming. The gay bars always seemed to have a story, good or bad, but on this occasion, it was good because Twiggy was very professional and treated us with respect. We did our shows and moved on to the next gig, but the image of Twiggy was almost impossible to forget. A couple of years later, I was booked back in Edmonton at a different gay bar. As I grabbed a drink, a construction worker came up to the bar, ordered a beer and sat down. He was wearing a white t-shirt and jeans, along with a baseball cap, and he had a long, scraggly beard. He looked over at me and said: *Hey Dalton!* in his deep voice. Surprised, I looked over and asked how I knew him. He said: *It's me, Twiggy!* I almost fell out of my chair. He had a totally different voice and an obvious makeover from the last time I saw him. We chatted for a little while and then went our separate ways—I realized that I could never be sure who I might be talking with. It's a small world, and what I had perceived him to be, ended up being someone completely different. I never knew his real name, but Twiggy was memorable and a genuinely nice person.

For the rest of the tour, when each show ended, I met up with Jenny because I was satisfied with what I had and wasn't looking for anyone else. The following week, we were back at the Club Malibu in West Edmonton Mall, and she surprised me by renting a hotel room for us at The Fantasyland Hotel. This place had multiple theme rooms, and she chose the Polynesian room with bamboo-lined hallways leading up to the door and a waterfall in the room that filled the hot tub. The bedposts were mermaid tails, and the ceiling was mirrored with lights inset behind them. It was beyond erotic with the reflection of her sweet body on top of me. The experience was off the charts, and she went above and beyond to create an unforgettable moment for us. Up until that point, I had never had a woman do anything like that for me, and I couldn't let it just be one night. I was addicted, and within a month, I decided to move to Edmonton, chasing this girl who fulfilled me with a deep sexual connection. I was looking for love and acceptance and thought I found it, but just because we had great sex didn't necessarily mean we experienced personal fulfillment within our relationship.

Before heading out to be with Jenny in Edmonton, I stayed with my folks in the camper they had parked in their backyard for a few days. I wanted to spend time with them before making my move further away from home than I had ever been. I had been dancing for a few years, and my parents saw me transition from the innocent little boy who hugged his father's legs when he came home from work to a man who worked in a world they had no clue about. The emotion my father could rarely express was a boulder in my mother's path of expressing her love. She just couldn't voice it, especially in front of him. They were depression-era people who had experienced so much turmoil and hid it from their children, except on the occasions when my mother drank, which I never personally witnessed but was told about.

My mother had a special connection with her daughter, and my biological mother, Gayle—different from what she had with her other children. There were times when they shared emotional moments that truly counted, usually through the haze of alcohol that occurred long before I was born. My biological mother shared this with me after my adopted mother's passing. I cannot imagine how hard it must have been for her to admit this because I know how impossible it is to feel true love without emotional connection. The love our family had for one another was always there, but it was expressed in a different way than most.

It was my last night at home before leaving to start an unknown journey with Jenny to a place entirely out of my comfort zone. My mother and I were out in the camper, and she was making sure the bed was set up properly—I could tell that she was procrastinating. She was concerned about my journey and didn't know when she would see me again. After fidgeting around for a few minutes, she finally broke and said the three words I had been waiting to hear most of my life. She turned, hugged me, and told me she loved me. As she turned to walk back to the house, I told her I loved her as well. She closed the door and went inside. At that moment, that 24-year-old kid broke, lying there in bed crying tears of joy and sadness. I was so happy she could finally express what she had always felt, yet so saddened that it took so many years to finally say it. Those words were so very important to me, and they made an impact. They were words I could not express myself for many years, and it was like 24 years of emotion poured out of me in one split second. She provided so much for me during her time on this earth, but she never gave me as much as she did that night.

The next day, I left for my new journey into the unknown, living my life as a jumper—the type of person who jumps at opportunities to explore new relationships in search of fulfillment. I couldn't seem to discover it within myself but always tried to find it through others. At the time, I didn't know how unhealthy that was, and Jenny made me happy and excited because she took me outside of my comfort zone, pushing the limits, even if most of those limits were mainly sexual. We stopped in Leduc and stayed with her parents for the first few weeks. Ironically, it was the same small town where I had the experience with the bachelorette girl and her friends in the hotel. When I arrived, Jenny's parents were not home, so we immediately jumped into her bed. We were so into one another that we forgot to close the bedroom door, and it was on. Thankfully, we were under the covers when her mom unexpectedly walked past her room. I was in her parents' house, who I had never met, and I was having sex with her daughter as she walked by! Later, when introduced, nothing seemed out of the ordinary, so I still wonder if she saw anything or not that day. It didn't matter, though, because nothing was holding us back, and we loved it. Jenny and I had a fantastic sexual connection that involved taking chances. One hot summer night, we went to a park, and with no one around, we decided to have sex on a picnic table. A group of kids rode by on their bikes, and again, I don't think they saw anything, but it was memorable. That passionate moment of being risky and naughty all at the same time was such a turn on for us both, and we seemed to feed off it.

Eventually, we found an apartment in Calgary, roughly three hours south of Edmonton. It was a crappy little place in an artsy district of town, and I think we must've cleaned that place for three days to make it somewhat livable. Our relationship started off great, but I believe we were more in lust than in love. From the moment we chose to move to Calgary, everything went downhill because our connection was one-dimensional with minimal understanding of one another's wants and needs. I was working as a doorman at a local nightclub while performing shows I got through my agent, and Jenny worked as a beer girl at a different club. It was a perfect recipe for failure, but we carried on, surviving on lust until the house of cards came crashing down.

As usual, we were messing around in the living room one day, and I picked her up to throw her over my shoulder, caveman style. She was laughing at me as I carried her into the bedroom, but when I started to take her clothes off, the laughter suddenly stopped. She said that she couldn't do anything right now, and at that moment, I didn't understand. Then she dropped the bomb that she had herpes and that she had been holding back telling me from the time we met. I was upset, not because she had herpes, but because she didn't tell me until that day. I had been having sex with her for over two months, and in my mind, I was at risk the entire time. In hindsight, I understood why she wouldn't have initially said anything because it's not generally something you share with someone when first introduced. However, I took it personally and made it all about myself. She tried to be open and honest with me, and I completely overreacted without considering her feelings.

Yet another lesson I learned about focusing on my exterior instead of addressing my internal issues.

Things got ugly in no time, and she started coming home drunk with bar friends, losing all respect for our relationship and herself. It was like self-sabotage, but I didn't help matters much. We tried to end it respectfully, but I took it hard. Living with someone after breaking up is not exactly a fun thing, and me being in my early 20s, I wasn't as mature as I could have been. I didn't take any accountability for our breakup, and she acted out because I was not being man enough emotionally to connect with her to find a resolution. So, to keep my mind preoccupied, I decided to sand and stain an old antique dresser. We were on the third floor of the apartment complex, and I had all of my tools with a can of stain outside the door to the balcony, planning to finish it by the next day. Jenny came home late with some people from the bar, and I woke up to a smash and the sound of one of her friends complaining about tripping over something. I got up to see that he had tripped over the can of stain and dumped it down to the floor below onto the neighbours' bikes. It also splashed onto Jenny's car, which was conveniently parked in the perfect spot. She started screaming at me and blamed me for having it out there in the first place. I was beyond upset because her drunk buddy should have been watching where he was going, but I avoided the confrontation and climbed outside down from the third to second-floor balcony to clean our poor neighbours' bikes in the middle of the night. Embarrassed, I went down the next day to apologize.

Thankfully, they were nice people and didn't really care...but I did.

It went from bad to worse when I heard through the grapevine that she was going home with the hypnotist guy who did a show in random clubs around town. Everything was breaking down around me, and I was lost and alone in a new city. My reason for moving there in the first place had moved on. What did I expect, though? I completely blamed her and would not accept responsibility for my part in our breakup. At the time, I thought it was all her fault, and I blamed her for everything instead of working to find a solution with a little more education and precaution. She buried her pain in alcohol, and I had my own pity party in my somewhat immature mind. I believed I was the victim, and my confidence took a dramatic hit.

Around that time, my father came to Calgary to visit relatives, and when I told him the story, he provided what he could for advice, which was a dose of reality and little emotion as usual. He said he was sorry I was going through it, but I had no idea what a bad day truly was. He painted me a picture of his experience before being deployed to fight in the North Atlantic in World War II. He said he was 18 years old, which was the legal age to fight in a war but not to buy a drink in Canada. He went into a bar to get a beer, and the bartender refused to serve him. He had to leave his wife pregnant at home and didn't know if he would make it back. Although my heart shattered, he made me feel just a little better as he told me his story of sacrifice. He always had a way of making me take a step back to think about what I had gotten myself into, whether good or bad.

A few months went by, and after finding a new place to live, I was back working the circuit and saw that Jenny had moved on to dating one of the other male dancers. Andrew was an entertainer from Florida who was touring with another group, and he seemed to be full of himself, which was typical of many of the dancers on the circuit. I saw him out at the club, and we got into a conversation about her that I wish I had never started. But I did, and I opened my big mouth, letting the cat out of the bag about her condition, which was none of my business in the first place. If I had taken the time to connect with her instead of making it all about me, things would not have gone sideways as they did. I told Andrew out of jealousy, and I wish I had kept my mouth shut. I can't say that I blame her for being upset, but I was still hurting inside from an overwhelming sense of abandonment. She never passed anything to me, but I never spoke to her again. I mistakened the sensation of lust for love, and this became a common thread for me.

The Naked Truth

My ego assumed that my exterior image could get me through almost anything, but my internal battles were never addressed and fed an ongoing struggle with my self-identity.

Not everyone perceives the world through my lens. Just because I disagree with someone doesn't mean I cannot respect the other person's perspective. In the current world of communication, people tend to see things as black and white, or right or wrong, with no grey area whatsoever. I may be living within a completely different environment or culture from someone else, which provides a completely different outlook. I may believe I am right about something, but there are times when it is best to simply let others know that I disagree while respecting their perspective. From their perspective, they believe they are right, so how can I disregard their point of view. Respecting another person's perspective provides a better chance that they respect mine even if they disagree.

I assumed that the bachelorette girl was just out with some friends, celebrating her upcoming commitment to her partner through the bond of marriage. I could not have imagined in my wildest dreams what I witnessed that night, similarly to my perception of Twiggy being based solely on the image I saw in front of me when we first met. Although he looked like a completely different person the next time I saw him, my initial perception of him was a flaming drag queen instead of the person I sat and had a beer with years later.

My perception of Jenny was the most significant of all. I perceived her to be this perfect woman with whom I had a deep sexual connection with. However, when she exposed her truth, that perfect image was tarnished, and although she was being vulnerable, I was not willing to reciprocate. Until I took the time to understand myself through honest introspection, I couldn't empathize and took offense blaming others for things they may or may not have had any control over in the first place.

Regardless of what I may have been thinking at that time, I needed to realize that I was fifty percent of the problem. When managing relationship conflicts now, I focus on making sure my ego isn't blinding me from the reality of the situation.

I was never able to break this cycle until being willing to accept my truth. I needed to be satisfied with the process of progression that included falling in love with my imperfections instead of unrealistically striving for perfection within my personal and professional life.

This didn't happen overnight. It took creating the space through detachment in my life without the distraction of an environment of clutter and mess around me. Simply stated, I got clear on what mattered in my life and got rid of everything else that didn't, regardless of how hard it may have been to break old habits that held me back from becoming the greatest version of myself. Without clarity, things that once seemed impossible would have stayed impossible.

Gratitude & Naivety

V

Climbing the Mountain with No Peak

Filtering through the residue of my relationship with Jenny, I chose to stay in Calgary, working at a club called Dewey Stevens. It was one of the most popular clubs in Calgary at that time and known for an amazing ladies' night. I was bouncing some nights and dancing the circuit on others. Most of the major stripping contests were held at this club, which was exciting and fed my hunger for friendly competition. Yes, we held stripping contests.

I believe it was around November 1994 when I crossed paths with Cassie. The timing couldn't have been better because we were both dealing with shit from the past, and it was good to have someone to lean on and vice versa. Life was so unstable and unpredictable at the time, and, ironically, assumptions were flying around the club that I was promiscuous, even though I was taking time away from getting intimate with anyone. I didn't want to put myself or anyone else through a rebound. However, she was such a down-to-earth, good person that I couldn't resist getting to know her. It didn't take long before I realized that the feeling was mutual and, surprisingly, she was a brunette!

She oozed sex appeal with an added touch of friendship. She was a girlfriend, yet our connection ran deeper than that. She was great relationship material—it just wasn't the right time for us. Unfortunately, we didn't date for very long, but we shared some sweet moments, which I will fondly remember forever. My road changed direction when I moved to Edmonton not long after Cassie and I met because I was offered a position in a dance review called *Total Ecstasy*. She came up to visit for New Year's 1995 and stayed in a condo I shared with three other dancers. Jessie, the manager, brought us all together to start a new group consisting of me, along with Rico, a black dancer who had long dreads and his friend, Julian, a well-built European entertainer. It was an interesting dynamic because we were strangers to one another, and then suddenly, we were roommates, each with our fair share of ego to pass around. It would have made a great reality show.

Cassie and I often sat outside wrapped around one another, sharing cigarettes and having conversations about life in minus twenty degrees Celsius temperature. Like so many situations in my past, I didn't know what sat right beside me. She was a total sweetheart, and I realize now that taking things for granted can be the hardest lesson to learn. She enjoyed watching my shows and took advantage of the opportunity to come out to a local watering hole in Edmonton. Unfortunately, we went in different directions, but the times I shared with her were nothing but positive. She was a shoulder to lean on, and I had no issue giving her mine. She was there for a reason, and I have nothing but respect and gratitude for that girl.

Total Ecstasy was a low point in my Canadian dance career. Jessie was a long-haired goofball who could carry on a normal conversation at times, but there were many moments when I wondered if his mother bumped him on the head when he was a toddler. However, he was also connected, and once he was able to get a few dancers to work with him, he got the accounts because the clubs desperately needed fresh meat. A few clubs in the area committed to working with us as an alternative to a revue called *Body FX*. They were a well-respected group with solid choreography and marketed well with a massive local following. Ironically, their manager, Pat, was the contestant who placed just ahead of me in my division a few years earlier when I competed in the bodybuilding arena.

When *Total Ecstasy* was created, I helped put together some simple choreography, and we went to work. Outside of the local shows, Jessie booked us in every shit hole town in Northern Alberta. He was a clown, and working the road with him was an experience, to say the least. The boys and I were tempted to punch him out many nights because he got drunk and turned into a complete moron. One night, while in a drunken stupor, he lost the keys to the tour van in about two feet of snow. We fortunately recovered, but he decided to get so annihilated that he barely knew his own name. Julian and Rico brought a couple of club girls back to their hotel room while Jessie sat in the corner of the room and watched them like a creeper. He was especially aggravating when he was drunk because he turned into a completely different person. Embarrassing as he was, his act was even worse. He entered the stage trying to be a rock star stripper singing Bon Jovi songs over an altered version of the original track, and the original vocals lowered while he sang into the microphone. It was cheesy and uncool, all wrapped up in one package. Some nights, we stood at the back of the room watching and cringing while he performed Whether he was on his high horse or just plain stubborn, he often did the last act of the night and tried his best to emcee, which was sub-par.

To top everything off, I experienced a couple of my most brutal injuries working with this group. At one point, we were performing to a very small crowd in a little club in Edson, Alberta. Dancers generally did two fast songs and then a slow one. If the tips were flowing, we added an encore. I always tried to create original performances, and when I began my slow song, I poured Pert Shampoo down my chest because it glowed bright green under the black lights and provided a unique effect. After the song ended, I cleaned up my mess but missed a large spot because the main lights came on, and it blended into the colour of the dance floor. Transitioning into my encore, I strutted across the stage, and my foot hit a wet banana just as the DJ turned the black lights back on. Flying into the air, I landed straight on my ass in a green pool of glowing shampoo. As embarrassing as it was, I sprayed a couple of girls in the front row. It was just shampoo, so they weren't upset, and they got quite a show. However, my tailbone hurt for days afterward.

The injury that topped them all off happened when we worked at *Barry T's* club in Edmonton. The house was packed, and the stage was set up *In the Round*. It was constructed with scaffolding material roughly six feet above the dance floor, and large sheets of plywood created an elevated stage at eye level with the audience. Making one of my most popular moves, I spun from one side of the stage to the other. Completing my last spin when I usually plant my foot on the ground and kick out in the opposite direction, I missed the side of the stage altogether, and my foot landed in the air. As my ankle dragged across the edge of the stage, the plywood scraped up the inside of my leg, and my crotch bounced off the edge of the scaffolding. I found myself lying six feet below on the main dance floor bleeding everywhere and writhing in pain. It was so brutal that the entire crowd dropped into silence. Rico came running up, thinking I may have broken my leg, but at that moment, most of the damage was done to my pride. Picking myself up, I chose to finish the show, and to my surprise, there was a massive lineup of girls throwing money at me while I performed my final song on a blanket. They may have been sympathy tips, but I wasn't about to turn the money down.

Living with three egotistical male dancers in a condo was far from easy. I made the gym my sanctuary to keep my sanity, and during that time, I befriended a couple of bodybuilders named Bruce and Nate. Nate and I got into a conversation about steroids one day, and I mentioned that I knew a connection in Spain who could get the best of the best. After some research, the three of us chose to invest in our own venture instead of paying a middleman to send over the product. I knew where my old partners got it from in the south—a small tourist haven called Torremolinos. I also knew what was involved but thought it was worth it to fly over there independently and make double the money. My three roommates wanted product ASAP, and they were willing to pay a high price for priority delivery. The risk was huge, and I needed to figure out a way to pull it off. Based on the contacts Bruce and Nate had, we would sell out if we could get the product back to Canada. So, I decided to sacrifice bringing some product back with me to get it home for their deadline.

It all became real when we arranged the flight to Madrid, and I was beyond nervous being the main man. This was long before electronic transfers existed, so I had to carry a bundle of cash with me. Irresponsibly, I arrived at the airport late and barely caught my flight, which added to my stress. Europe was a whole new world to me, and I am not the type to turn down an adventure, so I pushed everything in my life to borderline insanity without officially crossing over.

*I was trying to find the glorious view
at the top of the mountain.*

Arriving in Madrid in the middle of the night, I exchanged my money and immediately took a bus to Torremolinos. I was oblivious to the possibility of what could happen—I was alone and didn't speak Spanish. However, I knew where to go and took the long, lonely bus ride to the southern tip of Spain, arriving in Torremolinos at roughly five in the morning. The party never stopped in Torremolinos, with people still stumbling out of pubs and bars. It was the start of a Sunday morning, and I took a moment to smell the fabulous fresh baked bread permeating the air from the bakeries.

Fortunately, I found a little place to stay above a British pub called *The Parrot*. I was quite the sight to see walking down the street with two suitcases in hand. In comparison to most of the Spaniards I witnessed, I was a freakshow. If only I could have recorded the looks on people's faces as I walked down the street with heads turning from all angles. After getting a much-needed rest, the first place I looked for was a gym, and I stumbled across a place called *Olympic Gymnasio* with both an indoor and an outdoor area to train. The outdoor area was a rooftop deck with multiple free-weight benches and dumbbells, along with a view of the Mediterranean Sea right in front of me. It was the most beautiful view I've ever experienced while working out—almost surreal.

My next mission was to find a local pharmacy, which was not hard. There seemed to be one on every corner, and I could access and purchase as much product as my budget would permit. I then proceeded to bring it all back to my room in a couple of huge garbage bags. Each tiny glass ampule was wrapped in a box that took up most of the space, so I discarded the boxes and spent hours in my little room sticking each ampule in a line onto a strip of duct tape. I then placed the strips in packages, and once each package was full, I carefully wrapped them in photographic paper to block the X-Ray machines at customs. I saw the way the middleman, Juan, delivered them for years, and it worked. So, the next day, I shipped them, anticipating their arrival at my door in Canada within four to six weeks with a fake return address attached.

I spent two weeks in the Mediterranean, enjoying the food, the culture, and the beach. I have always found people who travel to be more interesting than those comfortably sheltered in what they know. There were times when I sat at a patio table having an espresso, and a stranger approached to say hello and have a conversation. At first, it shocked me because it was so foreign compared to what I experienced back in Canada where my guard would have come up instantly. But it was common at that time in Torremolinos, and I enjoyed the authentic human connection. It fascinated me because so many young people there spoke multiple languages, and they wanted to have a meaningful conversation with no other intention. This was long before cell phones decreased face to face interaction, and I am grateful I had that experience.

I was so very naive, and although most of my interactions were very positive, I remember a few incidents that got me in trouble. Somehow, I struck up a conversation with a young man who seemed relatable and trustworthy. We decided to visit a cool little cafe with signatures on almost every wall area from past satisfied customers. After we finished our meals, he asked me if I took offence to him smoking some hash. Although it wasn't my thing, I had no issues with it. I expected him to pull out a little chunk, but instead, he pulled out the biggest hash brick I had ever seen and used a knife to cut a piece off. I respectively declined when he offered me some, and I'm glad that I did.

We left the café, and he told me that he lived in an apartment just around the corner and needed to go up to get something. When he invited me up, I felt no threat whatsoever, so I followed along. I should have been more cautious, but I was young and not thinking of the trouble I could get myself into with a stranger I only knew for a few hours. As we entered his place, he went into the bedroom and returned with a pair of night-vision goggles and a few different maps of the Mediterranean Sea with markings on them between Spain and Morocco. He said he was a hash runner, and he and his partners were running hash by the ton from Morocco into Spain. I will never know why he opened up to me, but it may have been because I was a friendly Canadian who he related to. Or maybe there was a different motive…

At that moment, my father's words popped into my head which always seemed to show up in the most critical times. Especially in my teenage years, he constantly told me that even if I was one hundred percent innocent, I could go down with the rest of them by being in the wrong place at the wrong time. I suddenly realized that this could be one of those moments, and I made up some excuse and got out of there immediately. The fear of what I knew or the prospect of being caught with him presented itself like a tidal wave rushing over my body. There were untold possibilities of what the Spanish police could do to me. *Thanks, Dad. You helped me at that moment, and you never even knew about it.*

After that experience, I chose to lay low, but as the days

went on, I met some of the most interesting people while frequenting the bar downstairs. The Parrot provided a cozy atmosphere, and the longer I stayed, the more conversations I had with the locals. And the first thing that stuck in each of their minds was that I was a stripper from Canada. One of them was Mario, a very likable, middle-aged Italian bartender who took the time to ask me stories about my life. We shared some great laughs over my two-week stay, with a classic moment coming to mind when I ordered a whole chicken for dinner. The place was packed as I sat at the bar with Mario who tried to teach me Spanish. He, along with a few others, laughed so hard when I made a mistake while ordering my food, but I didn't care. I said the word loudly, and if I messed up, I messed up.

My dinner came out, and I stripped that chicken down until there was not one piece of meat left on it. The server came from the kitchen and yelled: *El Pollo Esta Muerto!* Or in English: *The Chicken Is Dead!* I attempted to repeat what he said: *El Pene Esta Muerto!* Suddenly, the entire room absolutely lost it. Mario was behind the bar at this point, chuckling so hard that tears poured out of his eyes. Embarrassingly, I discovered that I had said: *The Penis Is Dead!* Looking back on that memory, it was the worst and the best thing I could have said at that moment as the male exotic dancer from Canada. To this day, I am trying to figure out how I managed to say *penis* instead of *chicken*. I'm glad I did, though, because I like when people remember me for something positive, even if it was self-deprecating.

Another memorable moment at The Parrot was when I struck up a conversation with a beautiful, blonde, Irish girl. People frequented Torremolinos from multiple European countries, and that created a stimulating cultural experience. Unintentionally, I made an impression on this girl, and as we left the bar, I casually mentioned it might be nice to try to meet for coffee later in the day, and she agreed. It was one of those moments when I realized the impact of the power of words because there was no set time or guarantee we would meet, and for some reason that I can't remember, I didn't make it back that day. I didn't think much of it, but apparently, her perception was completely different from mine. The next day arrived, and while I sat downstairs having breakfast, an Irishman burst through the door yelling at me for standing up his little sister. My guard went up immediately, and although I was sitting in shock, I was forced to fight fire with fire. I stood up from my barstool and told him I didn't realize she and I had an appointment. I then noticed his sister standing behind him with tears in her eyes. Going over and apologizing to her for the misunderstanding, her brother continued yelling at me. I suppose it may have been a cultural thing, but I made no assumptions, and although I didn't want the conflict, I had no other choice than to put him in his place. Calmly, I told him that if I had to walk across the room to deal with this, I would smash him into the ground, and neither one of us would win. He turned and stormed out, muttering something under his breath.

I learned never to assume what the other person may be thinking. What I thought was casual was completely different in her eyes, and my words were regretfully misinterpreted. In this era of social media, I fully understand how quickly conflict arises through impersonal posts taken out of context. I have seen many people become warriors of the keyboard because they are not communicating face-to-face, and in many cases, would never dream of sharing some of the things they do online. Before I post or text someone, I think about this story and send it to myself first to explore what emotions arise when I receive it. I then adjust it if necessary because I don't want to hurt or piss off any followers online, especially someone's brother from Ireland.

My two weeks in Torremolinos were ending, and I was getting a little stir crazy hanging out at The Parrot. So, I checked out this one nightclub down the street called the Palladium. I was drawn to it and wanted to explore it because it looked pretty spectacular. I walked in and heard electronic music for the very first time in my life. At that moment, it sounded terrible, but I was fascinated by the inside of this three-story club. There was a bar and dance floor on the bottom, separated by a thick glass wall with a swimming pool on the other side. I stood there intrigued by the scene in front of me: crazy Australians running around naked and jumping into the pool with people on the dance floor right next to them. I never experienced anything like the borderline mayhem in front of me. Then, up a flight of stairs, the atmosphere was even more unbelievable as people dove into the swimming pool from the third floor. The crowd encompassed people from all over the world, and they were partying like rock stars, having the time of their lives.

Standing there entirely out of my element, a young Spaniard approached me who introduced himself as Juan. Being in Spain, many people were named Juan, but I wondered what the chances were that this could my old partner's middleman. Could my luck be that bad that the one *Juan* I met was *that* Juan? Then, he asked where I was from, and I told him Canada. He then asked specifically where I was from in Canada, and, fortunately, I lied because I wasn't hard to pick out in a crowd. We carried on with some small talk, and then he dropped the bomb. He mentioned that he did business with a friend in Canada by the name of Cade, and he used Cade's correct last name. Even though I am a horrible liar, I managed to keep my cool and denied knowing Cade or anyone else he mentioned. I remember laughing it off, diverting the conversation by saying there were as many guys named Cade in Canada as there were Juans in Spain.

Instead of leaving immediately, I waited around not to set off any alarms. However, when I left the club, I saw him and his crew outside sitting on Harley Davidson's. They looked organized, and I remained emotionless, walking by them down the street while they stared at me. I kept looking forward with the worst thoughts running through my head; I was alone in Spain, and two drug dealers from Alberta, Canada, were the only people on the planet who knew where I was. It was a dangerous situation, and my life could have ended in an instant. I was incredibly stressed the whole time, thinking to myself: *I could get a bullet in the back of the head, and if so, I may never be found.* I could have vanished off the face of the earth with everyone I ever knew being tormented, wondering what happened to me for the rest of their lives. I went back to my room and stayed there with all the *what if's* running through my head. I truly believe that at that moment, I put myself in a place that could have been beyond tragic for a young man in his early twenties.

> **I was risking my life all for the sake of money, and I could have been lost forever—a mystery to everyone I ever loved and who ever loved me.**

Reflecting on this experience pushed me to call my parents the next day, and the sound of my mother's voice put my stressed mind at ease. I explained that I was in Spain and my agent sent me there to do a tour. She knew that I toured as a dancer, and I was compelled to let her know I was alive. Although she was somewhat shocked to hear I was in Europe, she really wasn't that surprised, given my track record. We didn't express our emotions to one another often enough, but I told her I loved her that day because I was afraid of the possibility of never having the chance to say those words to her again.

On my last day, I shipped most of the product through airmail, but as insane as it was, I decided to carry a certain amount with me on the plane back through Frankfurt, Germany and then back to Canada. In the present, I would never consider doing this, but I was young and not thinking straight. During my five-hour layover, I stressfully waited at the Frankfurt airport with armed guards walking around in twos around me. I had multiple strips of glass ampules attached to my body, and it was beyond uncomfortable, but I needed to get them home. I confidently walked through customs to get my passport stamped, saying hello to the straight-faced agent while playing the role of the happy Canadian tourist. Without saying anything, he pounded the stamp into my passport, and I boarded the plane for my long journey home. The risk I took was massive, and it could have been worse in more ways than one. However, roughly a month and a half later, our shipment arrived at my door in Edmonton. Julian didn't believe it could be done until that doorbell rang. His skepticism vanished immediately when I opened the package. *Can't* simply wasn't in my vocabulary. In the end, my partners and I made a huge profit, and everything was good. For all the stress I went through, the payoff was worth it. However, little did I know at the time that this wouldn't be my last trip to Spain.

Out of pure frustration a few months later, Rico and I chose to move out of Jessie's place, and we rented a two-bedroom apartment in downtown Edmonton. It was mid-winter when we dumped the steroids from our first shipment, and although I almost got myself killed the first time, I chose to go again. I planned to fly into Barcelona this time and figure everything out when I arrived. The architecture was beyond anything I imagined, so I toured around the city for a couple of days. Just like the last time, there was a pharmacy on every corner, so I picked one and asked for a couple of different types of steroids. Although he spoke broken English, he understood I was looking for quantity, but he only brought me one vial of each. He wrote the name *Luis Roblas* on a piece of paper along with an address and told me to go to Benidorm roughly 500 kilometres away. Fortunately, I had two weeks to work with, so I stayed the night and then took the train to Alicante and cabbed from there to Benidorm.

After getting booked into a hotel, I took a taxi to meet Luis. As soon as I walked in and introduced myself, he knew what I was looking for. He took me into the back of the pharmacy and asked what I needed. I took my pick of the best steroids on the market and ordered thousands of dollars' worth in one purchase. I then rented a little place above a pub and went through the same process of putting together my boxes to be sent back to Canada. However, I stayed out of the spotlight this time. The craziest thing I did one night was going to a small club up the street called *Zanzibar*. It was a gay club recommended by one of the locals who said the drag show was very entertaining. When I walked in, I witnessed some of the ugliest drag queens imaginable. From the lens I was looking through that night, Spanish men dressed up as women didn't work very well, but they were entertaining, and another memory was created.

People from multiple countries across Europe flocked to Benidorm for the food, music, clubs, and beaches. Also, since the fishing boats pulled right up to the restaurants to drop off their fresh supply of flavourful seafood, I tasted some of the best calamari I've ever eaten. It was a fun vibe, and my ego was boosted during my daily jog down the boardwalk with my shirt off. I sensed eyes on me everywhere I went because I was huge and ripped to shreds, unlike the vast majority of Spaniards I crossed paths with. I took advantage of the clean, made-for-humans anabolic steroid *Winstrol*, readily available and easily taken through insulin needle injections directly into my quadriceps. The results were off the charts, and I was gaining muscle and leaning out more and more every day. People stared at me like I was an alien, but I smiled back and took it as a compliment. Even though I was used to getting attention as a dancer exposed to the public for quite some time, I found the response amusing, entertaining, and a self-confidence booster. I also explored a beautiful nude beach and found a smooth rock there half exposed out of the water. It was the perfect setting to swim out to and lay naked, relaxing while watching a film crew shoot a Spanish fitness show on the beach. It was so picturesque that I regretted not doing a photoshoot when the opportunity knocked.

After spending two weeks in paradise, I mailed off my product and took the long train ride back to Barcelona. From there, I would catch a flight to Frankfurt in the early morning, and the next stop was Calgary, where I planned to board a smaller plane to fly back home to Edmonton. I began my trek back, and when I boarded my train car, I met a friendly traveller from Russia; we bought a couple of beers and shared some stories about our countries. However, I was low on cash because I spent almost every dollar on product. I had my train and plane ticket home, so I was satisfied because I was going to double what I put into it for every amp sent back.

I invested as much as I could with no safety net.

In the middle of that night, I fell asleep and suddenly woke up to the crash of thunder. We were going through Valencia when the train slowed to a crawl, and we discovered it was struck by lightning! I was concerned because we were travelling all night to get to Barcelona, and this delay was going to cut it close for my connections. When we finally arrived at the next station, the entire train was unloaded, and we were forced to wait for another train to arrive. I became nervous when I saw it was full, but thankfully there was room on the floor, so I had no choice but to leave the comfortable train car to take a seat there. Although it was overwhelming, my new Russian friend and I carried on with our conversation and laughed at the insanity of the situation.

When we finally arrived in Barcelona, it was five-thirty in the morning, and my flight was leaving at seven-thirty. When I got off the train, my anxiety increased dramatically because I suddenly realized I was not even close to the airport, and I was flat broke without a credit card to back me up. There I was, looking distressed, standing alone in the crowded train station when my Russian friend tapped me on the shoulder and asked if I was alright. I told him the mistake I had made, and he asked me if I could help him carry his bags up to his room where he was staying at the hotel across the street. With a million things running through my mind, I figured it would distract me, and there was nothing to lose. As I brought his bags up to the door, he smiled and congratulated me on doing a fine job. I stood there confused, still wondering how I would get myself out of this mess until he pulled out his wallet and some cash. He then told me that this would pay for my taxi ride to the airport and provide me with enough to cover food for my trip home.

I offered to pay him back, he refused. The fact that he chose to help a stranger from halfway across the world hit me so hard that I almost shed a tear. I don't remember his name, but I still remember everything he said next. He made me a deal, asking me to tell this story to as many people as I could. He went on to say that, stereotypically, his people were perceived to be what the Russian government historically represented, but realistically, it didn't depict everyone in their country. He said that there are good people all over the world, and he was one of the good ones. This memory stuck with me for all these years, and I have told this story countless times, holding up my end of the deal by sharing this now. I learned the old adage to never judge a book by its cover; it's a small world, and even if only in my life for a short time, I will never know what kind of an impact someone can have on me.

With massive gratitude in my heart, I boarded the plane for the long journey home. I was up for at least 15 hours, and it took me another 19 and a half to get to Calgary. From there, I had a short flight back to Edmonton in a little prop plane. Being up for about 37 hours straight, I boarded that little prop plane for the flight back to Edmonton with no idea what was about to come next. Because of everything I went through, I was wired and could not sleep, and as we reached maximum elevation, we hit a storm, and the turbulence was insane. I saw the look of fear on parents' faces as their children cried beside them. The exhaustion overwhelmed me so much that I simply didn't care anymore. Finally, I came to the resolution that if I was going to die, then I was going to die. However, all ended well with the plane touching down safely back in frigid Edmonton. I took a taxi home, and when I arrived, my roommate, Rico, was hanging out in the living room stoned on the couch. He looked over at me and asked if I was alright, but

I didn't have the energy to explain, so I told him I would talk to him in the morning after I got some rest. I still had my clothes on when my head hit the pillow, and that was where it stayed.

And then, after everything I went through, the worst thing that could have happened, did happen. My package never arrived, and with each passing day, I hoped and prayed for it to show up, but it never did. To this day, I have no explanation as to where my shipment went, and that was hard for my two partners to understand. The threat of being killed became a reality again, but in a different way. I tried my best to explain to Jay, but he didn't take it very well, and I couldn't blame him because our whole investment vanished into thin air. I will never know if he believed me. However, I could only tell him what I knew, which wasn't much. Shortly afterwards, Jay went into a downward spiral and started using meth. Sadly, we lost touch as he went into a deep hole, which dramatically changed his personality. Eventually, he turned his life around from what I understood, but we never reconnected. I carried along, hoping that I wouldn't end up paying the ultimate price for a situation that was out of my control.

On the other hand, Bruce was working as a doorman at one of the local nightclubs, so I went by there in person to explain what happened the best that I could. I know he believed me when I told the story, but it still didn't change the fact that we all lost out on a massive profit. The loss was in the tens of thousands of dollars, and it was a very bitter pill to swallow because I couldn't trace the packages since they were full of drugs. I also exchanged large amounts of funds without considering if the government would track what I was doing. Things could have ended up far worse, but I was still alive, and my life was about to head in a completely different direction. From that incident on, I tried not to take each day for granted, knowing that tomorrow is not a given.

The Naked Truth

Many people take today for granted with the expectation that tomorrow is simply a given. My lack of experience, wisdom, and judgement could have easily ended my life while I tried to climb a mountain with no peak. There was no amazing view at the top, and I was disappointed when that boot of life kicked me back down that same mountain. Now, more than ever, I am grateful it did because I may not have made it to this moment, writing these words. There were many times when I perceived my road was paved in gold. However, I was not looking within myself for the happiness created from the memories of meaningful relationships, regardless of the cards I was dealt.

I have never been the type with one foot in and one foot out the door, being all in no matter what I am trying to create. Forever the optimistic artist, forming his clay, I find that life is short, and everything is temporary—it can all be gone in an instant. I learned that the hard way when the next chapter of my life was almost not written.

One word that comes to mind when I think about this time in my life is gratitude. I am beyond grateful to the kind man from Russia who helped me from the goodness in his heart. I am also thankful for the struggle I went through within experiences, good and bad. I find it essential to recognize these things in order to appreciate what life has given me. I am even grateful for the mental and physical pain I have endured because pain is necessary. It is like a fire alarm that goes off, warning me there is something wrong. In my opinion, covering up pain only exacerbates the situation, whereby addressing it clarifies what I need to heal, both mentally and physically.

There are times when I don't recognize what I am normally grateful for, and as a result, I take them for granted. One simple step I do to vastly improve my life is writing down a minimum of five things I am grateful for at the beginning of every day. I express and journal a new gratitude statement daily. Along with taking the time to acknowledge the best thing that happened to me at the end of that day, this practice is often a game-changer for me. It resets my mind to a place of positive momentum within the negativity in the world. Normalization depletes my gratitude but being aware of and appreciating the things in my life reduces that same normalization.

There is more to life than what I was programmed to think. Value is not determined by what I have but instead by what is in my soul. I appreciate my lowest moments now more than ever because they brought goodness into my life. When I cannot see the light at the end of the tunnel, I know I must be the light, especially when social media tends to sell lies. Like everyone, I have made mistakes and fought silent battles. However, the sun is guaranteed to rise and set every day presenting a chance for a new beginning with or without me. I have learned not to carry my pain into my present day or allow the repeated domino effect of yesterday's worries to become today's troubles. I can control my attitude and use gratitude and appreciation to stop allowing external things to determine what I believe is worthy. I can paint my own imperfectly, perfect picture filled with my mistakes, flaws, and beauty when I do this.

It has taken me a long time to provide myself with the same love I give others. But when I chose to love and be proud of myself and to be thankful for the life I was given, my life changed. I realized that the simple things in life are sometimes the most important.

Everyone has their own story. However, mine changed when I began reflecting: What if this was my last day or week on earth? Would I spend all the gas in my tank and die empty of everything I desired in life? Or would I leave some reserve in the tank of regret to be written in my obituary? It didn't take long to realize that I wanted to run that tank dry as a bone.

Relationships & Connection

VI

A New World

Within the connections I make, I always find new roads to explore and experiences to create, whether presented in small steps or gigantic leaps. The chapters in my life that required educated risks, including the one I took in Spain gave me clarity that everything can be taken away in a split second. Florida was my next chapter, where I became fully aware of this reality. I had an overwhelming desire to move in a different direction, so I followed a different path that provided me with new relationships without being normalized—I was very open to embracing change for more than one reason.

AJ Hamilton was the creator and agent for one of the best male dance revues in North America at the time. When we first met, I was working at the door at Casablanca's, and although he wasn't looking for anyone at the time, he gave me his card. He asked me to put it in a safe place, and if I ever considered moving to the Southern U.S., he would help me out. This was that time. When I called him, he was excited to hear from me and mentioned that his entire group had walked out on him to form another revue in Myrtle Beach, South Carolina. AJ then created a new group of ten dancers, and five of them were scheduled for a three-week tour in Canada. He made me an offer that was hard to refuse. He guaranteed me a permanent position if I learned the choreography and ensured the dancers would arrive at the shows on time. This was a new door opening into something I knew nothing about, but it excited me because it was an opportunity to dramatically expand my creativity.

Then, when I found out that my best buddy Cole was joining us on this adventure, it escalated the decision from good to great because I was taking a huge step out of my comfort zone, and he was a top-notch wingman who would support me. Along with Cole, AJ hired Johnny, another Vancouver dancer with many years of experience on the solo circuit. We had worked together a few times, and although he had a large ego, I appreciated his stage presence and ability to get a rise out of the crowd. However, he had no previous choreography experience, and dancing in a ten-man revue is a whole different beast. With that being said, I couldn't understand why AJ put him in a position to manage the group, but he did.

My new crew arrived in Canada, and it was like the first day of school, awkward yet exciting as we began touring throughout British Columbia from one small town to another. They were fascinated by the surrounding beauty, which I had taken for granted to a certain extent. Going into the final leg of the Canadian Tour, I held up my end of my deal with AJ—I felt confident with the routines, and the group was never late. As a result, the door was open to the states, and I stepped through with both feet, carrying the fear of leaving everything I knew running around in the back of my mind.

Club Lavela was known as the largest beach club in the U.S.

at the time and home to an electric Spring Break scene. The kind of show that AJ offered through his contract with the nightclub took far more than tying your dick off and dancing around a stage for 20 minutes while collecting tips. It took teamwork and dropping one's ego as much as possible. It was pretty obvious that AJ was hungry for new faces. However, although some dancers were more experienced than others, all-in-all he chose a top-notch group of men. Fatal Attraction and Ultimate Fantasy were highly regarded in the industry from touring across North America and Europe. We were all aware we had deep boots to fill.

Before I went down this new road and left Canada, I had to take one other very important step; I had to visit my parents to say goodbye because this wasn't going to be a short stint. I had no idea if or when I would be back, and I was aware of how emotional my mom was, seeing me leave towards an unscripted future again. She took the time to hug every one of the dancers before we left, and I don't believe it was just because they were good-looking. She wanted them to take care of me because she couldn't anymore. It warmed my heart to see the dancers' smiles as she expressed this emotion because they saw something rarely shared with them. I know they welcomed her hugs, but I appreciated the respect the crew gave her as well. They loaded up into the tour van, while my dad and I rode in his pickup, heading to the border. My usual butterflies came up in my stomach, and my dad gave me his usual words of wisdom on the drive across to the U.S. He told customs that he was going to get gas. It wasn't a lie as he simultaneously supported me to begin a three-day drive across the country with eight male exotic dancers all jammed into a tour van, along with a bed in the back to rotate sleeping and driving shifts.

As we travelled through Montana, the exhaustion from

stress took control, and I chose to sleep for a few hours while the American dancers each took two-hour turns at the wheel. Billy, a dancer from Tampa Bay, Florida, was driving on an interstate highway in North Dakota when I woke up to the van sliding sideways in the snow. He had never experienced snow before, which was a recipe for disaster, considering he was also pulling a loaded trailer behind us. I jumped out of bed and told him to get off the brake and gear it down. He straightened the van out, avoiding inevitable disaster. From that day forward, I was never comfortable with others driving. But there was no choice. Driving for three days crammed in a small space with seven other dancers tested our patience, but when we arrived in the southern states, some relief came when the plan changed. A few of the dancers were picked up in Birmingham to do another show while we carried on to Panama City Beach the next day. Birmingham was a whole new world for me, but it was familiar to Rio, one of the dancers, because he lived there. He missed his wife and understandably chose to stay at his house instead of a hotel room. They had a trailer like many people living in that area, and when they offered for me to stay with them, I gladly accepted.

They did everything they could to make me comfortable in this strange new world, including taking me out to a local female dance club where his wife introduced me to a few dancers. As nice as it was, I was uncomfortable being out of my element because Alabama was very different from what I was used to in so many ways. My stay was short because we needed to continue our journey to Florida the next morning. When we finally arrived in Panama City Beach, I was awestruck. Hurricane Opal had hammered the Gulf Coast just a few weeks previous, and this city had taken a direct hit. I had never visualized the devastation created by a hurricane before, with houses torn apart and their remnants lying everywhere. Yet, remarkably, the beach was still incredibly beautiful.

Young Jason Lee who I believe was 21 was rooming with Billy in a condo, which was a short walk to the Gulf of Mexico. He was gracious enough to offer me his couch until I could get on my feet to find a place of my own. They were still out of town with the other group, so Jason instructed me to knock on their door, and his girlfriend, Tanya, a Hawaiian Tropic model, would be there to greet and let me in. When I arrived, Tanya and her cute friend, Tara, opened the door, welcoming me with hugs. I assumed I would be sleeping on the couch, but they were not about to let that happen. They were staying in Jason's room and offered to share the bed—I wasn't about to turn down their generosity, especially after three days in a tour van and a night on Rio's couch. I slept comfortably with each of these beauties on either side of me, and although we only slept, it was a very cool experience crammed between two very appealing strangers of the opposite sex. Most men dream about having an opportunity like this, but I fell asleep and woke up with no regrets.

Even though it was late October, Cole and I took full advantage of our first days in what some like to call *The Redneck Riviera*, lying on the beach taking it all in. We were so excited while we were tanning that we called a couple of friends in Canada just to let them listen to the waves crash to the shore, along with the warm wind blowing off the Gulf. Of course, the locals looked at us like we were out of our minds because they thought it was too cold to be lying out in our G-Strings. But we paid no attention being more than happy to be out of the Great White North, enjoying southern paradise.

On our first night out in Florida, AJ invited us to a club and introduced us to one of the new dancers he brought in from Mobile, Alabama. Danny was a good-looking young cat with a ripped bod. He had all the physical qualities of a male dancer, but he couldn't dance a lick. He had massive potential but zero experience. When we were introduced, I bought him a drink, and we connected instantly. Cole and Danny rented a condo right across the street from where I was staying with Jason and Billy. They knew I had a thing for Tanya's cute friend Tara, so they offered their place to be alone and as romantic as I could with her. Instead of using the bedroom, I used the kitchen and cooked her dinner, making the best of the situation while living with just the clothes on my back and no real home. Tara was the first girl I dated in Florida, although it was short lived. She was attracted to me, but only because I reminded her of Clint, one of the former dancers who left with the old group. She had her own set of drug issues that I initially had no idea about, which was a road I wasn't willing to travel down with her.

Putting together a new group of dancers with their share of ego, personalities, and addictions isn't easy, and a few of the dancers from the Canadian Tour didn't work out. So, AJ started recruiting to fill the empty spaces. I formed a bond with almost everyone I met, but there always seemed to be one bad apple in the bunch, and his name was Curtis. He had a huge ego and came across as an asshole who only looked out for himself. Even so, I could see why AJ hired him because he was good-looking with a decent body and had been working in Chicago for quite some time. It was just unfortunate that he brought his crappy attitude with him to Florida. We all made an effort to get along with him, but eventually, we got fed up with his bullshit. Although AJ had a 500 dollar fine in place for anyone getting into a physical altercation within the group, it was tempting for some of us, including myself, to knock his lights out. Luckily, Jason and Billy decided there was another way to deal with him.

As the winter set in, our bookings were few and far between because, normally, groups are booked on the road, but since we were brand new, we were forced to take whatever we could get locally to keep food on the table in the offseason. Jason, Billy, Cole, Curtis, and I were booked at a small local show in what seemed like a ghost town in the winter but turned into a tourist mecca in the spring and summer. On most nights, Curtis did an act to Rubber Ducky, the old Bert and Ernie skit from Sesame Street with an adult twist. He got into a bathtub, lip-syncing the song with his little rubber ducky and a scrub brush under his robe. After the skit, he stripped out of his robe to Closer by Nine Inch Nails and gave himself a bath with a bucket of water and sponge.

On this night, the crowd was small, so the boys and I decided to get our revenge. As the emcee, Jason brought Curtis's bucket and sponge out for his act and placed it in the tub. While Curtis was getting changed, we all decided to pee in his bucket. We stood there, watching his act, anticipating the moment he would grab his soap and pee-covered sponge to lather up his body. As nasty as it was, we watched him give himself a urine bath without looking like he realized what we had done. For all the frustration that had built up inside us, there was a brief moment of satisfaction. I think of this moment as a reminder to treat others with respect, even when frustrated, because karma usually comes back to bite in many different forms. It unfortunately also bit my Canadian dancer friend, Johnny, due to his inability to be a team player. When AJ put him in the role of manager, Johnny's ego expanded even more than it already was, and along with his inability to learn choreography, animosity started building within the dance group. He was set in his ways being a solo dancer for so many years, and I couldn't blame him for looking out for himself because this industry can chew you up and spit you out if you let it. However, learning dance routines was mandatory, and frustration built after multiple failures at practice. Assumptions were made because he never revealed that he had dyslexia, and we didn't realize it affected his ability to learn the routines. We resorted to giving him the job of walking out after we finished the choreography to present a rose to a lucky lady in the audience. I genuinely believe he had no idea what he was getting himself into when he joined the revue, having been very successful in Canada. Unfortunately, his ego took a dramatic hit when he moved to Florida, and I felt for him because, although he was misunderstood by many of the U.S. dancers, I had known him for years, and he always treated me with respect. He was just trying to fit in like everyone else, but the pressure got to him, and many of the dancers were relentless, even though he tried to change their perception of him.

We were booked for a show in small town Opp, Alabama around this time, and the memory of this booking is burned in my mind for more than one reason. As we pulled into town, I was disturbed to see a sign on a gas station door that read *Whites Only*. I told the boys that we were moving along to the next station because, as someone raised in a diverse and predominantly inclusive area, I was not about to support anyone who condoned blatant racism. This was definitely a more backwoods area, and when we arrived for the show at the local community hall, I witnessed the epitome of a *redneck* situation when a lady drove up and parked her tractor with a bunch of girls who were so wild, I swore they hadn't crossed paths with a man in two decades. All ten of us from Ultimate Fantasy and Fatal Attraction were in this show, and these girls were ready for a good time.

Billy was not only known as the slut of the group but also

affectionately labelled as *The Scraper* because he scraped up any girl he found who was still hanging around the bar when the *ugly* lights came on. As per usual, we had a long line of women, including the gal with the tractor, standing with money in their hands, waiting for Polaroid pictures after the show. Billy arrived late with a dirty smile on his face and whispered to a couple of us that he had been getting a blowjob in the change room. The line kept moving along as one group of excited girls after another vied for their position to have their picture taken with us. Finally, Johnny made his move and grabbed the cutest girl to sit on his knee, and after the picture was taken, he gave her a kiss—she reciprocated by full-on making out with him. Billy never said a thing in the moment, but later, he mentioned that she was the same girl he had been with not 30 minutes prior. I'm not sure if Johnny even cared, but I'm glad he never knew then because times were already hard enough for him at that point.

This was the reality of an era when male dancers were very popular and political correctness, dependent on someone's perception, had not yet reached the degree of today's advocation. In many cases, women escaped their boring relationship reality and being taken for granted of. Some took it to the next level with the dancers after the lights went down. Our wildest and craziest crowds tended to live in the bible belt areas where ideology restricted some women from cutting loose at home. However, when they got to ladies' night, they turned into hungry wolves. We also toured through military towns where husbands were overseas fighting for their country while their wives took dancers home to break the monotony of loneliness and disconnection. Although I had many opportunities to take advantage of these situations, I rarely did because sex was more about sharing the combination of emotional and physical connection for me. In those moments, I wanted my partner to focus on me and vice versa without experiencing guilt. I also didn't want to be part of the stress that those actions would create for the person waiting at home. I would never want someone to do that to me, so I didn't want to be part of a woman cheating, regardless of the temptation in certain circumstances. I believe my upbringing influenced this integrity mindset, and I carried it with me through most of my dance career. However, I was not perfect.

Our first spring break in Northwest Florida was just around the corner, and it was a foreign experience for most of us and beyond exciting. We rotated through three main clubs during this dance season with a few other local shows to fill in the gaps. Club Lavela was one, and Cash's and Nightown were also massively popular nightclubs located roughly an hour away from our home in Ft. Walton Beach. The expectations on us were extremely high for a group of newbies trying to perfect dance routines that the previous group had almost flawlessly done for years.

There was an unforgettable moment as we drove into the parking lot for our first official practice at Club Lavela, passing the enormous life-sized billboard of the entire ten-man revue. As excited as we were, reality set in when we saw they were still promoting the old group. However, they replaced it with our picture a few weeks later. It was a surreal moment because, in my wildest dreams, I could never have pictured myself on a billboard being promoted as a male dancer. Perhaps, due to my lack of self-confidence and diminished self-love, this was like a dream come true in a form I did not expect. When the first night of the season officially opened at Club Lavela, there was a long line-up across the parking lot, and we were treated like stars as we walked by people waiting to get in. Once we passed the doormen to enter the club, we were introduced to the *VIPs*, Hans and Gunther, two brothers who owned and ran such a prestigious establishment. It was so exciting to be recognized and accepted as one of the *crew*. Hans was a charismatic playboy who wore the most expensive, trendy, and up-to-date clothing. He was a little cocky, but I understood because, in his position, he had an image to present, and he did it very well.

Gunther seemed more down-to-earth and easier to talk to, and he asked me if I wanted to go up to the MTV tower to do some *scoop and rolls*. I had no idea what he was talking about, so I asked AJ to translate, and he told me that scoop was GHB, often referred to as *The Date Rape drug*, and rolls were ecstasy, an emotional stimulant that combines a speedy adrenaline rush along with a dramatically enhanced sensory experience. I was 26 years old, and up until that time, I had never experimented with any drugs outside of alcohol. In this new world, there was not a soul who would judge me on my actions, and I was about as free as a bird could be at that time. However, I didn't take him up on his offer that night. I had no idea what GHB was, and I was never introduced to ecstasy back in Canada. The only time I even heard about it was when Jessica told me she took it during her travels in Europe said she loved it. The electronic music scene was at an all-time high in 1996 and walking into this place was overwhelming at first. There were thousands of people having a spectacular time with little to no conflict—the scene is nearly impossible to describe. I was used to the bars back in Canada that, in many cases, were filled with drunk people, thinking they were invincible.

Spring break arrived, and this winter ghost town turned into mayhem overnight, with every hotel room on the strip filled with college kids having as much fun as they could for the short amount of time they were visiting. Once the party started, it didn't stop. The massive three-story building had multiple clubs with different musical formats, all built into one 35-dollar cover charge. The Thunderdome was the club's heartbeat, with DJ, Jerry D, playing the most progressive dance music of the 90s, along with a top-notch laser light show. During the day, this was our practice area with a stage that rose above the dance floor where we performed in the evening. The DJ booth and our change room were located directly behind the stage, which was a perfect setup for ladies' night. This club also had two levels with large, suspended cages hanging over the dance floor and a small pub as an option for customers to take a break from the mayhem.

Next to the Thunderdome was the Darkroom connected from both levels, and it provided some of the craziest, trippiest music I have ever heard. The upper level of the Darkroom was our official meeting spot once ladies' night finished, with the male and female dancers dominating the area most nights under the black lights and glowing stars on the walls and ceiling. After we had our fill of the Darkroom, we took a trip down to the Underground located in the basement of the building. It was filled with gargoyle statues, modern, comfortable couches, and hardcore industrial electronic music blasting through its multiple speaker boxes with a dark and evil ambience. The Galaxy was a small offshoot of the Underground that played the same music with an unforgettable visual of bright pink walls and planets hanging from the ceiling, along with a colossal popsicle flying smack dab in the middle of the made-up galaxy.

When we wanted to have a change of pace, dropping over to the Rock Deck was a great option where we were entertained by some of the best up and coming live bands in the Southeastern U.S. Sometimes, we toured the pool deck outside to take in the breeze coming off the Gulf of Mexico. The pool deck area was always active during the day with male hard body and wet t-shirt contests, and there was a waterfall that drained into the swimming pool for the tourists to cool off in. When dancing in the Thunderdome during ladies' night, men could occupy the pool deck to take in the Fantasy Girls. This female dance revue took the stage where many top bands of that era played during spring break and summer. Last but not least, The Pussycat Lounge had a high-end appeal with a dress clothes requirement for access into its unique retro environment. It provided a relaxing place to connect without having to scream over club music. The capacity of all the rooms was roughly 8,000 people at the time, but I know they exceeded that on more than one occasion. I had never experienced anything like it, and I haven't since.

Creating our first spring break show was satisfying, and once we experienced success and acceptance, the party began. One night, I was backstage getting changed when Danny showed up with an excited look on his face. In his thick southern accent, he explained that, like me, he had never taken drugs in his life, but took this one little pill, and the experience was like nothing he ever imagined. He told me if I was ever going to consider doing anything, this was it.

My life in Canada seemed so far away, and even though my parents warned me to stay out of shit, I thought to myself: *What could one little pill do?* My friends and family were so far away, and I was on my own journey. So, I popped that little pill, having no idea what was about to be released inside of me.

About 40 minutes went by, and Danny and I were up at the main bar chatting with a couple of girls from the show. We were back-to-back in conversation when suddenly, he grabbed my shoulder and squeezed it. I turned to face him, and he asked me if it had hit me yet, but I just laughed and said: *No*, jumping back into my conversation. Then, it suddenly hit my clean system, and I felt a rush of tingling from my head to my toes. The first-time serotonin release was like nothing I had ever experienced. The music in the club compressed and sounded different for a few seconds as the rush of energy hit me with a speedy, emotional, in-depth perception of everything going on around me. My heart rate increased when all my senses went into overload, and the block of emotional expression I had carried for so long disappeared in a split second. The most significant deprivation I experienced my whole life was instantly released, and I fell in love with this new sense of freedom. It was like every cell in my body went into emotional overdrive—similar to always being deprived of a sense, and then, with the flick of a switch, it was suddenly turned on. Unrestricted emotion sat on the tip of my tongue, and it tasted amazing.

Whether with complete strangers or the individual dancers in our little group, I had deeply bonding conversations when my emotionally blocked walls broke down. It was almost always a great time. And if we needed to bring it back up, we would finish off the night by heading down to the Underground to dance nonstop with no regard for what anyone thought. This indescribable feeling came in waves when the speedy side kicked in, and we rode the wave by dancing to some great beats—the higher the beat, the higher the wave.

DJ Mad Martin spun certain tracks, and he used an effect called a data flash that created such a bright flash that the entire club lit up for a split second when the song hit its peak. Then, using perfect timing, he added a thunderous sound effect just before the track dropped back into a medium beat. People jumped for the ceiling, hitting the ultimate high as that crash of thunder struck hard every single time. It was a raver's dream, and I soaked up every second of it. However, when the lights came on at four in the morning, I hit a brick wall. There were many nights when I danced so hard that I had to take my shirt off and ring it out like a sponge being pulled out of a bucket of water while exiting the club. On this particular night, I arrived back at our condo on the beach, and Tanya and Jason were upstairs in his bedroom loft, coming down off some pills while listening to Pink Floyd's *Dark Side of the Moon*. As I lay on the couch watching the sun rise off the Gulf of Mexico, I had a whole new understanding of *Comfortably Numb*, having no regard for my future because the present was so very satisfying.

Night after night, we relived this experience differently, and as the spring turned into summer, the united bonds the male and female dancers created became stronger and made me more at ease in this erratic, chaotic, yet exciting environment. The summer of 96 was one of the best I ever experienced while working in the largest beach club in the U.S. I had many new friends, and I was treated like an absolute superstar with minimal responsibilities. My main priority was entertainment, even if it was just lying out by the pool in a G-String, tanning while chatting up the ladies to draw them in to see the show. The gym was our next stop, and then we showed up back at the club for practice, grabbing some food and returning by seven in the evening to start all over again.

The dancers in Ultimate Fantasy and Fatal Attraction were a team, and when we were on stage, we got down to business. However, when we were off stage, we all partied together like no one else. For most of us, our ego was left on the stage, and we had each other's backs. It was a tight-knit crew of newly formed relationships that I had never experienced before. Although the former group was long gone, some of the regulars who adored them came out to see what this new group was all about. In this situation, I understood the hesitancy to embrace change because the old group had been respected for many years. They were truly loved, not just by fans in the audience but by those who had worked directly with them. AJ's girlfriend Kassie, a true Southern Belle, had former experience in advertisement and promotion. She coordinated our photoshoots, costuming, and promotional marketing material. Her partner, Janice, assisted her in the process and was more directly connected to the group due to her role and personality. She was kind of like the sister, and Kassie was the mom. From the first day I met her, Janice and I had a vibe in sync with a special connection and respect for each other that carried no judgement. We became good friends, and in a world of mayhem spinning around me, she made me feel at ease.

When the former era of the revue reached its peak, there were 11 custom-made pendants designed for them. Ten were created for the dancers, and the last one was given to Janice. We were in the Thunderdome, dancing to the groove of some raunchy electronic insanity, when she stopped me in my tracks and expressed how significant receiving the last pendant was. She told me that during that summer, she made a promise to give her necklace to the one entertainer who reminded her most of the former group's overall ability and persona. She then took it off and put it around my neck while goosebumps rose up and down my arms. I knew them personally, and I had mad respect for their entertainment ability and unity as a team. It is still an honour to wear that pendant around my neck to this day, and I will probably be buried with it. It represents a moment in my life when I experienced the peak of my confidence and acceptance. Although I was experimenting with ecstasy, I remind myself every time I look at it that my self-worth was at an all-time high, positively impacting others. We were real friends when I truly questioned who my real friends were. You were so very appreciated, Janice.

The summer of 96 had everything from the girl doing her best Sharon Stone impression in the front row of the crowd, spreading her legs in a miniskirt during our dance routines to the mayhem on full display during the day with Wet T-Shirt contests on the pool deck. There were some beautiful people and some not-so-beautiful people letting go of all inhibitions and having the time of their lives. Some nights, the ecstasy pills went down my throat like candy—one pill often turned into four or five, and I found myself going to bed at seven in the morning, only to wake up a few hours later to start all over again. It was in the middle of these fabulous yet borderline insane times that I found myself lying on a couch in the corner of the underground with my first hit of ecstasy starting to kick in. The emotional rush flowed through my body, and I saw a woman enter the club with sex appeal written all over her. She got in line at the bar with four male friends surrounding her. I walked up to the bar, and without a shred of doubt, introduced myself without considering she could be with any of them. I found out later that one was her ex-boyfriend, but that didn't seem to matter to her because she didn't hide the instant attraction between us. I must have had a good eye because it turned out she was a model through an agency in Atlanta and appeared in a couple of rock videos in the 90s. We also had the commonality of taking our clothes off for a living because she danced at a local strip club called *Show and Tail*. I knew she was trouble, and I was playing with fire, but she was irresistible. Hannah had long, blonde hair, green-blue eyes, and a body that didn't stop. She was a feminine bad girl with a confident yet dirty side that turned me on in a big way.

Dating Hannah became a wild, short ride of explosive fun with destined heartbreak. After popping a tab of ecstasy, we made an appearance at the club but chose to leave early since

Billy and Jason were out of town, so I wanted to take advantage of having the condo to myself with Hannah. Ecstasy can make the mind race so hard that, in my experience, it is almost impossible to concentrate long enough to keep an erection—but not on this fateful night. Our senses were overloaded, and our conversations were intensely connected as we lay there in Billy's bed, listening to a thunderstorm blowing in from the Gulf of Mexico in the distance. As the storm moved upon us, the humidity rose in the air, with lightning flashes getting closer and closer. We opened the windows to let the breeze come through, smelling the salt air coming off the water.

I have experienced the difference between making love and fucking, but this was a perfect combination of both, including the emotional connection we shared. We laid there naked in silence with the faint sound of our hearts beating and the stimulating touch of our hands running up and down one another's bodies. I stared at her as the downpour of rain started to batter the coast; I was fascinated by her beauty, and even decades after this night, I have admittedly paused a few of those rock videos she was in just to see her face again. It was an experience I wish could have lasted forever with an almost perfect backdrop. We were focused entirely on one another and came together like two actors in a movie scene. As a perfect fit, we laid naked in the open window of the condo, watching the storm blow off in the distance. It was heaven until shortly after when it all went to hell.

Everything came crashing down on my twenty-sixth birthday. The night started out great with the boys in the group pulling off what seemed like every practical joke in the book on me during that show. Wendy and Wanda, two regulars who quickly became friends, came out for the show, and I had no idea what I was in for. That night, my act was a routine to

Michael Jackson's *Smooth Criminal* with a gangster skit similar to the original video with the choreography to match. My set was about to start, and I opened the door on cue to make my entrance to the stage, but it was empty. The entire ten-man revue, along with my agent, were sitting in chairs on the dance floor below, waiting for me to do the act by myself. I stood there embarrassed for what seemed like an eternity, and then AJ brought a box up on stage with a turtle in it. When he took it out, I noticed it had a dollar bill taped to its shell, so I played along and took the dollar bill off its back with my teeth. Then, I jumped off the stage to the dance floor below, and something didn't sit right. It didn't take me long to notice that those bastards had put thumbtacks on the bottom of my boots, which made it impossible to move without landing on my ass. When I was finally able to get off the dance floor, Jason threw me my *Daisy Duke* shorts, and the first table I visited was Wendy and Wanda's, where they immediately covered me in Silly String from head to toe. Like so many things at the club, it was over the top, but at the same time, it was appreciated because I knew they cared enough to do it in the first place, even if it was somewhat humiliating.

Simultaneously with that memorable moment came a horrible one on the same night. Hannah showed up at the club and split with me before taking off to Miami. Her addictions got the best of her convictions, and I never saw her again.

Being heartbroken on my birthday was no fun to start with, but then, in a desperate attempt to find party pills, Danny and I broke the golden rule of never buying anything from an unknown source. With the combination of regular ecstasy use and my scattered emotions, I wanted to compartmentalize the breakup for the night and try to move on. So, once the purple pills Danny scored in the club started kicking in, we knew they weren't ecstasy. Instead, it was ketamine, used in anesthesia. Having the brutal realization that I was about to go on a bad ride, I went outside to try to get my shit together. Standing there staring at the spot where Hannah and I broke up, I started to cry, and I couldn't stop.

As much as I had lost control of my mind, Danny was in worse shape as he lay on the floor of the balcony a few feet away from me. He had his back against the side of the club, fearing his head was going to fall off. We were both helpless and unable to control the insanity running through our minds. Then Jason and Cole showed up and tried to calm us down. They tried to explain to me that after I came down off the shit, I would laugh so hard at myself, but as much as I tried to relate, nothing helped. The tears flowed for what seemed like hours. So, I left the club with a couple of party buddies to lay on the beach before making too much of a fool of myself. There was an angel among them who helped me gradually come off the emotional rollercoaster. She simply pulled her hairbrush out of her purse and told me to lay back on her and relax. So, I did, and she ran the brush gently across my head while I listened to the sweet sound of the waves breaking on the shore. It took time, but whoever that girl was, I greatly appreciated her assistance out of hell.

Moving on from that dreadful night, I made the best of living just off the beach in the little two-story condo with Jason and Billy, along with Danny and Cole located in the condo across the street. Eventually, a couple of new revue members from Las Vegas, Dallas and Jay, moved into another condo in the same complex. At times, it reminded me of touring with a band because the boys in the group were constantly fucking with one another on and off the road. If we were on the road and booked into a hotel, I often found my hand in shaving cream or toothpaste when I turned the knob to open the door. The pranks started to get out of control at home when Jason and Billy toilet-papered the van that Dallas and Jay were using. The battle continued when they got revenge by breaking into our condo and writing *Don't fuck with Vegas* in shaving cream on Reno's bed. When Billy walked into his room and saw it covered in shaving cream, it ended in an argument when the alcohol took over. It was getting stupid and quite immature, so I jumped at the opportunity when Wendy and Wanda mentioned they had an extra room for rent in the city.

Living with those two girls was like a 90s version of Three's Company at times, with each of us having our struggles with addictions and relationships built into the package. Not only were they fabulous roommates, but we formed a great friendship in a time when so much of my life was fun yet in complete disarray. An example was when I was invited to an after-party on a night when everyone I knew had left the club, so I showed up alone at a complete stranger's door around three-thirty in the morning. I was pleasantly surprised when a super cute blonde girl was on the other side. After introducing myself, Allison welcomed me in with a stipulation that everyone had to wear boxer shorts and nothing else. I laughed and mentioned that I only had a G-String, so she provided an instant resolution by offering a brand-new pair of her husband's boxers. She walked me into their bedroom, grabbed them from the drawer and pressed them up against my crotch, saying: *They should fit well.* She was aggressive, confident, and sexy as hell. Her husband, Oliver, came in and introduced himself, and although he seemed a little average for her, I could see what she liked about him—it was obvious that they had an open relationship. I walked out of the bedroom, and there was a very touchy, feely vibe as they introduced me to the rest of the crew, who were all lying around high on ecstasy. I met her friends, Jim and Thomas, and quickly realized that this was a group of locals who were the life of the party in Panama City Beach, especially in the off-season when it became a ghost town.

Jim was a talented, gay hairstylist who worked at his family's salon just off the beach, and Thomas was a very kind-hearted yet crazy party animal who everyone loved. He had a million one-liners always running through his brain and a good sense for when to bring them out, making the entire room fall into a laughing fit. They were best friends who loved their ecstasy. I formed a unique bond with this alternate group of party friends who were open to expressing emotion and being vulnerable. Partying with this crew after the bar started to become a regular thing, regardless of where we chose to land. The environment was always comfortable, the music was always spot on, and the dimmed lighting melted into the created space.

One party night, in particular, stands out when we all chose to land at Oliver and Andrea's place. I was chatting with Oliver on the couch when Andrea came out of nowhere and started giving me a perfectly-timed back massage. She was an expert at hitting all the right spots while in our party state of mind. It was just before sunrise, and I was so relaxed and enjoying myself when we suddenly heard a scream come from the bathroom. A girl I had previously only crossed paths with a few times had taken an overdose of GHB and was found flatlining and turning purple in the bathtub. The ambulance was called, and the paramedics arrived and knew what to do immediately. Whatever they gave her, it brought her out of her state, and all was good again. We were all in shock as the reality of the situation set in, but once she recovered, the party continued with renewed ease. We hadn't slept, and as the sun rose, we carried on to our next adventure because our minds were racing a million miles an hour.

Andy, one of the members of our little group, offered to take us swimming at a massive freshwater spring on his family's property that serviced one of the largest bottled water companies in Northwest Florida. The trees along the shoreline had rope swings attached to them and swung down across the crystal-clear water with about a 20-foot plunge after letting go. I took full advantage of the situation and experienced the incredible adrenaline rush with my heart beating rapidly as I dropped down into this little piece of paradise. Rising out of the water, I looked over to the shoreline, and although I still had the party pills in my system, I witnessed the reality of how brutally addictive GHB indeed was. The girl who had flatlined only a few short hours earlier was standing there, draining a shot of GHB down her throat. Unlike anything else I had seen, GHB seemed to make people experience instant memory loss, or even worse, put them in a state of mind where they just didn't care what happened to them. As a result, the chance of overdose is very high, and over the years, I saw multiple people overdose on GHB, which was a wake-up call for me. Dropping pills and staying up all night was one thing, but this scared me. However, I eventually made it home safe, and another cycle of partying was in the books.

On another occasion with this same crew, we gathered together, all loaded up with our party pills at Jim and Thomas' place. The plan was to go all night long, spend sunrise on the beach, and then grab a pontoon boat in the morning to venture out to Shell Island, which was unpopulated and only accessible by boat. It was about five-thirty in the morning when I reached into my pocket to grab one of the two pills I had left; I planned on taking the last one on the island. However, I somehow lost them and stood there disappointed in the kitchen because I didn't want the party to end. Jim could tell something was wrong and came over to find out what was going on. When I told him I had lost my last two pills, he put out the alert to everyone in the room, and they started stripping the couch cushions trying to find the pills—with no luck. The emotional drug-induced rollercoaster went up, down, and then right back up again when my birds-of-a-feather came through in a big way. Thomas contacted his *guy*, and out of the goodness of his heart, he bought me a couple of replacements for our little island adventure. Having friends who helped me in this way is incomprehensible to some, but at that moment, I realized they wanted me to be there with them as much as I wanted to be.

As the sun came up, roughly 15 of us took the pontoon boat to the island, where we ran around, wearing whatever we wanted and doing whatever we wanted to. Andrea and I had been going back and forth with each other all night, laughing and messing around. She was such a cool and attractive party buddy who I admittedly gravitated toward. She and Oliver were swingers, but as much as I may have been tempted, I never went there. Watching her chatting with a few friends in her G-String, I decided to strip down to my G-String and lay on the beach, checking out her beautiful body. There were hundreds of jellyfish washed up on the shoreline, and for some reason, I grabbed one and stuffed it down the back of her G-String. They were harmless, but she absolutely lost it, chasing me around that little island, screaming at me and laughing hysterically with that dead jellyfish in her hand on a Friday morning when most of civilization were at work.

This was a crazy, out-of-control, and irresponsible time in my life that created memories like none other. I lived completely in the moment, whether good or bad, forming some genuine relationships with a flock of local Floridians. There were no boundaries, and the lens I looked through was unrelatable to many, but I have no regrets. These people may only have been in my life for a short time, but when I was with them, I was a truly free bird, flying with birds of a feather, who still remain in a special place in my heart.

The Naked Truth

Leaders work with others by example, gently guiding the team in a positive direction with a will to walk beside them through the fire, while karma can bite a bad apple—like Curtis, without realizing that it even happened. My lack of relationship commitment was due to a combination of leaning on drugs to bring out emotion and being induced by a passionate sexual experience with Hannah that ended in heartbreak. This led me to take women for granted expecting that someone else would be around the corner. Hannah may have also had this expectation due to my career, or maybe she didn't. I found a sanctuary with my alternate friend group that formed a connection without expectation. By living in the moment, I was able to create unforgettable experiences, even through the altered reality of my addiction to ecstasy. I learned that tomorrow is not a given, and I was liberated from the systematic lifestyle that most of us are required to abide by. And I took full advantage of it with no regret.

Positive attracts positive, and negative attracts negative. Misery loves company, and the more misery is passed on to others, the more karma can bite when least expected. However, by leading with positive actions and respecting other's perceptions, I found that acceptance and respect came with the territory, and it was on full display when Janice gave me the pendant. More importantly, I found respect for myself.

To truly connect, I need to be authentic to my values and live harmoniously with them. Although it's impossible to always be in perfect harmony, the more I honour my values, the better connection I have with myself and, in turn, within my relationships with others. Taking the time to clarify these values has given me the ability to attract others into my life who have this same clarity naturally because like attracts like. Regardless of career, it is essential to respect my partners and vice versa, whether personally or professionally, and anything less is non-negotiable once that door is opened, which again is a key element to self-worth.

Summer of 1996—Club Lavela, Panama City Beach, Florida

Smooth Criminal—Club Lavela, Panama City Beach, Florida

1998—Corey, Jason, and Billy, Unchained Melody, Club Lavela, Panama City

YMCA—Club Lavela, Panama City Beach, Florida Beach, Florida

Corey, Billy, and Jason, Smooth Criminal—Club Lavela,
Panama City Beach, Florida

Corey and Cole, Unchained Melody—Club Lavela,
Panama City Beach, Florida

1998—Corey taking a tip from Wendy, Club Lavela,
Panama City Beach, Florida

1998—Corey, Smooth Criminal, Club Lavela,
Panama City Beach, Florida

1993—The Early Days—Corey, AKA Dalton Strong,
Promo Shoot in Vancouver, BC, Canada

Jason and Corey as Pinocchio and the Fairy Godmother,
Club Lavela, Panama City Beach, Florida

Unchained Melody—Club Lavela, Panama City Beach, Florida

Growth & Instability

VII

Pleasure and Pain

I was living the single life to the max, and it didn't take long to move on from Hannah to yet another stripper. I met Launa on a hot, sunny afternoon on the pool deck at Club Lavela, and I offered to take her for a walk down the beach. Walking by the parasailing booth, I asked her if she wanted to go since the dancers could parasail for free as a trade-off for the parasail staff receiving free entry into the club. She accepted, and we both enjoyed the initial rush as the parasail rose high above the speedboat. We rode tandem with her long black hair blowing in the wind, sweeping across my body. We rose to 500 feet, and I made my move, kissing her and creating a more than memorable, exhilarating experience.

Although we only dated for a short time, it was a good time. The sex was hardcore yet passionate, and whether we were screwing around in the middle of her kitchen or in the back of an old 70s van I bought off Wendy's uncle, we had a lot of fun together. Unfortunately, she started wanting more, and I was in playboy mode, taking someone for granted who frankly deserved more than I was willing to give at the time. Even if I was just out doing random things like shopping at a drug store, my confidence was at an all-time high that summer. For example, one day, when I went to pay for items I was buying at the local drug store, I consciously picked the cashier with a beautiful smile and, based on her interactions with customers, seemed to have a great personality. Making my way up to her, I pulled out a couple of tickets for an MTV concert being held at the club and asked her if she wanted to join me. She accepted, and when we arrived at the club that night, I sensed her excitement as we walked past the long lineup, holding hands ready to experience one of the best shows in MTV history.

Bush, Collective Soul, and the Goo Goo Dolls blew the roof off the place that night, and as a VIP, we had the best available spot to watch the show. A storm blew in off the gulf, and it poured rain, but that made the experience even better because as crazy as we were watching the concert in the rain, Bush was crazy enough to play in it without missing a beat. Respectfully, I dropped her off after the show and gave her a kiss goodbye with no expectation and no follow-up. I'm sure I could have tracked her down, but my priorities were all over the place. I took so many of these times for granted, and sometimes I wish I could turn back the hands of time to rewrite the story, but that's not my reality. My world was borderline insanity, but I still wouldn't change it because I lived experiences many cannot comprehend.

It seemed like me and the guys were on a permanent vacation with something new going on every day. This was our new home and working the club day and night was part of the package when tourist season was in full swing. When we weren't at Club Lavela, we were roughly an hour away in Fort Walton Beach, dancing at Cash's. It provided the most insane wet T-Shirt contests I had ever witnessed. It was crazy during spring break, but there was nothing like it on a long weekend during the summer. We performed for the ladies at the main stage on the bottom floor while the men hung out on the second-floor balcony, where our show could be viewed from above. The main stage was set up theatre style about six feet above the dance floor with three speaker boxes at the front and stairs going down each side to the dance floor below.

It was the Independence Day long weekend in 1996 when my group, Ultimate Fantasy, was chosen to judge the wet-T shirt contest at Cash's. The club was packed as Jay, Dallas, Cole and I entertained the audience from the main stage. Our show was great, but in the end, it was more entertaining for us when the real show started after ladies' night was finished. To put it into perspective, all four of us had picked different poisons to take, and by the time the contest started, they all started to kick in. Jay was drinking the hard stuff, Dallas was doing the white stuff, Cole was smoking the green stuff, and I was taking my party pills. We sat on chairs behind a fold-out table at centre stage, judging the contestants with numbered cards, ranging from one to ten based on their originality and the crowd's reaction. Each girl walked up and had a pitcher of ice-cold water poured over her by the club DJ—the crowd got louder and louder as the drugs kicked in harder and harder.

An actual mayhem moment happened when a tall, good-looking black girl jumped up on stage in her G-String and heels with a lollipop in her mouth. She took the icy water like a champ and then proceeded to do the splits over two speaker boxes while pulling her G-String to the side, taking the lollipop out of her mouth and shoving it inside of her. The crowd went ballistic with her finale that included pulling it out and giving it a lick. I assumed she had stage experience as a stripper with a performance like that, but I will never know. The whole place lost their shit, and based on crowd reaction, she had a near-perfect score. I felt for the poor young girl who followed her because she didn't stand a chance. As nasty as it all was, it had been signed, sealed, and delivered. We all had quite the visual judging that show, and we chuckled about it for quite some time afterward, but the story didn't end there.

Cole and Dallas had been looking for Jay and were concerned because he was drunk and had the van keys in his bag. We all began the hunt, searching the club from end to end with no luck. When we met back up, we all figured there was only one place he could be, so we walked around to the back where the tour van was parked. When we looked through the window, we noticed movement in the back, so Dallas swung the side door open to find Jay having hardcore sex with the contest winner. Drunk and surprised, he turned to look back at us, pulled out a little too far and missed as his dick hit a brick wall. The look on his face was unforgettable, and as much as we felt for him and what happened, it was funny as hell.

After poor Jay was so rudely interrupted by us, we decided to grab some food across the street at The Waffle House. We were kind of a hard crew to miss, especially as messed up as we all were, but the staff also knew us well because we stopped in regularly after shows. The 24-hour restaurant was almost empty when one of the off-duty staff members decided to get silly and throw a piece of food at our table. So, the battle began between the strippers and the Waffle House staff with food flying by my head and my emotions in overdrive, high as hell on ecstasy.

Most of the time, working with that crew of dancers was nothing but a pleasure, but Jay could be a little over the top. He was constantly picking on me, calling me Gump for taking girls to The Waffle House after shows to get to know them instead of just fucking them and moving on. This progressed to a Thursday night at a club called Nighttown, in Fort Walton Beach when the group tried to humiliate me by getting me a *Gump* Waffle House name tag and presenting it to me in front of the enthusiastic crowd of women. Although they never knew it, I took it as a compliment because *Forrest Gump* was and always will be one of my favourite movies. Old Forrest was a little slower than most, but his heart was also bigger than most.

It was all in good fun,
and although they had a good laugh,
I knew that they were doing it out of love
in their own strange way.

As the summer of 1996 ended, I started to miss my family and friends back home, even though I was living the dream in so many ways. I lacked connection and was relying on the drugs to keep me emotionally satisfied. The partying got to a point whereby I was stressed from constantly entertaining on and off stage. The erratic emptiness of the club scene started to become overwhelming, and I began desiring something more. Then, being in the middle of yet another night dropping party pills and wandering through the club, an angel of a woman walked past me, and we locked eyes with one another. Out of the thousands of people roaming around the club that night, we happened to pass by each other at just the right time. Without speaking, we stood there in the middle of mayhem and read each other's minds. I could tell from the dilation of her pupils that she had dropped ecstasy as well, so when I asked her if she wanted to go outside with me to get away from the music, she accepted the invitation. Emotions surged through my body as we walked out of that smoke-filled insanity to the pool deck. We took off our shoes to dip our feet in the water, and minutes seemed to turn into hours. Julie was not only beautiful, but she had a good head on her shoulders, even though at the moment, she was out having a good time. She was a college student from Mobile, Alabama, who worked as a Hawaiian Tropic Model on the side.

We dated for the rest of the summer and into early fall. If I could paint a picture of one of the most romantic moments I've ever had, Julie and I standing waist-deep under the moonlight in the warm waters of the Gulf of Mexico would be the one. It was near perfection, holding one another in silence under the moonlight away from all the others, absorbing everything we could. The people who wanted a piece of me seemed nonexistent as we focused on a rare moment. Being in the now, we were not thinking about the past or the future, and we were beyond satisfied without any drug inducement.

Although now a distant memory, if there was a moment I could turn back the hands of time to recreate, that would be it. She accepted who I was with my imperfections fully exposed, and although she enjoyed the dancer on stage, she had real, true emotions for the person offstage. I drove that old, nasty 70s van out to stay with her, and she didn't blink an eye. The last time I visited Julie, our group was leaving to go on tour to my home province of British Columbia, and as I kissed her goodbye, something inside of us knew that it might be our final kiss. I was homesick, and she sensed it.

The tour was a mad success and as we neared the end of our stint in Canada, my world was flipped upside down in the blink of an eye. As usual, Dallas, our emcee, was whipping the crowd into a frenzy before we made our entrance to center stage in a popular nightclub on the outskirts of Vancouver. We were doing our opening routine when I was startled by a group of girls chanting my name. I turned my head and noticed they were all from my high school. One of them stood out above all the others—Jessica, the girl of my high school dreams who, in my mind, I never stood a chance with. It was exciting that they all came out, and it was fantastic to reconnect with them after so many years. Cole knew them as well, and they quickly realized that we were no longer the kids they knew from high school. We had developed into charismatic entertainers with more confidence on stage than ever before.

When I pulled out my photo album of pictures I had collected from my new life in Florida, I saw a different look in Jessica's eyes when we reconnected that night. As we turned the pages, she asked me about the picture of the beautiful brunette girl lying on the beach, and I told her that was my girlfriend, Julie. She complimented Julie with her words, but as we spoke, I noticed that she was looking at me through a different lens than she had in the past. When we all exited the club, the girls participated in signing our little prop trailer that we towed behind the van. Earlier in the tour, one of the women at a show signed it, and the tradition continued until the very end. The rest of our group, along with Jessica's friends, went their own way, leaving Jessica and I to catch up after so many years of being disconnected. We always seemed to cross paths in one way or another with no lack of conversation when we did. We talked about ex-boyfriends, girlfriends, and then us.

I waited for this moment most of my adult life, so even though I knew Julie was back home in Alabama, I decided to finally put it out there and let the chips fall where they may. We were like two kids nervously trying to test the waters without hurting each other's feelings. I boldly suggested we try kissing, and if it wasn't right, it wasn't right. When I kissed Jessica for the first time, it definitely felt right, and when we arrived at her place, it was everything I expected and more. We had a non-drug-induced connection because she was enough of a drug for me at that moment. I remember thinking that being in her bed was like a dream come true, and within hours of being just distant friends who hadn't talked in years, we experienced a mutual attraction. The bar of expectation I had set came down, and she was the one. This was the first of two butterfly effect moments that dramatically changed the direction of my road. Until that night, I had been flying by the seat of my pants, but then, I decided I wasn't about to let her go.

For the second time in my dance career, my buddy, Cole, witnessed me leave everything for the love of a woman, but he understood because he knew that what I felt didn't happen overnight. I chose to leave behind my Florida life to stay in Canada while abandoning someone I cared deeply for, but my decision was made. I called Julie to tell her the news that I was staying, and she assumed that it just made sense since my family was there, but I didn't tell her anything about Jessica. My heart sunk when I had that conversation with her because I let go of someone who accepted me for the person I was to pursue a woman from my past who had never given me a second look. This choice wasn't easy for more than one reason. Cole was my closest friend, and I was saying goodbye to him and Dallas and Jay, who went back to Las Vegas, never to be seen again. So, in a way, I was breaking up with more than just my all-American girlfriend—I was leaving my team behind.

I sometimes wonder what could have happened if I had taken the road back to Florida, but I chose to go with my heart, and it was with Jessica. She was a friend, but now being together with her was a new reality. But was it? Was I still that kid back in eighth grade with no confidence, trying to solidify a dream from my past, or did I leave behind an amazing woman who accepted me for the imperfect person I was over a one-night love affair? But being together with Jessica really was like a dream to me. She was the girl I always knew as a friend, but now I got to understand her affectionate side, and we had so many things in common. We laughed at stupid shit for hours over coffee and truly just enjoyed each other's company. In many ways, she was still the girl who motivated me back in high school, but now she motivated me in a different way. She did the little things, those things that most take for granted. I don't think I truly appreciated them as much as I could have because I was focusing on being with her, not about her. She was doing live theatre at the time, and I was totally impressed with her performance. I had heard her sing years before, and she still had an amazing voice in the play she was performing in. She seemed to enjoy entertaining for similar reasons I did—the audience reaction.

She was a nurse at an old folks' home, and it wasn't exactly an appealing job. I noticed she had a way with the elderly when she interacted with my parents because she could make them both laugh which wasn't easy for most. I was back, working the Vancouver circuit, and Jessica came out to support me on many occasions, but then one night, when it truly counted, I didn't support her. I had finished a show, and she had a health scare that went straight over my head, even though she mentioned it to me days before. She was very concerned about ovarian cancer, and I responded with little to no emotion. She had to go outside with me to let me know how upset and shocked she was that I simply didn't seem to care. I later realized that this was somewhat of a defence mechanism I used around emotional expression, passed down from generation to generation in my family. I saw the same type of reaction from some of my family members when they experienced tragic moments in their lives. However, placing blame on the past does not excuse my actions at that time. The truth is that she needed someone to give her a hug and stand by her, and I failed miserably. My lack of communication with her was understandably not appealing, and it made her rethink our relationship.

She decided that it would be best if we broke up,
and although it hurt my heart,
I tried my best to understand.

Then a few days after we split, she asked me to come over, and it seemed like everything was fine. We started fooling around, and suddenly I was back in bed with her, assuming we were continuing our relationship. But she had different plans because the next time we made contact over the phone, she was on a completely different page. She put it to me straight, saying that we were still broken up, and that was just sex. Even though I had more than one experience in my life that was *just sex*, I honestly thought it was different between us, and admittedly, those words hurt in a big way. So, we ended it, and I chose to move in a completely different direction. My agent wasn't booking me as often as she had in the past, and she suggested that I go back to Alberta because I could make more money as a top dancer in a circuit with far less competition.

I followed her direction and moved back to Calgary for the second time, working the solo circuit and reuniting with my old buddy, Rico, from my former review. It was good to be back with some of the Alberta dancers, and once again, a new experience appeared around every corner. A few Calgary dancers invited me to join a revue they had put together, and although it was short-lived, we had a great time. The one night that really stood out was a charity event we did to a packed house in downtown Calgary. Each dancer always left at least one item of clothing on stage for some lucky girl to bring backstage to him because he *forgot* it.

As I left the stage, the other three dancers were preparing to be introduced to do a quick routine, and I heard the emcee pick a girl from the crowd to bring the shorts I forgot back to me. She came up on stage, grabbed the shorts, and I waited for her in the hallway by the entrance to the change room. I assumed she would give me a hug or kiss like most women did, but not this girl. Instead, she threw the shorts on the ground, pulled my G-String down to the floor and started going down on me. I was shocked yet extremely turned on in that split second. Then, I heard the music ending and the dancers getting ready to leave the stage, so I suggested we go into the bathroom.

I admit that I was in a bit of a dark place at this time. A side of me came out that had never revealed itself before. Whether it was because of my experience with Jessica, telling me that it was *just sex* that made this come out, or not, I cannot say. But once we got in the bathroom, she stopped and said she couldn't continue. She said she was married and realized through her drunkenness that she had gone too far with me. I looked down at her and told her that she had already started the job, so she might as well finish the job. I had absolutely no heart or consideration whatsoever for this woman's feelings. She finished the job, cleaned herself up and walked back out into that crowded bar.

After the show ended, all the dancers donated our time to charity by serving shooters and drinks to the crowd left behind, and I figured this girl was long gone. Then, I turned around, and she was standing right in front of me with a smile on her face. She said she wanted to buy each of us a shooter and one for her husband, who stood right behind her. We downed the shooters, and she introduced me to him. He obviously had no idea what had happened only 30 minutes prior, and as they walked away, never to be seen again, I was once again in shock. It was another moment that tested my faith in the opposite sex.

I worked everywhere between Alberta and Ontario in that next year or so. During my travels, I hooked up for a short time with a female dancer named Jackie. I could tell she was bad news, but again, I was drawn to a bad girl. She wasn't hard to look at, yet I was attracted to someone I knew wouldn't take me in a forward direction. But, it turns out, there was something about her that opened me up to trying something I had never tried before—marijuana. Although I had multiple experiences with ecstasy when I was in Florida, I had never smoked weed. It was taboo to me because my biological mother had smoked it in front of me with her boyfriend when I was only ten at the drive-in theatre. As I mentioned, I led a pretty sheltered childhood being raised by my grandparents, so I took issue with it most of my life up until then.

Although my friends, Julian and Rico, smoked it regularly, they could never convince me to smoke with them. They were in the room when Jackie convinced me to smoke a joint with her, and they were astonished when I did. Of course, the laughs and the munchies kicked in, so Jackie and I walked down to the local convenience store to stock up. After grabbing a stupid amount of garbage food and leaving it on the counter, we both found ourselves in front of the ice cream cooler in silence, trying to make a decision about what to buy. The same thoughts went through our minds, and we both started laughing hysterically. Decisions, decisions. When we approached the counter, the poor man was trying his best to bag up all the shit food we had stacked in front of him, but Jackie couldn't stand there anymore without absolutely losing it laughing. She bailed on me and left me to pay up the bill. It was a fun experience for the first, but not the last time I smoked weed. And even though, in some cases, weed is supposed to make you lose short-term memory, I could never forget the look on that man's face as we left the store. It was priceless.

Calgary adventures continued with Jackie as my sidekick when she was around. But our relationship was more about having a good time when we saw one another, and when we didn't, I didn't worry about what she was doing. I was at a point where I just didn't care anymore. My self-worth had depleted from everything that had happened since I came back to Canada, and I was just out looking for a good time with no expectations. Heading out on the road with Jackie was a true test for our short-lived relationship. We lived separate lives, and suddenly being together every day in different hotels with each of us booked doing shows was a strain. After working in Winnipeg for a week or so, we moved on to Thunder Bay, Ontario, where she connected with one of her biker buddies, who was very obviously interested in her. She seemed to give him the same signs back. I was at a point where games were not in the equation, and once again, I was breaking up with another girl who I knew was bad news and looking for something that wasn't there.

I was searching for acceptance and was full of self-doubt so, I settled for someone who didn't love themself because I didn't love myself.

As time went by, Jessica and I started reconnecting. She was tired of working at the old folks' home, and I couldn't blame her. She wanted more out of life than wiping butts and considered entering the dance arena, but she didn't know where to start. At first, I was very reluctant because I saw the harsh side of the industry when I was in Alberta, and so many other female dancers went down the wrong path. But who was I to question her? My path hadn't exactly been paved in gold. I wasn't going to be a hypocrite, but one cannot measure apples to oranges when comparing male and female dancing. In my opinion, female dancers deal with far more crap than men do. Back then, the clubs ran multiple female dancers all day and night in most cities. On any particular day, the first girl on stage could do a show for hardly anyone. The people in the crowd were more likely to focus on the burger they were eating than the actual show. It was a hustle from the beginning till the end of the day.

The guys in the crowd were mostly there just to see some girl take it off and spread her legs. Unfortunately, in Alberta, the laws were not favourable for women either. At that time, they had a crazy law spearheaded by the biggest buzzkill on the planet, Audrey Jensen. Believing that *the lust* caused by exotic dancing created many of the great evils in society, Jensen set out to ban stripping in Alberta. She was an effective advocate, organizing letter-writing campaigns and showing up in front of strip clubs with protest signs. Over time, she earned the ear of many politicians in the right-wing government.

Aside from all that, when female dancers had good shows, they paid very well. In fact, they made much more money than most of the male dancers simply due to the frequency of being on stage, but they worked their asses off, mentally and physically. Even the skills required to work the pole on stage take a lot of work, and society, in general, tends to be more critical about a woman's appearance than a man's, which is no different when it comes to being under the lights.

Then came the lizards that constantly frequented the female strip clubs—the organized gang side of the equation. It was a major concern for me as Jessica's boyfriend. What could I do if one of these assholes tried some crazy shit on her? In comparison, the male dancer wasn't pressured the same way, not having to hustle as much as the women who had to do five or six shows a day. All we had to do was keep in shape, have a few good dance moves and be half-decently good-looking. I saw multiple male dancers over the years who I didn't think should be on stage, but they blew the crowd right up. Being in my dance shoes, it wasn't as mentally hard to deal with as some thought.

Jessica didn't want to work in BC because of her family and friends, which I understood, so we chose to get a place together in Calgary for her introduction to the industry. I wanted to support her the best I could, and one thing I knew about Jessica was that if she was going to do something, she would do it right. So, she worked hard on getting in better shape and researched the best doctor she could find to get her breasts done. It was far from cheap, but it was a good investment. We agreed to do what it took to start her off on the top. Since I had spent time in Florida, I introduced her to all the agents as Ms. Nude Pensacola. It was total bullshit, but from day one, she had what it took to get that feature dancer pay. She did her audition at The French Maid, a local strip club in Calgary, and I was nervous as hell watching her for the first time. She was understandably nervous as well, but she had a look that knocked their socks off. The crowd went wild as she took it off, and her confidence began to grow. From that point on, we were basically starting her from scratch by doing photo shoots for her promo and gathering as many costumes as possible. In the beginning, I overheard a couple of other dancers talking some shit about her when she was on stage in one club. I guess they could tell she was a rookie, and they were jealous and upset that this new girl was getting paid more than them. Whether the clubs knew it or not, she pulled it off and pulled it off well.

Jessica was always a very strong woman on the outside. She decided she was going to take the reins and make the most of it. I was beyond proud of her, but as time passed, I could tell it was changing her. It was also changing us. She wasn't the nurse I fell in love with anymore. Now she had the body, the looks, and everything that most guys dream of on the outside, but they didn't know the real person inside. I like to think that I did—to a certain extent anyway. We moved into a little condo together, and everything was going well, but that didn't last long. It seemed like I couldn't do anything right, and although I screwed up a few times, it wasn't intentional. One night right after she had her breast surgery, she asked me to grab a painkiller out of her purse because she couldn't get up, having to stay in bed. She was in quite a bit of pain, and I made the stupid mistake of giving her the wrong pill without checking the bottle first. The one I chose made her sick, and there was nothing I could do about it. To top it all off, in my haste, I left her purse in the bathroom sink, and the faucet dripped directly inside of it. She was beyond upset, and I couldn't blame her. I felt absolutely horrible and spent the rest of the night downstairs with a pit in my stomach.

Overall, things were more positive than negative because we had each other's backs in those early days. She experienced instant success, but for me, it was very hit and miss. One of the best achievements I accomplished around that time was when I competed in the Mr. Nude Western Canada contest. It was held at Dewey Stevens in Calgary, and the best of the best dancers were competing for the title that they narrowed down to five guys. I had done a couple of other contests in the past with disappointing results. Having a thing for originality on stage, I guess I pushed it past the limit of what was considered appealing in those shows, but on this night, things were very different.

We all drew for positions to make things fair, and I chose fifth. This was the best place to be because the judges were girls in the audience who were drinking, so the later the pick, the better. I copied a show from one of the Vancouver dancers who had a killer act based on Billy The Kid. Nobody cared because I was in a different city. It had a voiceover from the movie Young Guns and then transitioned into Blaze of Glory by Bon Jovi. It was a different kind of show because it started with a slow song that I stripped to on stage in front of a fire pan. I lip-synced the song while stripping down to my tearaway jeans in front of the fire.

Before the show, I gave the DJ my music, and he told me that the fourth dancer was late because he was stuck in traffic due to another show across town. I needed to get ready to take his place because he wouldn't make it in time. So, I went backstage to begin the task of tying my cock off and putting my costume on. I took my time to make sure I got a good tie-off because the crowd was huge, and this was a big contest. I accomplished the tie-off, but there was only one problem: just as the third dancer finished his show, the dancer who was supposedly stuck in traffic came running in and threw the DJ his music. They put him on immediately, and I was left standing with my full costume on and an elastic band wrapped around the base of my dick. I had to make a decision…should I pull the elastic off my cock and try to get it up all over again, or just wait it out and hope for the best?

I chose the latter.

Standing there in that change room tied-off in my costume, my nerves were at a maximum and the pain increased by the minute. I stood there for 20 minutes waiting for this guy to finish his set, and it got worse and worse. By the time he finished, and I was awaiting my entrance, the pain was beyond intense, but I had no choice. I had to perform. Then I heard the crowd chanting my dance name: *Dalton, Dalton, Dalton.* Walking out with my cowboy hat tipped down and my intro music blasting, the girls were literally losing their minds. The screams were ear-piercing. My confidence was high, and I knew I wasn't going to lose this one. Little did the audience know that the pain I experienced while entertaining was excruciating.

Going into my third song, Bed of Roses, I spread out a white sheet on the dance floor and lit a few candles. From there, I grabbed a bundle of roses that were sitting side stage and dropped them on the sheet one by one while circling the bed. The fuck scene began on the roses I had dropped, which I later gave to the girls when they tipped me. The line-up seemed like a mile long, and I was forced to do two encore songs, extending my set to well over 25 minutes. As I left the stage, they still wanted more, but I had to get backstage. My cock felt like it would fall off, and it probably would have if I didn't get that elastic off me. I had been tied off for a little over an hour.

Going back to the change room with the sound of screaming women in the background, I took my towel off and snipped that elastic. I fully realize that most people have not had an experience like this, and for that, they should be thankful. As I unwrapped the elastic, the pain became more and more intense. When it finally released, I almost hit the roof, and then came the next level of dramatic relief, and I was completely numb. I quickly put my clothes on because they were going to announce the winners and I didn't have much time. They started with third, then second, and by the time they were about to announce first, they didn't even need to say it—the crowd had already. Finally, it was over, and I was Mr. Nude Western Canada for 1997. I stood signing promo posters for what seemed like an eternity. Girls offered five dollars per signed print on a piece of paper. They gladly paid, and I had no issue taking their money. However, over and above the money, I experienced an elevated sense of accomplishment. It was a job I carried through to the finish, numb dick and all.

I won my first big show, and I was dating one of the hottest female dancers on the circuit. Life was absolutely amazing, and later that year, Jessica and I decided to make a road trip to Winnipeg. It was November, and the weather was beyond frigid. I introduced her to my agents there, who were a gay couple by the names of Rick and Mitch but affectionately known as *Dick and Bitch*. Jessica was booked solid, being new to the scene, but it was my third trip out there that year, and my bookings were few and far between, so I was pretty much along for the ride. I was in a strange place at that point. Although I was very happy for her, I wasn't making the money I needed to.

The animosity started to show,
and I could understand why because
she was pulling most of the weight.

Next, I was entered in the Mr. Nude Canada contest in Brandon, Manitoba, and I did the exact same act that night, but this time, something felt very different. It wasn't the same kind of crowd. I could tell that the local dancers were supported, and I was almost unknown in that town. Pulling off the best show I could, the crowd went wild, and there was one more dancer to go. I really thought I had it in the bag, but this young kid came out and danced his ass off. He had a large group in the audience cheering him on. This was the first and last time I ever crossed paths with him. He just came out of nowhere and disappeared right back from where he came from.

I placed second, and I know it sounds petty, but I should have been first. The judges picked him because the deck was stacked against me. The kid knew it, and as soon as he won, he bailed out right away. I was pissed, but it was just one of those nights, and it even got better when we left. Jessica and I were at a gas station, and while I was paying for the gas inside, a couple of assholes started harassing her. I came out and told them to fuck off, but the damage had already been done. Now she was upset, and the high hopes I had for that night turned to shit. It just felt like things with us kept going downhill, and we were having more bad times than good. I knew I needed to make a change, so I contacted the owner of a revue in Myrtle Beach, South Carolina and expressed an interest in working with his group. Going back to the U.S. also seemed appealing because I had been working in this ice-cold environment for far too long.

Matthew, the owner, was familiar with my group in Florida and figured that if the Florida crew had hired me, I must be quality. Jessica supported my decision, so we put a plan together. I would fly down to Myrtle Beach, and she would come down after me when she finished the bookings she already had scheduled. When I arrived in Myrtle, they put me up with one of the other dancers until I could find my own place. Right from the get-go, it just didn't feel right. I was bounced around quite a bit, and the money wasn't very good. I was back, living on someone's couch, and when we were booked on the road, the tour van didn't even have air conditioning. At one point, it broke down on the side of the highway, and a couple of us had to hitchhike home.

Jessica made her way down, and through the male revue, I was able to connect her with a local female dance group. She didn't really hit it off with the dancers, and at one point, she found herself at an orgy that she wasn't about to have any part of. However, we did get some awesome promotional material put together, taking pictures on Myrtle Beach. The promo shoot was most likely the best part of the Myrtle Beach experience for us because shortly after that, all hell broke loose. I was at the wheel of a loaded tour van, pulling an overweight trailer, driving down the interstate when we came upon a construction zone. I couldn't stop in time to avoid the vehicle in front of me; the momentum from all the extra weight had a part to play in it, but I should have been more careful. When I tried to turn into the center area, I slammed on the brakes, and we ended up skidding right into the vehicle ahead of us and totalled the van.

The hole was dug so deep that I felt like giving up. I had little to no money, no American driver's license, and no social security number while working in a male dance revue. I gave the police the information I had, but I was trapped, unsure what to do, and desperation began to set in. The owner of the revue was out of town for a few days, and I had to get out of there. Fortunately, the following morning, one of the guys in the group was leaving town, and he said I could jump in with him. He was going to Houston, Texas, to work at a club he was connected with from the past. I took him up on his offer after speaking with Jessica about it. She arranged to go to Calgary to work the Stampede for a few weeks, and we would try to figure things out from there. However, when I drove off that morning, the look on her face said it all. We had a short window to get out of town, and I had no choice but to leave a horrible situation spinning out of control.

I thought it was my most desperate time, but I never felt so alone and lost when we arrived in Houston. The bar was a straight hustle and a far cry from what I had experienced one short year earlier. The sound of the crowd chanting my name back in Canada had faded, and the reality of standing on *The Meat Rack* set in. The dancers all had their girls frequenting the bar, so they were always first pick to dance. You see, we would stand in a line up on a long platform, and the girls chose who they wanted to do a 20-dollar private dance. We also rotated, doing the occasional stage show, which paid next to nothing. I stood there watching all these girls, asking this one long-haired, skinny guy for dances, and when he turned around, I saw why. The guy was indeed hung like a horse. This, once again, confirmed I was definitely not in the right place. I suspected prostitution, and I got my ass out of there.

I called Jessica and explained the situation, and she was kind enough to send me some money to help me out. I told her I wanted to catch a bus back to Panama City and explained that my old agent in Florida agreed to hire me without pay to start, but I could keep my tips. It was better than nothing, and even though I had quit on him before, he did his best to help me when I needed it. He came to the bus station in Panama City and picked me up. He brought me over to my old roommate, Wendy's place, and that was where I would live. Wendy was happy to have me back. We had a great friendship, and it kind of felt like being home again.

Things seemed to be moving in a positive direction, with Jessica planning on coming down to give dancing a shot in Florida. Even after our crappy Myrtle Beach experience, I was excited to see her and hoped to introduce her to The Fantasy Girls female revue that worked at Club Lavela because she wouldn't have had to hustle as much or show as much skin. We had discussed shipping her costumes down when she crossed the border to make sure she didn't set off any alarms for intent to work, but she chose to take a bus across the border and carry her costuming with her. She was caught at the border and unable to cross. It was the straw that broke the camel's back. On the phone that night, I actually broke down in tears. We got into a pretty good back and forth, and it was justified on both sides. She told me I had to grow up, and she was right. My life was a mess, and I was dragging her down with me. I was living in the past, hoping I could have that sweet nurse back I knew when we first got together. But we both changed so much, and after the call, an overwhelming sense of relief came over me. I burned every picture I had of her in the backyard grill that night. I was done, and so was she.

I started over by reuniting with my old buddy, Cole, and was introduced to some of the new dancers in the group. My first show back at Club Lavela was quite the experience. The group had definitely changed quite a bit, but the main components were positive overall. The night before I arrived, a few of the other dancers did a show with the usual Polaroid picture-taking session. It was the beginning of spring break, and the crowds were huge, but the money wasn't the best because most college students spent their money on booze or cigarettes before tipping male dancers. I arrived at the show and went back into the change room to prepare for the night. However, just before the show started, the police arrived and arrested three of the five dancers. They literally cuffed them in their costumes and escorted them out of the building in front of the eager crowd waiting to see us perform. It was nuts! Supposedly, the night before, they took a picture with an undercover cop. The officer claimed she was touched inappropriately during the picture session. It honestly wouldn't have surprised me if she had been. I think the dancers got a slap on the wrist, but the embarrassment of being arrested at the club was enough punishment. We didn't have issues after that, but the police did drop in every so often to *check* things out.

Our agent, AJ, had to bring in a couple of replacements that night to string a show together, and Jason, Lee and I killed it, doing his Pinocchio act. It was one of the best dance revue comedy acts I had ever seen. The emcee brought out this little, yellow plastic chair and placed it at centre stage. Jason then came out to this voiceover of Pinocchio singing a song about wanting to be a real boy and not just a wooden toy by wishing upon a star. After that, I arrived as his fairy godmother, all dressed up in a little pink tutu, along with a halo and magic wand. Of course, a 220-pound, six-foot, two-inch male dancer wearing a pink tutu and G-String was quite the sight. The girls fell out of their chairs when I showed up. The fairy godmother granted Pinocchio his wish, and then Jason looked down in his G-String and displayed a huge smile—cheesy but funny as hell. The other dancers then went into a quick little bit of choreography, and the crowd went nuts as soon as Jason tore off his shorts.

Sometimes the best people in your life show up at the most detrimental times. I tragically lost my best friend, Jamie, in a car accident when he was 17, and since then, I have refused to call anyone my best friend. Except for Cole; for as long as I've known him, he's been my best friend—bar-none. And at this time, I needed his ear. So, as I settled back into a somewhat *normal* life, I spent quite a bit of time with Cole, getting baked in his carport surrounded by his wall-to-wall fish tanks. He bred fish and sold them to local pet stores around Panama City. He also knew Jessica from school, so talking about our situation with him was real. He always had my back, and as part of his support, he offered me one of his Labrador's puppies. Animals heal even the worst wounds sometimes, so I had a hard time refusing because I needed something more in my life, and she was the perfect solution. The puppy was so needy, and I bonded with her immediately. I chose to call her Baby for some reason, and the name seemed to fit. I took her out walking every day and treated her like gold. That dog knew every trick in the book. I loved her with all my heart; we were destined to have a long-term friendship.

Cole was also working at a sex toy and porno movie rental shop called Night Movies to make a few extra bucks. In conversation one day, he mentioned that he could get me a few hours if I wanted them. I was getting show pay by then, and things were starting to look up, but I took the job knowing that shows could be sporadic, and I was tired of struggling. It was great to be back and working with Cole was a pleasure. About a month after I got back to Panama City, I heard the news that Jessica had married one of our mutual friends from high school. I was not only blown away, but I felt betrayed. However, I could have been more grown-up about it because when her new husband called me at work looking for the money I owed her, I tore a strip into him.

I'm not going to get into what was said, but he knew I meant every single word. I was acting out of pain at that moment, but I refused to pay her back and told him to get her to call me if she wanted to discuss the situation. I was also just getting back on my feet, and him calling my work when I was in that state of mind was the last thing I wanted to listen to. She eventually had to sue me to get her money back, and I had to give her credit. She was smart enough to send me a registered letter to the post office that I signed for. It served me to be in court in Canada or be presumed guilty. She stood her ground for justice within the situation, and she was right. I should have paid her back, but I also assumed they got together prior to her cross-border bus experience. We had broken down to the point of no return, and she got every penny I owed her back. It took a few years, but it was paid. Then the downward spiral began.

The Naked Truth

If I knew then, what I know now... This is a statement that I have said many times based on the growth and wisdom I've gained through the inner struggle of instability. Hindsight is truly 20/20 and the wisdom gained through my struggles with instability provide a clear view of how and why I went from the top to what I thought was the bottom in such a short amount of time.

Although I had the status of receiving the title of Mr. Nude Western Canada, I mistakened status for worth and assumed that my status would carry me through. I made uneducated decisions, choosing to take a position in a group with no idea where that road would lead. This decision put both Jessica and me into a situation that forced me to leave a trail of damage beyond repair due to my legal and financial position at the time. Although I created this mess, she still supported me when I desperately needed her the most, trying to keep my head above water; I was looking to find my way back to the only place I knew as home at the time.

She was irresponsible for making the attempt to bring her costuming across the border, but it's no surprise we chose to break it off because I was more irresponsible than she was at the time. My jealousy and rage held me back from doing what was right, and although stability started coming back into my life, financially, I chose to avoid paying her back, which was morally and selfishly wrong, all things considered.

We had broken up, and she moved on. However, I could not accept the reality of the situation and chose to blame everyone but myself for the failures that brought me to this place. But it wasn't about failure as much as the learnings and growth I received as a result of it. Looking back, I am grateful for my struggle because I appreciate the stability I have in my life now more than ever. I wouldn't respect the stability I have as much if I had not experienced the loneliness, fear, and loss shortly after experiencing adoration, comfort, and status in my world of minimal responsibility.

Addiction & Control

VIII

The Downward Spiral Toward
the Light at the End of the Tunnel

Life was becoming somewhat normal again in a place of security I once knew as a second home, but I still had a massive void in my heart. The painted picture of what was supposed to be was destroyed, and my hunger for filling the emotional void turned into starvation. I was grateful to have caring people surrounding me, but there were many who were acquaintances at best and only acknowledged me for what I had instead of who I was. Many of them only saw the entertainer on the billboard as they drove into the parking lot, or they tried to get something they wanted through me, assuming I was well connected.

The person they didn't see was suffering from lack and stuck in a state of victimhood, searching for acceptance and love. But I didn't love myself, so anger, guilt, and sadness coursed through my body while blaming all my recent problems on everything and everyone else but me. How could I expect anyone to provide me with love when I couldn't love in return due to my own inadequacies? I didn't even realize who my closest friends were or acknowledge them through the haze of my entertainer life; I wanted to be appreciated by someone so very badly for the real person I was offstage. I had thousands of people in my face daily, yet I felt completely consumed in my ego and self-pity, drowning my reality with another pill going down my throat.

At the end of another night of partying with thousands at the club, I decided to detach from the mayhem and leave alone. I was consumed with disconnected emotions, trying to deal with the path I had taken and where it was leading me next. As I walked across the massive parking lot to an unknown destination at three in the morning, I heard a female voice calling for help. I was the only person in the vicinity, and looking over to see what was going on, I saw a girl hanging out the side door of a vehicle, displaying all the familiar signs I had seen so many times before. She was left to fend for herself, vulnerable and helpless from the effects of the GHB someone had slipped into her drink—it was taking over her body.

As I approached the vehicle, she looked up, and I discovered she was a girl who owned a clothing store across the street from the club. I had no idea how long she had been crying out for help before I happened to cross her path. Although we didn't know each other, I extended my hand and assured her that she would be alright, and I would make sure she was safe. At that moment, I was so helpless, consumed by my issues, but there was no way I could leave her. She could have died in that parking lot, and it was a sad situation for more than one reason. It was a brutal reminder of the side of humanity I saw around me, opening my eyes to the likely reality that not one person stopped to help her. She wasn't the first person I saw fall victim to being dosed with this drug, and unfortunately, she wasn't the last. Without proper medical attention, she may have only been remembered as a casualty of drug abuse without anyone knowing the reality of what truly happened to her.

After that incident, Anna and I became party buddies, partially out of mutual trust, but also because we both loved having a good time, blocking our reality by expanding our emotional beings through the little magic pills. In addition, we discovered we had mutual friends who were locals, and there were many nights when we found ourselves out on the dance floor, living in the moment while staying within the security of the people we knew.

We partied for one full night in the Underground club and then went to the most comfortable place we knew to wind down. It was four in the morning at our old friend Tim's house where, as always, the crew was lying around in their underwear, connecting by doing whatever it took to make each other feel good, including deep conversation and the occasional deep-tissue massage. Getting a massage on ecstasy brought things to a whole different level, and we all willingly gave and received them without any alternate expectations. It was sunrise when Anna asked me if I wanted to go back to her store to do some Whippits, otherwise known as nitrous oxide. Since we were still high as hell, I walked right through that door. I had seen people inhale laughing gas, but I'd never tried it myself. Although it was foreign to me, through the haze of multiple ecstasy hits and my trust in her, I was open to trying it. Conveniently, she had a large stock of it under the counter at her store.

Alice's White Rabbit was one of the most original stores I'd been in, with multicoloured shag carpet covering the walls, insanely cool New York club clothing, and incredible electronic music playing in the background. She catered directly to the club scene, and at the time, her store was beyond popular with tourists and locals, who shopped for original club gear with the intention to stand out in the crowds of thousands who frequented the two massive nightclubs across the street. On this early morning, when most people were heading off to work, we locked ourselves in the store, and Anna went behind the counter to turn on the stereo. She then grabbed a few boxes of whipped cream cartridges and a couple of balloons. We sat on the floor, crossed-legged and face to face as she cracked open one of the cartridges and filled up one of the balloons. Laughing gas provided a rush to my head with the emotional release that sent me into a brief yet intense laughing fit. Adding the element of being high on MDMA, what I experienced is impossible to describe.

We found ourselves on the beach, coming into what most would call early morning after having finished three boxes of Whippits, and we finally decided to go sleep it off. As fun as that moment was, I was playing with fire, trying to fill a void with anything I could to drown the pain inside of me. While in my little world, the rest of the universe outside of drugs and the club scene kept moving along without me.

I was in a downward spiral,
being beyond selfish and irresponsible in the process.

On more than one occasion, while partying with me, my roommate, Wendy, tried her best to talk me through some of the crazy shit going on in my head. I neglected my dog, the one thing I had in Florida that gave me unconditional love, leaving her for days on end, assuming that Wendy would take care of her. She woke me up when she finally had enough by informing me I hadn't fed my own dog for over a month. That reality hit me and pierced my heart. I realized the damage I was leaving behind to this sweet pup who got the crappy deck of cards dealt to her. I was the selfish owner who only cared about the next pill I would swallow, trying to stay in my emotional *comfort zone*.

I started having clearer and more realistic nightmares than I had ever experienced, which brought me to tears. The guilt I had about neglecting my dog drove these nightmares to a place I never imagined—twisted enough that I would shudder to think of them for days. I was dropping ecstasy like it was candy, and the hole I was digging was so deep I could barely see the light anymore. The mutual friendships I valued were now only intermittently in my life and staying at the club until four in the morning after doing a show was my new normal. When I was high at the club, I felt like a rock star because everyone who didn't know me wanted to know me, but for all the wrong reasons. Cole told me years later that he tried to talk to me, but I wasn't listening.

My *Rock Bottom* moment came one night around four in the morning while searching for somewhere to go since the party was still raging in my brain with hardly anyone I knew left at the club. Some guy mentioned an after-party being held in a massive mansion on the water in Panama City, and of course, I was open to going anywhere at that point. When I walked in, the only person I knew was the guy back at the club who suggested the party, and loneliness started to hit me. I had the clothes on my back but no savings, no plans, and no genuine friends surrounding me anymore. As the sun began to rise, I went into the bathroom to splash some water on my face. Looking in the mirror, I was disgusted and shocked at what I saw. My eyes were black and sunken from having little to no sleep, and the morning sunlight gave me a cleansing reality of what I had turned into. I saw the vision of a person who had once looked after himself but had thrown everything away to drown his life into a false sense of reality.

I started thinking about my family, who gave me everything they could, and I felt reduced to a shell of my former self. What would they think of this person I was looking at? My father's words began ringing in my head, hearing him tell me I was in the wrong place, and I was in trouble. Florida was a no-tolerance drug state, and I can only imagine what some of the people at that party were doing behind closed doors, not to mention the fact that I had MDMA pills in my pocket. Even taking that out of the equation, my life was a mess.

My father never knew it, but he saved me with the words he embedded into my soul from a very young age. Moving from the mirror to the bathroom window, I watched the neighbour hug his kids goodbye and leave in his suit and tie for work. He had a purpose, and although I didn't know him, I envied him for the love in his life and the responsibility he gladly took on. That was the picture I painted, but I was a million miles away from that reality with no one to blame but myself. As I watched him drive away, I looked back in the mirror at my deteriorated exterior and felt the gaping hole in my heart. I called a cab and headed home to sleep off the insanity of the night before. I decided this was not going to be my life.

Although my drug phase was far from over, I made it an occasional instead of a daily thing. However, there were some new dancers in the group, and comparing myself to my original crew, it was hard fitting in at times. There was a brotherhood but just a different one, and as messed up as I had been, it wasn't a surprise that we didn't have the same kind of connection. I still felt swallowed, rarely paying for drugs while simultaneously living the dream and the nightmare. It was the summer of 1998, and although it wasn't the same as it had been previously, there were still some amazing memories to come.

We were performing at Club Lavela, and while I was on stage one night, one of the Fantasy Girls, Tanya, passed me a note, pretending it was a tip. It said: *Cassidy wants to know you... really know you.* Cassidy was a tall, blonde knockout married to Randy, the DJ of the radio station that broadcasted live out of the club. They were an odd pair, at least on the outside, because she was strikingly beautiful, and he was a short, slightly overweight loudmouth DJ. She had trouble written all over her, and I knew nothing good could come from it. Not only because she was a married woman but also because her husband was good friends with the club's owners. I tried to avoid her at first, but she made a point of walking by me while holding her husband's hand and staring right through me with obvious intent. And then, it came to a head on a night when all the male and female dancers met backstage after our shows for an *ecstasy toast*, clinking our pills together and dropping them at the same time. We were all going on the same ride, and it was sure to be an eventful evening. At 11 o'clock sharp, we met up at our little comfortable couch section to the good vibe beats of the Dark Room. Wearing my best *Club Kid* attire, sporting a massive Jiminy Cricket hat and ridiculous sunglasses, I instantly sensed the electric energy in our little VIP section of the club.

Our pills started kicking in at the same time, and the fun, crazy insanity began. Looking across the room at one of the Fantasy Girls, I told her to get down on the floor and meow like a cat. The whole crew started chuckling as she got down on her hands and knees, crawling across the floor, meowing with her ass up in the air like she was in heat. She proceeded to rub up against my leg, and I got down on the floor behind her and started barking like a dog. She quickly scrambled on hands and knees under one of the tables and started hissing at me. The entire room absolutely lost it, and I looked up to see Cassidy standing there with a smile on her face, watching us entertain everyone with our drug-induced stupidity. Getting up off the floor, I sat back down, and she walked over to show me the tan lines she had worked so hard to get earlier in the day. She bent over, pulled down her shorts and sat her bare ass down in my lap. After a few seconds, she hiked them back up and asked her friend to stand guard as she grabbed my hand and pulled me around the corner outside of the room. As we walked out, she turned me toward her and leaned in to kiss me without saying a word. It was really hot but playing with fire can truly get you burned. It didn't take long before her friend came around the corner to let us know that Randy was coming up the stairs to where we were. She pulled away without saying a word.

Cassidy had supposedly dropped acid the next time I was at the club, and when I walked up the stairs, I heard her yelling at one of her friends, expressing that she wanted to see me. She said my name over and over, and the heat of that fire started to get a little too close. I carried on with my night, and when I went out to the pool deck to get some air, Randy approached me from out of nowhere to formally introduce himself. I took a step back but held my composure because, in my eyes, I had done nothing wrong and was prepared to give him a dose of reality if necessary. He held out his hand, and I shook it as he explained that he wanted to shake the hand of the first man Cassidy had been interested in other than himself. Playing off that he had accepted what was happening, he pretended that he wanted to be buddies and we should go up to the Dark Room as new friends to surprise her. I played along, knowing he was going to try something, but when we arrived at the VIP area, he made the mistake of pushing me into her while she sat on the couch. I was face to face with her when I told her I was sorry for what I was about to do. I turned around and pushed him back, and he flew halfway across that little room. I wasn't about to hit him because I didn't need an assault charge, especially as an illegal alien. Shortly after that incident, she was hired as a VJ on MTV, moving out of town never to be seen again.

The constant circus of fun was in full swing, but I found myself stressed from partying too much as the summer moved on, still holding onto the residue of memories with Jessica. On the upside, one of my former revue mates, Julian, came down to Florida after I recommended him to AJ, and it was nice to have someone from my past to talk to. He had met Jessica a few times, and he was a good listener when I opened up to him about my struggle, living without her in my life. It was hard to admit I had given up on myself to a certain extent. I still had the confidence to perform on stage but accepting myself for who I was offstage was a different story. Because he had not been with me through this journey, he had an unbiased opinion. I appreciated his ear more than anything, and realistically, I just needed someone I could communicate with who I could trust.

Summer went on, and my struggles continued when I rented a Toyota Forerunner from one of the dancers in my group. He gave me a good deal to help me out, which was appreciated, but I had no idea what I got myself into when one of the tires flew off the truck while driving down a busy highway at 45 miles an hour. The vehicle came crashing down on the street as I watched the tire fly off, bouncing out of control into another car coming toward me in the opposite lane—the truck ground to a halt. Cody had put the wrong sized tires on the truck, and it was fortunate no one was killed. In a way, Murphy's law seemed to be kicking in, but it could have been far worse.

As erratic as my life was at the time, Cole and I created one of my best acts inspired by the pain that I was feeling. *The Executive* was based on a man who lost everything and was left destitute after living the dream. He drowned in his sorrows after the loss of his partner, and although I was far from destitute, I related to the loss, which allowed me to pour my heart and soul into the act. The entire costume was created from clothes bought at the second-hand store. I trashed an old suit I found and attached a beard with long hair to a baseball cap. We set the scene by building a park bench, and I beat up an old metal garbage can and attached a fire pan to the inside of it with chains. We created the voiceover that started after the emcee introduced me as a random person found wandering the streets who was given a shot at being a dancer. After my introduction, I stumbled onto the dance floor, holding a bottle wrapped in a brown paper bag. I began complaining about how I lost everything and only had two possessions left to my name—a picture of the partner who left me and my wedding ring to remember her by. I explained to the crowd that these were my last two possessions, and I threw the ring on the floor. Then, pulling her picture out of my pocket, I sat on the bench with my head down in shame.

The intro music faded in as I lip-synced the lyrics to Aerosmith's *Don't Wanna Miss A Thing*. As the chorus line approached, I took the lid off the garbage can and lit the fire pan inside. I used flash bombs created with different coloured powder to provide the reveal effect, dropping them into the fire. It was the perfect transition that always triggered a reaction from the crowd when the flash went off, creating a brief smokescreen for me to strip off each layer of my costume. After stripping off all the layers of my nasty outfit, I did an oil show in front of the fire on the park bench, with my tear-away pants being the last to remove. As the song finally built up to the famous Steven Tyler scream at its peak, I tore away the pants, and the house came down. For the grand finale, I took the picture I carried for so many years and threw it in the fire to burn her memory forever.

I had no issue expressing the emotion of that act on stage, but I had butterflies before I did it almost every time and goosebumps when I performed it on more than one occasion. That act meant something more to me than the others because I was portraying a part of me. Some nights, the sound would be deafening by the time I dropped that picture in the fire. My creativity brought a level of excitement back into my life that I had not experienced in quite some time. The show was an inspiring creation from my heart, similar to my purpose for writing this book. It isn't just about the past relationships I had with all these different women, but the value created by the failures and learning experiences I received from them. In some cases, the mistakes I made are obvious from the outside looking in. However, at the time, they were developed without being aware of why they were even happening in the first place. I had so many lessons to learn, and I still do. A significant portion of this book is based on relationships because, to me, creating memories and forming relationships is what life is all about, regardless of how they begin or end. Everything is temporary, so making an impact on others is where the fulfillment is born by leaving a legacy far beyond my dance career.

On the one hand, I turned a corner, but on the other, I kept following the entrenched rut that I didn't even realize I was in due to my ego. Through my experience, some of my best ideas were developed from the pain I felt inside that I was simply not willing or even able to face. I covered it all up with a smile and played the role I was being paid for. It was similar to being on a rollercoaster that never ended; it was fun at times, but the highs were really high, and the lows were really low.

Stability was a word that was not in my vocabulary at this time, but I had a deep desire to have it.

Just before we left to go on the road in 1999, the rollercoaster came to a grinding halt as I tragically lost one of my friends, Ashley. I was the last person to see him alive as he sped off on his motorcycle, leaving me at his house until he was to return from delivering a few MDMA pills to a buddy of his. The accident was spurred on by him running from the police when they tried to pull him over. I assume that his fear of going to jail in a no-tolerance drug state was what made him run, and I found out later that when he tried to make a corner with his headlights off, he misjudged the turn and hit a mailbox—he was instantly killed.

I waited in his living room until finally giving up, assuming something had come up. I was awakened the next morning by the tragic news about a young man who was taken from the world far too early. This gave me a front-row seat to understanding that tomorrow is not guaranteed, and everyone has an expiration date. I left with the group on tour, carrying a heavy heart, and eventually landed in a popular country bar by the name of Whisky River in Macon, Georgia. We arrived at a packed house and walked in through the back door of the club. I stood there with Jeff, one of the new dancers from New York, evaluating the crowd to see what this night was about to bring.

There must have been 500 women in that place, and she immediately stood out with her long blonde hair, sitting in a little red, white, and blue Tommy Hilfiger dress with four or five ladies at a table. We locked eyes, and she stared at me with a drink in one hand and a long, slim cigarette in the other. She was stunning with a face like a porcelain doll, and I could tell she was young. The attraction was obvious, but little did I realize that she had just celebrated her 18th birthday only one week before. I took my performance up a notch that night, and when I broke into the crowd with women waving dollar bills all around me, I made my way over to her table. She held up a bill, and I jumped up on the empty chair in front of her, looked down, and asked her to put her money away. It was the first and only time I didn't accept a tip. Instead, I leaned down and whispered in her ear that I had to know her and asked her to stick around after the show. Jenna was definitely a diamond in the rough compared to the other women at the table that night, but my focus was all on her because she had sex appeal written all over her.

Budweiser had sponsored the event, and the club had asked us to give away some signed shirts as part of the promotion. We chose to wear them on stage for our closer with the intent of throwing them in the crowd after we took them off. After signing mine with *Love and Kisses on all of your Pink Parts*, I threw mine out into that insane crowd. She may have only been four feet, ten inches, but nothing was stopping her from getting that shirt. After the show, we had our usual lineup of ladies, waiting for Polaroid pictures, and I was on cameraman duty for the evening. Danny, one of the dancers, kept falling asleep in the middle of the session due to taking GHB. Not only was it unprofessional but also aggravating because I wanted to talk with this girl, and we were taking forever due to his state of mind. Looking over, I noticed that she was sitting alone, so I took a second to let her know that I had to finish up, but I would be there as soon as I could. She waited patiently, but by the time we finally finished, some random dude sat down and was chatting her up.

Walking up without introduction, I took control by looking over at her and saying: *Babe, what can I grab you to drink?* He got the point loud and clear because his chair was empty by the time I got back. As sexually appealing as she was, I wasn't looking for a one-night stand with her. I authentically wanted to get to know what this girl was all about, so we decided to leave the bar and go to the Waffle House where we could be one-on-one without distraction in a 24-hour greasy spoon at the exit of an interstate. She mentioned that she lived with her cousin, and I could tell she had a hard life, but I had no idea to what extent. I really liked her, but we were two completely different people from two different worlds. Small town Georgia was like middle earth in comparison to where I was raised. However, that didn't matter because there was a connection that strangely filled the void of instability I was experiencing when we met. After we finished, we both went our separate ways, but it didn't take long before we connected again over the phone.

The next night and we chatted for three hours, and although I lived almost five hours away, I told her I was tempted to drive back up there to see her, but it was already nine at night and, it would take me until three in the morning before I could get there. She called my bluff, and I asked my neighbour, John, if I could borrow his car for the trip. I drove a little robin's egg blue Ford Festiva all the way back to Macon, and she met me at the interstate exit in front of the same Waffle House. Embarrassed, she immediately warned me about her place, which I understood because it could have been condemned. We slowly walked through a penned-in area surrounding the old farmhouse, which led to the front door. Vicious Chow dogs were surrounding us, and although none of them bit me, I was admittedly nervous entering this environment for more than one reason. I was taken back a bit when we initially walked in. She mentioned that a snake had dropped through a hole in the ceiling of her room one night, and Georgia has some really big snakes. She was staying with her cousin, Sandra and her niece, Jennifer, who were in bed sleeping by the time I arrived. We pulled out the living room sofa bed and decided to put a movie on, but before the opening credits finished, sexual attraction took over. It was an awkward place to be with someone for the first time, but it was sweet regardless of the less-than-perfect surroundings.

As unstable as my life was, I wanted more for her than the cards she had been dealt, and even though we barely knew one another, she gave me a reason to look out for someone else other than myself.

As I was about to leave the next day, the sun was setting in the Georgia sky, and I held her in my arms under a peach tree in the front yard. I told her that regardless of whether we ever saw each other again, she was better than this place, and I saw bigger things for her. I fully realized we were from two different planets and that opposites attract. However, we had commonalities that connected us. We communicated over the phone for the next month or so, but it didn't take long until she made a trip to Panama City Beach to visit me on New Year's Eve. She brought a friend along for the trip, and that night, I brought them into my rock star world for the first time. When Jenna met the other dancer's wives and girlfriends, she was intimidated by the scene but up for the experience. I introduced her to the crew as my girlfriend, and everyone welcomed her with open arms. However, I don't think Jenna or her friend truly knew what they were getting themselves into.

The friends in my circle were all dropping ecstasy, and she wanted to try it. She decided to take it with me because everyone else around us was doing it, and she trusted I wouldn't give her anything to harm her intentionally. Her friend was not into it, but Jenna wanted to take it. So, without considering her body weight, I irresponsibly gave her the same amount I would take, and I was double her size. When it kicked in 45 minutes later, she was overwhelmed and so afraid that she wanted to leave the club. We went outside, and she wanted to go back to my house. When we pulled up into the driveway, she asked me where she was. Although it was hitting her hard, her friend assured me that she could take care of her while I went back to the club to the party. I helped her into my bed and knelt beside her, trying my best to make her comfortable because her mind was racing a million miles an hour. All her emotions poured out as she told me that she wanted to be the mother of my children. It may have been the drugs talking to a certain extent, but I knew she meant it. Through all the instability around me, she gave me a sense of ease when she said it. Although I didn't want to have children, I knew that she loved me enough that she would go there. Then, in the next breath, after baring her soul to me, she demanded I go back to be with my crew instead of babysitting her. My brain was racing as well, and once I knew she would be ok, I went back to make my appearance at the club. Admittedly, she was a little surprised that I left but understood I was also messed up and not thinking straight.

She told me later that she thought she saw grass growing on the floor of my bedroom, but for all the ecstasy I had taken over the years, I had never hallucinated.

I came home in the morning, crashing out after a night of dancing mayhem. Jenna was sound asleep, and we took the entire next day to recover, and the next night was far better than the one before. I am obviously not a rabbit, but we fucked like rabbits that night with a bit of fetish role play incorporated into the program. Sexually, we were on another level, and we didn't leave the bedroom for hours. My roommate, Wendy, and Jenna's friend sat out in the living room, saying they wished they could have sex like that. They made their way back up to Georgia the next day, and Jenna was clearly still dealing with the effects of the MDMA because her cousin pointed out that something was different about her. She got a dose of the Panama City party life, and she wasn't about to let it go. She knew that I was going to be her ticket out of the borderline poverty she was living in, and I gladly accepted.

Roughly a month later, we got our first place together, which was one side of a duplex near the beach that one of my dancer buddies, Alex, offered us to rent. We moved in, but after a couple of days, I was booked for the biggest money-making road trip of my life. The tour would take us from Panama City to Fort Wayne, Indiana, north to Peoria, Illinois, then to Erie, Pennsylvania, finishing off in Jamestown, New York. One group would stay at home to do the local club circuit, and the other would hit the road. Everyone was aware that AJ had booked a show that was to be one of the biggest and best of our careers, and he could only send five dancers out of the ten in our two groups. At times, AJ had to make hard decisions because he knew that all parties could not be satisfied, but he had to deal with addictions, bookings, promotions, and sometimes even babysitting. I would be gone for a week, leaving Jenna alone in paradise in comparison to her former environment. For her, it was a whole new exciting world, living so close to the beach, but she was too scared to go there by herself.

Ultimate Fantasy was a talented group, but AJ chose to hold them back, and fortunately, Fatal Attraction, which was my group at the time, was to go on this tour. We only had so many emcees, so the way things worked out, he was forced to send a rookie on tour with us with barely any previous experience, and a few of the veteran dancers were not happy about it, including me. Chaz was beyond irritating, and I understood the frustration of the dancers left behind, but Ultimate Fantasy had previously been booked for a European Tour, so I assumed it was our turn, and I'm grateful it was.

We arrived in Fort Wayne early and witnessed a massive lineup of eager ladies outside the club as our tour van pulled into the parking lot. We made our way up to our change rooms located on the top floor, overlooking the entire club below. Standing, looking down through a one-way mirror as the club doors opened, we were shocked at what we saw. Even though there was still an hour before we took to the stage, like concert fans rushing the floor to find the best spot, they jockeyed for position because they assumed it was standing room only. We immediately put a plan together to get as many dancers in the crowd as often as possible so that when the main dancer performed his act, we would have up to three other dancers in the crowd, collecting tips right from the beginning of the show. Our only concern was our rookie, Chaz. He was sub-par at best, and we had no other choice but to give him the final dance spot. We figured that by the time he went on, the ladies would be drunk enough that it really wouldn't matter, and we were correct.

Outside of our show pay, we had three ways to make money based on tips, selling promotional posters, and taking pictures with the ladies after the show. Our agent took half of the promo and picture money while we kept 100 percent of our tips and show pay. There was so much money being waved in the air during the show that we had to empty our G-Strings in a bag at the back of the stage and get right back out there as soon as possible. It was absolute mayhem with a grand total of 1800 women, so we chose to pool our tips to make things fair.

By the time Chaz hit the stage, the crowd was going insane, so to ensure his show was successful, we gave him the one act that anyone could pull off. It was the standby act that had been done a million times before but never seemed to get old—YMCA. It was obvious he was the odd man out, but the crowd's reaction didn't show it, and we didn't care. They were so fired up by that time that he could have done almost anything, and they would have been screaming. I have danced for many crowds over the years, but that crowd was like none other.

We finished our closing routine, and Christian, one of our more popular entertainers, sent the crowd into a frenzy when he opened his G-String and snapped a picture of his crotch. He then handed it over to Cody, our emcee, to give away to the first girl willing to throw her bra or panties on the stage. I stood there in awe as the pile got higher and higher, eventually reaching about three feet high, all said and done. If I had not been there to witness it, I would never have believed it. In a little over two hours, I raked in over 1300 dollars, which I believe was the most I ever made in one show throughout my entire 25-year career. After the show, I chose to go back to my room and call Jenna while the other dancers tried to find a hook up for the night. I was beaming with excitement while the money was being counted. I promised her that I would take her to Victoria's Secret when I got home to pick out the most badass outfit we could find. She was beautiful, and it was time to level up.

Bloomington, Indiana was our next stop, and we found another packed house waiting for us with a perfect set up for ladies' night. A long catwalk extended from the main stage right down the middle of the audience, similar to a fashion show experience. Cody emceed the first half, and I took over for the second half with the added pleasure of introducing Christian as the final performer of the night. After pumping up the crowd, I did my usual intro for him: *Ladies! Welcome to centre stage, six foot four and hung to the floor, Mr. Christian Styles!* The crowd went wild as he came out to his slow, sexy act that made the ladies melt. However, as I watched him, I could tell something was off. He strutted down to the end of the catwalk and slid up between a girl's legs to accept a tip. He then proceeded to pass out right in her lap, and I did my best to smooth over the situation. His addiction to GHB got the better of him, but I wasn't about to let the crowd know it. I made out that he was diabetic and asked the crowd if anyone had sugar at the table. It was the only thing I could think of, but nothing was going to cover up the visual of dragging his lifeless body in a G-String backstage in front of a shocked audience.

With the feature dancer passing out, the club manager was obviously not happy. The paramedics arrived when the rest of us attempted to have our usual picture-taking session; Christian was screaming over the club music while pictures were being snapped. After the paramedics shot him up with something, he began fighting them off with the IV in his arm while coming out of the coma he was in. What started off as an amazing show finished as an absolute disaster. Making my way back to the change room, this huge man was lying on the floor with his back against the wall, looking like a little kid who had just lost his best friend. He immediately apologized, but he just didn't get it. His drug issues were affecting our business to the extent that we were never booked in that club again. The damage was done.

Trying to put everything behind us, we drove north the next day to Peoria, Illinois to another large, enthusiastic crowd, which was, fortunately, a success with nothing going sideways. Then came the college campus in Erie, Pennsylvania. Even with the debacle in Bloomington in the rear-view mirror, the tour was a success, with only one show to go in Jamestown, N.Y. the next night. However, the show in Erie was hard to forget. We were obligated to watch out for one another on the road because anything could happen. Jeff and I were chatting after the show when we realized that the rookie had not been seen for an hour or so. We went on the search because he was new and bound to get into trouble. Concerned, we looked around the club with no luck, so we resorted to checking the tour van parked in the back. We opened the side door, and there he was, snoring in one of the middle seats with his mouth wide open, drooling all over himself. Without even making it to the bed in the back, he was yet another story of a dancer being wasted on GHB. This kid needed to learn a lesson, and as brutal as this was, I chose to give him one. I decided to make him really think about the consequences of his actions because although I wasn't exactly fond of him, I didn't want him to end up as another statistic for his stupidity.

I asked Jeff to go to the back of the tour van and grab the camera as I unzipped my pants and put my cock as close to his open mouth as I could without touching him. Jeff snapped the picture, and I zipped up my pants and headed back into the club, leaving the chips to fall where they may. The following day, we were all having breakfast in the hotel restaurant when I asked him how his night was. He couldn't remember anything after the show, but I slid the picture across the table, and he got the picture in a literal sense, almost throwing up. It was a hard lesson for him, but that was the last time I saw that kid do GHB. He was lucky to have had the opportunity to be on that tour in the first place, and he messed up. He had witnessed Christian being revived by the paramedics only two nights before, and I assumed he would have learned from that, but he had not. Although I was far from an angel with all my ecstasy use, GHB was a whole different thing. I saw countless people over the years flatline and brought back to life taking that garbage, including some of my party friends. The addiction is indescribable, but from what I saw, people simply didn't care what the consequences were.

I saw some of the most amazing people struggle with it, along with other substances— substances they thought they were doing, but the substances were doing them.

That kid may have been upset with my actions that night, but in the end, it may have saved his life.

The snow was falling as we made our way into Jamestown for our last show, and we were all hungry to get back to the warm Florida climate. Fortunately, the show went well, and I called Jenna to let her know I would be back with some stories to tell. When I mentioned I was coming back, she took five showers that day, wanting to look and smell good for my arrival. When I made it back, I was beyond excited to see her as I opened my bag and dumped the dirty money all over the bed. We rolled around in it, laughing hysterically, which made the road struggle worth it, and this girl who had lived a life of hardship that most cannot comprehend was beyond excited, living in a dream. We had a nice little beach pad away from the city, and she had enjoyed a full week alone to soak it all in without distraction. She had a perfectly painted picture, living in the present moment with a man she considered a superstar.

As promised, I took her to Victoria's Secret, and when we walked into the mall, passing the full food court, it seemed like every person turned to stare at us. We were a bit of an odd-looking couple, with me being 28 years old and six feet, two inches, and her being 18 and four feet, ten. It was the first, but not the last time we had all eyes on us. Going into Victoria's Secret, she had no idea where to start, being overwhelmed, never having anyone do something like that for her.

She looked amazing when she tried on the sexy little outfit I picked out for her, and a new image was created. She was a girl who came from nothing, and at that moment, she was something. Regardless of being self-conscious about her body, she wore it well, and her excitement was written all over her face.

The next night was when she got to show off this new look at Cash's in Fort Walton Beach. She walked in with me from the back and sat down at the bar while I went upstairs to the change room. The intimidation she felt from the other dancer's girlfriends and wives was gone, and she instantly exuded confidence and sex appeal. Even Jason, my old roommate, tried hitting on her before he knew who she was. But after she told him, he apologized to us both out of respect, and we all had a good laugh about it. Around this time, I experienced one of the most original exotic dancing experiences of my lifetime. I was contacted by a gentleman by the name of Will, who was serving in the U.S. military. He had a unique request, looking for a dancer willing to embarrass his female captain retiring from her long-standing position of authority. From what I understood, there was a large group of military men who had taken orders from her for quite some time, and they were looking for some playful revenge.

I walked in, and the room was filled with male officers, waiting for the big moment. Entering the stage, the captain was playing along, waiting in her chair while the crowd of officers enthusiastically supported my entrance. As the tease began, they started getting louder and louder until the noise was almost deafening. She played right along with it, sitting there as I did my best to embarrass her to their delight. After the show concluded, multiple military men kept entering the change room, throwing me money, showing their gratitude at the same time. The massive enthusiasm was obviously based on taking orders from her for quite some time, but I could tell it was out of love and respect for who she was.

After the show, I met up with Will outside to get paid, and somehow our conversation turned to the subject of working out, and he mentioned that he really wanted to get in shape but didn't know where to start. So, I worked out an hourly fee whereby I would help him with his training along with providing a diet by calculating his calories like my old trainer, Lou, had done for me back in my bodybuilding days. Will had the self-discipline to show up and follow every step in the process, and I was truly proud of his accomplishments. Once he found his wings, I dropped the fee and continued to train with him when needed. He appreciated the help I provided, and he showed it by dropping by before one of my shows and giving me a really cool jacket. I was surprised yet very appreciative, and that wasn't the last time he showed up when it counted.

Jenna and I had moved out of Alex's duplex and rented a

little place in the city, but we only had one piece of furniture, which was a blow-up mattress. However, it was a start, and we went to the Salvation Army to buy a couple of used couches. Although we couldn't afford end tables, we used cardboard boxes with towels thrown over them. I let Will know that we just moved in and barely had anything to our names. He shocked us both when he showed up at our place with a moving van full of furniture he wouldn't use anymore because he was being deployed to Germany. We were grateful and astonished at the reciprocity. This was one of the key moments in my life when I truly understood the value of giving back and how it can affect others' lives.

Our new little place had very thin walls, and we were in that *honeymoon* phase, exploring all aspects of a new and exciting person in your life. That exploration was very sexual and vocal at times. Our bedroom was located right behind the thin wall we shared with our neighbour's living room, and we could hear a pin drop on both sides. We had exchanged phone numbers with the nice young couple who lived next door when we moved in just in case of emergency. One mid-afternoon, while having some really intense sex, the phone rang. Our neighbour, Dave, was concerned, standing outside of our front door with a knife. Jenna opened the door, and there he was, making sure she wasn't being attacked. He was embarrassed but relieved that it was just us having freaky sex; we all had a good but awkward laugh at the time.

Jenna's 19th birthday was approaching, and I wanted to plan something special. So, I arranged a surprise party for her that she would never forget with all ten dancers in our revue, along with AJ, our agent, and a few other close friends. It was almost shocking that they all showed up for a girl's 19th birthday party because even getting them to perform was hard enough at times. Everyone waited patiently as I went to pick her up from work. They were all inside, sitting in the dark when the door swung open, and the balloons dropped from the ceiling with the most unexpected surprise she had ever had in her life. Having no clue what had just hit her, we started the music, and I sat her down on the couch. The dancers lined up in formation just like we did for our opening routine to Janet Jackson's *If*. She sat there in our living room in utter shock. When the music stopped, Dave from next door came in with her cake, wearing a silly clown outfit I had in my costume trunk. The cake was custom made with Winnie the Pooh and Tigger, wearing tiny icing G-Strings on top. She felt loved and appreciated, but the best was yet to come.

I had a connection through the group who was a massage therapist with a side gig, cleaning some of the most high-end apartments on the Emerald Coast in Navarre Beach. It was winter, and the building was empty, so she gave us the key to the penthouse suite for a private weekend in paradise. Walking through the door, we had two options: the door to the left was the entrance to a little guest suite about the size of a shoebox, or there was the main unit through the door to the right. I opened the door to the left just to get her reaction, and it was priceless. Enthusiastically, I showed her around the little suite, and she was beyond happy and appreciative. Next, I gave her the option to stay where we were, and then I opened the door to the right. When we entered the main unit, her chin hit the floor because she saw the fully stocked penthouse with a massive kitchen, living room, master bedroom, and a bathroom with a huge marble tub and shower. Even though it was a rental, it was all ours for the weekend, and we took full advantage of it, dropping MDMA together while listening to some kick-ass beats in the monstrous king-sized bed and connecting on a whole new level.

She opened up about how badly she wanted to be reunited with her little brother and sister, with who she had lost touch so many years before. She allowed herself to be vulnerable after battling so many demons from her past. She didn't want to expose them before out of fear of losing me, and through her vulnerability, I started to truly fall in love with a young woman who had been starved of love for most of her life. It was her and me against the world, and we were ready for the battle with an attraction that was beyond sexual. We had time to make up for the past, with the two of us experiencing another level of understanding. I had a deep desire to give her a life she was robbed of in her childhood.

I tried to be the knight in shining armour
who rode in to save the day,
giving her a life she deserved instead of the shitty deck of cards
she was dealt from the start.

We took up every inch of that king-size bed and absorbed as much of the experience as we could. And then, we took advantage of our empty surroundings the next day by grabbing a few blankets off the bed and bringing them outside on the balcony to create a sexual experience to be remembered. We were 23 stories from the ground with a view of the Gulf of Mexico in front of us, loving every second of it as we pulled the covers back, exposing ourselves in broad daylight. Even as a helicopter flew by the building, we didn't miss a beat because it was all about us. She was not like any other woman I had met, and I had zero complaints. I had found a four-foot, two version of Pamela Anderson with even more sex appeal. She came into my life with no expectations and by fate. No matter our pasts, nothing else mattered because we were living in the moment, and it was absolutely spectacular. It was erotic and naughty being physical, and yet, it was emotional for her and the happiest she had ever been.

The Naked Truth

This path of self-destruction came with the view of my relationship with Jessica in the rear-view mirror, but still on my mind. Although I was back in Florida, I was still living in the past at times, trying to find the emotions I experienced with my former group by consuming myself with the party lifestyle and dropping ecstasy to heal the pain artificially. Being out of control attracted people who were also out of control into my life. I was on a constant search for connection, and although I made some good friends along the way, it took the visual of my broken-down exterior to realize how far I had fallen.

When I met Jenna, I not only saw an extremely attractive young lady, but also someone who had minimal life experience outside of what she had learned through the hard times of her past. I loved how she showed her appreciation for the things I did for her, and although I barely had control of my own life, I had control of our path forward with her support every step of the way. She adored me, and at times I took it for granted, even though I enjoyed blowing her mind through my actions.

Although she wanted me to go back to the club and enjoy myself on New Year's, I was responsible for almost overdosing an 18-year-old girl, giving her a foreign substance that was unfamiliar to her. Although I was high, and it was her decision to drop ecstasy with me, it was my responsibility to take care of her at that moment. Instead, I selfishly went out, leaving her to deal with the effects of this experience without me. I brought her into this new and exciting world, and anything could have happened to her, but I was so consumed with the drugs and partying that I never considered that. We started our relationship based on sex and drugs without forming a true connection as a team. She was naive to what this world was all about, and if I had been a truly good partner, I would have stayed by her side to help her get through it and not worried about my status, making an appearance back at the party. Although she was under the influence, she mentioned that she wanted to be the mother of my children; having a kid was the last thing on my mind, especially at that time. I was not even close to being responsible enough to have kids, but this was something that she wanted, and it should have been discussed. We were communicating but not connecting.

Integrity & Empathy

IX

Walking the Tightrope in the Land of the Free

The *Butterfly Effect* moments I experienced in my life had me wondering what would have happened if I'd taken a different path than the one I did.

Overall, I did a good job avoiding the temptations of women throwing themselves at me while I was on the road, especially having the sexual connection I had with Jenna. However, I was not perfect, although, at times, she thought I was close to it. When we crossed paths, I knew I found something special, regardless of our imperfections. Her life was riddled with abuse, neglect, minimal education, and disappointment before she met me, and I was not about to have any of that in our future. At times, our relationship had sexual addiction and drugs incorporated into it, but we had meaning with a deep trust and ease that I had never experienced before. My status had attracted partners in my past, but she recognized my value in more than one way, and I knew she loved me with every part of her being. She left everything she knew to start a life with me, walking through the door I opened for her into this new, unknown world. However, one occasion put me to the test at the most unexpected time, which could have changed everything in an instant.

Our group was booked in Little Rock, Arkansas, and although I had been faithful to Jenna from the moment I laid eyes on her, I never expected to hear my phone ring with a very familiar voice on the other end. But again, this was long before any type of social media existed, so it took far more effort to find someone rather than doing a simple search on the internet. So, Kaitlen's unmistakable voice shocked and surprised me as memories of our past simultaneously flooded my head. To this day, I still have no idea how she tracked me down, but she did. She asked: *I don't suppose you would happen to be booked in Little Rock, Arkansas tonight now, would you?* Whether intentional or not, she was booked as the feature dancer at a club down the street and wanted to drop by to see our show. The red flags were everywhere, but I hadn't seen her in years, and although I knew it was trouble, I was happy to hear from her and opened the door.

When she arrived, Cody, the emcee, burst into the change room, mentioning that one of the hottest women he had ever seen was at the front entrance asking for me. I walked up to the front of the club and saw her standing at the top of the stairs, and everything I had blocked for so long came rushing in like a freight train. She watched my show but was scheduled to be on stage, so she asked me to drop by when I was done, so we could catch up. My mind was racing with excitement and fear because I knew that my amazing new relationship would be put to the ultimate test if I went to see her. But we had unfinished business, so I walked right in.

As I approached the club, I knew she was on stage based on the music playing. It was the music we shared a love for when we were together. I like to think that she had an appreciation for the sweet moments possibly taken for granted in the past, but at this point, they were far back in the past. She may have been a stripper, hustling a bunch of guys for money back then, but I got the message. Watching her finish her show from across the room, I waited for her to sign promo pictures and wrap everything up. It was ironic to watch a long line of men excited to have a few seconds to chat with her and get an autograph. I had been in the same situation multiple times myself, but I thought about that girl I knew in our younger years, working in that little shoe store. That girl had so much natural beauty long before the surgeries and the costuming I was witnessing now. The men in the line were willing to wait to have a brief conversation but had no idea what I was looking at. They only saw the fantasy, not the reality. She looked stunning, but she was so far away from the girl I knew based on her exterior. I was looking at Kaitlen from the inside, not the stage persona assigned to her.

We left together, and when she asked me to go back to her hotel room, I sensed my morality bending. We arrived, and she had to make the call to check in with the father of her son. As I listened to their conversation, guilt started coming over me, along with a sense of awkwardness for a couple of reasons: he had no idea I was standing there and neither did Jenna. She ended the call with: *I love you.* Then it was just us, standing in a hotel room hundreds of miles away from anyone we knew. We both had the same desire pulsing through us but didn't know where to start. Lying on the bed, Kaitlen turned on the T.V. to break the silence and reached out to hold my hand. We were older with more experiences behind us, good and bad, but it didn't really matter because the desire for one another had not gone away. It may have been stronger than ever before at that moment, and I slept with her that night, but we didn't have sex. We laid in bed wrapped around one another, but it wasn't about sex. I missed her in my life, and I was beyond conflicted.

The question became whether we would throw away everything to start a new life together or take the moment for what it was and go back to where we were a short 24 hours before. She had money, but I could tell that it had not brought her happiness. We woke the next morning, and I had to leave because we were scheduled for the next show. I took the time to look over at her lying beside me with her eyes closed, admiring the beauty of her face in comfort and at peace. I got up to head back to the hotel with a cloud of regret and guilt enveloping me. What would I have thought if Jenna had done this behind my back? How much pain would I have experienced knowing that for one night everything was put to the side to release emotions from the past with someone who didn't work out in the first place? I kissed her goodbye, looking back to see this picture-perfect woman lying naked on the bed while walking away with multiple thoughts running through my head. She seemed to be bound to an unhappy relationship with a young child, and I had a fabulous relationship that I was not willing to jeopardize. Jenna may not have had the money or the *fame*, but she had never wronged me, and she didn't deserve yet another heartbreak in her life. I couldn't even consider breaking her heart because she was stone cold in love with me—most people don't find that kind of love.

We were driving out of Little Rock when my phone rang, and it was Kaitlen. She expressed her vulnerability after seeing me again, and I could tell she needed stability. She was willing to throw everything away with the hopes of starting a family with me, but the timing was off. I explained that I was with someone I truly loved, and if it had been a year earlier, I would have tried again. She could afford anything she wanted, but it wasn't about the money at that point. The vision she had was not possible, and she started crying as my heart broke for her. I often wonder what would have happened if I had taken the other road. What would my life have been like? I will never know the answer to that question, but I often thought about it. I knew that if it truly came down to one moment, one decision could alter my life completely. I chose the road of morality and integrity in a world with so little of it, leaving behind a woman from my past who most men would fantasize over.

Coming home after that tour was challenging in more than one way. The guilt was still sitting in my mind, but I could live with the actions I took and didn't take—I left that skeleton in the closet where it belonged. However, another factor came into the equation; the dancers were conflicted with our agent, AJ, and there was talk of breaking off and forming a new group without him. But I wasn't in the same situation as the rest of them because I was illegal and had been in the U.S. for far too long without a social security number. If things got nasty, there was a high possibility I could be deported back to Canada, and our house of cards would fall.

Jenna and I were concerned, and we didn't want to take any chances, so, although we had not been together for very long, we chose to get married. This was spurred by desperation to a certain extent, but we both made the decision with no regret. Even though we were very different in so many ways, there was a mutual love for one another. Our wedding ceremony consisted of a small group of friends, and of course, the dancers. It all happened so fast that our families didn't even know, and our pictures were taken with a disposable camera. I asked Cole to be my best man, but he couldn't make it, and although I was disappointed at the time, he made up for it years later, inviting me to be the best man at his wedding—I was honoured to be part of it. Cole had been a road warrior with me for so many years, and he helped me come out of a downward spiral that may not have happened without his support.

At the time, a mutual friend of ours, Austin, filled in as best man, and Cole's girlfriend performed the ceremony. While reading the vows, instead of saying *lawfully wedded wife*, she mistakenly said *awfully leaded wife*, and we all had an awkward chuckle at her mistake. Nevertheless, it was a beautiful ceremony with our closest people surrounding us on the white sand beaches of Panama City.

My new wife was more beautiful than the sun setting behind us, and when I looked into her striking eyes to say those vows, I meant every single word.

The only downfall was the image of our friend Christian stumbling around in the background on the beach, oblivious to what was happening. He was once again high on GHB and making a fool out of himself, which may have been a bad omen to a certain extent.

We walked with our heads held high, being treated like a couple of celebrities, with the doormen and bartenders clapping as we entered the massive club for ladies' night. For me, the only lady that mattered that night was Jenna, and I dedicated the show to her. With a perfect follow-up, we went to a small local bar, and one of our friends sang a wedding song to us while we had our first dance. Jenna was so small that she resorted to straddling me as I held her up in the air, and the moment was sweet with a large crowd of strangers watching us celebrate our day. I married a small-town girl from Middle Georgia, and we made a pact that night bigger than

214

the vows we expressed hours earlier. No matter how much it hurt, we agreed to end it if either of us ever strayed because the bond would break beyond repair. We agreed wholeheartedly, both believing it was beyond comprehension that it could be a possibility.

Through trust, Jenna became vulnerable and confided in me about everything she went through as a kid. I knew it was rough, but I didn't fully realize until she broke down and told me the whole story. She had dealt with sexual trauma at times and was forced to take a shower with a garden hose sticking through the bathroom window from outside as a kid. Being constantly teased at school for the rags she wore was a common occurrence, and she was, unfortunately, put in the position of a fill-in mother for her two siblings at a young age. Her mother had substance abuse issues on a whole other level, and Jenna was dragged around like a gypsy from town to town throughout her childhood. She eventually landed in middle Georgia, with the closest family she knew. At this point, she hadn't seen her mother in years, and her biological father lived in Oregon, but she didn't know him. Her brother and sister were out there somewhere, but she hadn't seen them since they were very young, living in Texas. Jenna had so much pain on the inside, but just wanted to be loved and had so much love to give. Even within her Georgia family, she dealt with a different kind of abuse. Her grandfather was a dirty old man who made sexually suggestive comments to her and her sister while they played pool in her grandmother's bar. When they brought it up, the excuse was that he loved them, and I was stunned how these things were considered acceptable because it was all so very wrong compared to the sheltered world I was brought up in.

I saw potential that she didn't see in herself because mental, physical, and sexual trauma just does that to a person. Having been told she was shit all her life, she started believing she was. I wanted to smash that deeply embedded limiting belief out of her. The problem was that she never faced these things head-on. She didn't seek therapy but rather dealt with her trauma on her own by sweeping it under the rug and flicking off the switch on her emotions when things got hard. She covered up most of it by playing tough to protect herself, and I understood why. When I look back, the red flags were there, but I was wearing rose-colored glasses to filter it out myself. But even though we had all that against us, we started a new life together, and it was very exciting.

I was her husband, but I was sometimes forced to act more like a father figure, trying to protect her due to her age and limited life experience. It was the beginning of a co-dependent relationship, which was healthy at times but unhealthy at others. It was the wrong thing to do, but she was 100 percent in love with me from the first day we met. I was a man that was kind to her, not some little boy she met back in Georgia, trying to be a player. I provided her with a dramatic life change in more ways than one, and I took control, guiding her in the right direction at times and the wrong way in others. By trying to be the *man* as the hunter and gatherer instead of supporting her to achieve her own goals and dreams, I took control, providing her with a safety blanket while also stunting her ability to grow as a person. Years later, she felt bad for me having to support her through this time in her life because she was still kind of like a toddler, never exposed to the lifestyle I led. And like a toddler, she needed to fall flat on her face to learn to walk.

Jenna a was ten years younger than I was, so I had an obligation to make her feel secure with my occupation while giving her the freedom to experience new friendships. So, she came out to the shows with the other wives and girlfriends, sitting in the back of the room, observing the mayhem of ladies' night. She always kept her composure, and I can only remember one time when she became upset with a woman who tipped me. As I moved to the next person holding up a dollar bill, she overheard this woman commenting to her friends that she was taking *that* home with her. Hearing those words set her off, and all four-foot ten of her wanted to beat that woman senseless.

However, as her new husband, I took their money, and when my G-String was full, I happily strutted up to her, smiled, and emptied it into her purse, giving her the confidence that it was all about her—that blew her mind. She came out to Cash's in Fort Walton Beach most of the time because she was still underage, but the bartenders still served her drinks. On one occasion, the other girls got her absolutely wasted on shots while I was dancing, and it was obvious when she approached me afterwards. She was out making *friends*, and my protection mechanism kicked in. Unfortunately, a person has to learn the hard way sometimes, and the pink Kamikazes she had been slamming came back to bite her; later that night, I was the one holding her hair back as she puked pink nastiness in the bathroom stall. It was far from appealing, but I couldn't talk because I had my fair share of party times, and I didn't judge her.

I have found that being in some relationships can be like walking a tightrope at times. One of the *friends* Jenna made was a female bartender named Candy, who had voiced that she was bisexual. I could tell almost immediately that she had the hots for my wife, but Jenna said I was crazy, so I let the chips fall where they may. Candy had been there for Jenna's 19th birthday, and it seemed like she was always around. I sensed that something wasn't right about this woman, and my perception was bang on. The date of April 19, 2000, will forever go down as one of the worst days of my life. It was my birthday, but we wanted to keep it fairly low-key, so we decided to make an appearance at the club. The plan was to stay for a while and then break away and return to our little duplex with a couple of friends. A new dancer by the name of Adam joined us, along with Candy, and the four of us dropped MDMA together. We enjoyed the whole experience in the little comfort zone we created—a safe, secure environment, or so we thought.

Candy went out to her Jeep to get some music and suddenly realized that it had been broken into. All her music was stolen, and in her emotional, upset state of mind, she called the police, and she and Jenna rode in the police car on a search for the little criminals. Their eyes were like saucers, and they were talking a mile a minute, so the cops had to know they were messed up. When they finally got back, we carried on with our get-together, trying to put the event behind us. Jenna and I decided to take our last hit of ecstasy at around four in the morning to keep us going until sunrise and then crash out. Adam had already left, but Candy hung out for a while, leaving shortly afterward. We went to bed at sunrise, and everything was fine until I started to hear Jenna moaning and groaning next to me. I thought she was just having a hard time getting to sleep due to the drugs, but I had no idea what was about to happen. She started getting louder, and I tried to wake her up, but she was in the middle of a bad dream that she couldn't get out of. Even in my drug-hazed state of mind, I knew something was going terribly wrong with all the signs of GHB woven in. She was screaming so loud that the 15-year-old neighbour kid came over and knocked on the door to check on us. He saw her writhing around on the bed and was scared shitless, seeing her completely out of control.

*She was gripping the bed so hard that she started
to tear the bedsheets with her fingernails.*

It was beyond scary because she was only 95 pounds, and this kind of reaction could have killed her. I saw others who had overdosed with GHB in the past, so I tried everything I could to get her to come out of it, but nothing worked. Finally, I turned on the shower, picked up her struggling body and carried her in with me, but it didn't work. So, I laid her on the bed and covered her body with wet towels to keep her temperature down—that didn't work either. Time blew by, and I felt utterly helpless, with my emotions in overdrive from the drugs still coursing through my body. I should have called an ambulance, but in my state of mind, I just kept trying everything I could to revive her while doing my best to monitor her heart rate.

I was scared and desperate, so I called Adam, knowing that he put GHB in his drinks from time to time with the possibility of Jenna grabbing the wrong cup. He swore to me that he didn't have any in his drink, and I believed him. I called the only person left in the equation, and when I made contact with Candy, I dropped a bomb on her. I didn't want an explanation or an apology; I just wanted her to tell me how to get Jenna out of this horrible state. She told me to put her in a tub of cold water and hung up on me. In an utter state of shock, I called her back, and when she answered, I told her to leave town, threatening her life before I hung up, and I meant every word. If Jenna was hurt as a result of this, there was going to be hell to pay.

I quickly turned back, attending to an out-of-control situation that I had minimal solutions to use. As her eyes rolled back into her head, my last resort was putting her in the tub of cold water. I was trembling with fear as I saw her starting to slip away. I was helpless and scared in my drug-induced state of mind, but I will never forgive myself for my obvious irresponsibility. My emotions were overloaded to start with, but this was beyond comprehension: *What was going to happen? Was I going to lose my wife of less than a year to a drug overdose that was no fault of her own?*

I held her hand with tears streaming down my face as I sat on the toilet with her convulsing in the tub. It had been roughly two hours since this living nightmare began, and I prayed for her to hear me, but she did not respond. She was shutting down as I begged for her to breathe, and I cried so hard that it hurt my insides. Then, one last time, I said: *Just breathe, baby. I don't want to lose you.* And with my head down, looking at a pool of tears on the bathroom floor, she suddenly took a deep breath, and her eyes rolled straight forward. I was about to finally call the ambulance when she looked right at me and was instantly concerned about me, not her. She asked me: *Why am I in the bathtub? Why are you crying? Are you ok?* Amidst a mix of laughter and tears, massive relief blanketed me as I replied: *Am I ok?* I held her and refused to let go while the dam broke and tears flowed down my face.

The nightmare was over, and although she had no idea what happened to her, for the next two days, every muscle in her body ached. I truly felt for her, especially when I had to help her brush her hair and teeth. We were oblivious to how dangerous this person we trusted was, and to this day, I have no idea why Candy did it. She may have been trying to dose both of us to take advantage of the situation in some way, but I had no clue, and quite frankly, I didn't care. It was a terrible experience I will never forget as long as I live, but I was just happy that my young wife lived to breathe another day. I shudder to think of what could have happened that night. What if she didn't make it? What would my life have turned into? Every beautiful memory created from that day forward would have been erased forever, and the regret of loss and irresponsibility would surely have been something I couldn't live with. I am beyond grateful I never had to live with that outcome.

GHB was rampant in Panama City, and it took its toll on our friend Christian as well. However, in his case, it was intentional on every occasion. Living up the street from us, we often visited Christian and his girlfriend, Catherine, and we all became very good friends. After a show one night, we broke off from the club to have a small get-together at their house, and one of Christian's friends, John, tagged along with a girl he picked up from the bar. The four of them had been taking GHB, but Jenna and I avoided it at all costs, especially based on what had happened to her. High as hell on GHB, Christian and Catherine decided to take a shower together while John and his girl had sex on the couch in the living room. Jenna and I chose the kitchen to have our usual love fest with one another, connecting on MDMA, with every emotion pouring out of us. Having some very good party pills that night, we eventually went outside to smoke a cigarette, and we stood there, holding one another in the backyard with our hearts pounding a mile a minute. I was so high that I couldn't control my jaw from locking down and chewing with my eyes rolling in the back of my head, which were all side effects from the speedy sensation of the uppers we were taking. Every time I took a drag off her cigarette, the high accelerated because something about menthol enhanced the experience even more. Jenna loved it when we dropped ecstasy together because I was sweet and attentive to her in a way that I wasn't when I was sober. For example, I constantly reminded her to drink water or orange juice during our deep, passionate conversations.

Christian and Catherine had a couple of dogs, so we chose to go to the bedroom next and hang out with the animals. They sensed the headspace we were in and accepted every bit of love we provided. Since they were still in the shower and Jenna needed to pee, she asked if it would be safe to come in. They agreed, and when she was in there, Christian's bisexual side came out for the very first time. He suggested that she and I get in the shower with them, but we respectfully declined and went back to the bedroom. Suddenly the door busted open, and they came barreling into the bedroom naked and soaking wet, ready for action. Christian asked me to grab the video camera as he threw Catherine down on the bed. He had a full hard-on, and to her delight, he slid his big cock inside her missionary style. I started videotaping as Jenna looked on with a look of utter shock. Christian was thrusting away while, simultaneously, telling me to feel Catherine's ass—I immediately turned to my wife for approval. She smiled and gave me the nod, so I felt her ass, but he still required my assistance. So, when he asked me to hold her ankle as he changed positions, I did while still holding the camera in my other hand. From what I could tell, one of the benefits of being on that drug is the ability to hit a higher level sexually, and they were definitely doing that. She was demanding him to fuck her, calling him daddy as we watched on in amazement. We kept looking back and forth at each other in complete disbelief because it was like directing a live porno without having to be in the movie.

Then, just as Catherine was about to give Christian a blowjob, she asked Jenna for advice. Watching my wife instruct another woman on how to give a blowjob was not only cool but a massive turn-on. Recording the scene, I stood there thinking to myself: *Ya, baby, tell her how to do that shit.* It was awesome, but we left the room to let them finish up on their own because, admittedly, we were all pretty messed up. However, Jenna and I were far more in control than the others. But then the real shit show began... It didn't take long before Christian came busting out of the bedroom buck-ass naked, stumbling around like a fish out of water. He had fallen deep into the GHB hole and was completely out of control while we all tried to restrain him before he hurt himself or someone else. At one point, he stumbled over to the front of his couch and took a massive pee, thinking it was the toilet. In the middle of trying to settle him down, he backhanded Jenna across the head, and it was beyond lucky that he didn't knock her out cold. After making sure she was alright, we chose to teach him a lesson instead of getting angry.

I went back into the bedroom to grab the video camera, and I recorded every second of him making a complete fool of himself. He needed to witness the mess he had created, and we left shortly afterward. The next time we saw Christian, he immediately apologized. He felt terrible after seeing what he had done, and in the next breath, said he would never do it *around us* again. I wanted to slap him so hard when he said those words, especially after hitting my wife. We were trying to get him to stop doing that shit, but to his detriment, he wouldn't stop. Jenna was traumatized by what she witnessed that night, and she wanted nothing to do with GHB ever again. It was a messed-up scene, to say the least, and he completely missed the point. The boys in the group even found him one night passed out on the dressing room floor in his G-String with the empty plastic bottle of GHB still in his hand. He was my friend, but like so many others, he didn't care and would do it regardless of what anyone said. For Jenna, Christian was everything that turned her off, being a womanizer and a drug-addicted idiot, but the saddest part was that he was a genuinely nice person.

He had the looks, but his addictions were far from appealing.

Many dancers were into GHB at the time, and some kept it under control, but that was not the case for the majority. We even had a photoshoot scheduled with Playgirl, but most were too messed up even make the session. Then came the straw that broke the camel's back.

We had a booking all the way in Grand Junction, Colorado. It was insane, but AJ was paid enough to send us out there, so he made us drive halfway across the country for one show. He estimated how long it would take for us to get there based on the route he provided, and as usual, I did most of the driving. At around three in the morning, just south of Shreveport, Louisiana, without an exit for miles, I was watching the gas gauge drop lower and lower until the van started to sputter, and I realized we were running out of gas. Pulling off at the next exit, I tried driving as far as I could, but it wasn't long before it died completely. Waking the boys up, I let them know what was going on. We were already on a tight schedule, so I desperately started running up the dark road with the narrow hope of finding an open gas station in the middle of nowhere. There was not a streetlight in near sight, but I saw a set of lights far off in the distance; I knew there was only a slim chance it was a gas station.

After 45 minutes of running, I thankfully discovered those lights were a gas station that was open with a police car parked outside. The officer was nice enough to help, grabbing a jerrycan and driving me back to the van. We gassed up and got right back on the road, but the delay affected us, and by the time we arrived in Oklahoma City, we knew we had no chance of making the show on time. Calling the nightclub, I spoke to the manager, and he was not impressed, but I mentioned we would continue moving forward if he was willing to reschedule for the next night instead. He had already promoted the event but accepted my offer, so we kept going, relieved that our adventure could continue. The show was a mad success to a full house of enthusiastic ladies who tipped very well. It didn't affect the owner's revenue at all, so we came offstage in great spirits, thinking all was positive, all things considered.

That all changed when we came out of the dressing room, and the club owner was standing outside with the local sheriff. He told us that he wasn't paying us a dime for the show because we didn't fulfill our commitment to be there the day before, and there wasn't a damn thing we could do about it. None of us wanted to get arrested, and the trip was already bad enough, so we took our tips, tucked our tails between our legs and went back to the hotel, angry as hell. We were taken advantage of, and regardless of our mistake, we should have been paid based on the verbal agreement we had. However, the contract stated that the show would be the day before, so driving almost 4000 miles altogether along with the struggles we endured along the way had us all beyond upset. The club paid for the hotel, so in my rage, I decided to grab a screwdriver out of the van to unbolt the coffee maker off the wall. I should have known that two wrongs don't make a right because karma bit us in the ass the next day.

We started our long trek back to Florida, and as we drove through Dallas, Texas, the rear end of the van blew out, leaving us stuck on the side of the road with no place to stay and little to no money between us. After contacting our agent, he covered the bill to get the van fixed, but we were stuck in a crappy little motel room for a couple more days. When I called Jenna to explain the situation, she was so upset that she considered driving out to rescue me with her friend, Ronda, but I told her the best option was to wait it out. We finally made it home, and I was greeted by a call from AJ, who was very upset, asking me what happened with the coffeemaker. I admitted to him that I stole it after the owner screwed us out of our pay, but he was far from impressed and decided to fine me 100 dollars for the incident. It was the final straw after everything I had gone through on this tour. I told him I wasn't paying his fine, and I quit the group. This was an example of when I wish we had GPS instead of manual calculations because he made a mistake in the estimated time it would take to get to Colorado in the first place. Based on when we left, we had no chance of making the show on time regardless of running out of gas in Louisiana, so all the stress we went through was unnecessary, which solidified my decision even more.

There were now only so many options available to me based on having no social security number. So, instead of being responsible and applying for it, I procrastinated, taking the *easy* route by working under the table doing construction.

I look back at this time with a deep sense of regret because my strong value of creativity was eliminated from my life, and the excitement that came with that territory diminished and greatly affected me personally.

I went from the stage that I knew like the back of my hand to the construction site that I didn't know, having no experience. However, our new neighbour, Danny, offered to take me under his wing and teach me everything he knew about laying ceramic tile. It was extremely hard work, but we moved in a forward direction. We struggled to pay the bills on more than one occasion based on what he paid me. But I continued to forge ahead, being the *man*, taking on this new occupation without choosing to gently guide my wife towards helping us with extra income. Just like my father, I went to work, and she was at home to greet me when I walked in the door from a hard day of breaking my body on the construction site. The struggle became so hard that we let a few bills slip and had to pay a mechanic in pennies for an overdue bill of 95 dollars for repairs because we were flat broke. The bill had to be paid, and as degrading as it was, he demanded payment, so I dropped the massive bag of pennies on his desk and told him to count it because it was all there.

It was perfect timing when we met a new group of friends through the kid next door, who ended up being some of the best people we crossed paths with during my time in the U.S. They lived a few blocks down, and when we met Kyle and Jeffery, they were a couple of 15-year-old skater kids who had no structure in their lives but wanted it. Their mother, Brandy, was an absolute mess with an addiction to hard drugs. She was so desperate at times that she faked being sick, asking the doctor to prescribe her something for pain. If it wasn't a pill she was looking for, she got her twin boys to sell the prescription on the street, so she could afford to get the high she really wanted. Of course, as friends, we wanted to do what we could to help them, but at times, we became replacements for the parents they barely had.

Walking into their house for the first time, I witnessed Brandy sitting on the couch, watching the T.V. that wasn't on, with no expression on her face. Then, the boys introduced me to their father, Ron. My first impression was that he was a cynical asshole. He avoided home life as much as possible by frequenting the bar up the street, drinking away his pain while sitting on a barstool. Based on what I saw, I understood why, but the kids brought me back to their room with a look of embarrassment on their faces. After describing this visual to Jenna, we agreed to keep them off the streets by giving them a sanctuary, an outlet from the daily insanity they had to deal with. We sat them down and offered an open door to them with a few very solid rules: they were to never steal from us, they had to treat our place with respect, and they were never to bring hard drugs into our home. They could also not bring anyone into our house without our approval first. When they agreed, a beautiful new relationship was formed. I was twice their age at the time, but Jenna was only five years older, and she formed a special bond with these two blonde skater kids, and they never took her for granted. They appreciated having someone who cared, and Jenna loved the company while I broke my back on the construction site. She was like the big sister who put them back in line if they attempted to step out of it, which rarely happened.

I eventually formed a friendship with their father, who was a very good man but believed that the whole world had screwed him over, and to a certain extent, he was justified with his perception. It was pure hell for him, dealing with an ex-wife who was still in the equation, sucking them dry for everything they had. However, he still accommodated it because he didn't want to leave the mother of his children destitute. He was a former Vietnam vet who earned a purple heart after being shot down in his helicopter and was considered a *Golden Boy* by the U.S. Navy. Unlike so many at the time, he had full medical coverage and was fortunate enough to have filled out the right paperwork while serving to get full lifetime benefits from the government. Unfortunately, he drowned his pain in alcohol and had not only given up on himself but also on his kids.

Jenna and I had our fair share of things to deal with at times, but we truly enjoyed having those kids around. We mentored them when it counted, even though we may not have been the picture-perfect example based on our issues with drugs. As time went by, my work started slowing down, and although we loved living in Panama City Beach, the ends were just not being met financially. I didn't have the experience to do my own installations, and with our bank account almost drained, we were forced to pack up and move to Macon, Georgia, where we were closer to her family, who offered to help us get back on our feet. This was not an easy transition, staying with the in-laws in a trailer with our animals, but eventually, we moved to the little town of Roberta, Georgia, with Jenna's cousin, Ethan. He was there when we needed him most by offering us a far better place to live, and we were both grateful to him for extending his hand. I really enjoyed getting to know Ethan, sitting out on his porch, talking sports and laughing for hours, exchanging random stories about the differences between Canada and the U.S. It was fabulous that a true southerner and a west coast Canadian could find common ground without bringing our political ideologies into the equation.

I was able to get work immediately through a family friend by the name of Kirk, and although he was a serious asshole, he was a master at his trade. His family had been in the tile business for years, and he was looking for someone to help him out. He taught me everything he knew, but it was painstaking because he treated me like shit. However, I hung in simply to get enough experience with the intention to go out on my own. He left me on job sites for hours on end, trusting I would get everything done to his standards while he was out *quoting other projects*. It didn't take very long before I discovered that he was addicted to crack and was looking for someone to do his job while he went out to get high all day. He was such a desperate soul that he stole our only wedding gift and pawned it off for drugs. We needed storage space when we made our move, and he offered his shed with what I thought were good intentions, but my assumption couldn't have been further from the truth. However, I left it alone, simply moving on because my immigration status held me back from doing anything about it. I now had experience, and through the grapevine, I found a company roughly 30 minutes south of Macon in a little town called Warner Robbins. They were willing to hire me to run my own show, paying me under the table. We rented this cool old house close to the air force base, but it was in a pretty rough neighbourhood. At first, we didn't have cable T.V., so we sat outside on the porch to watch in-person live-action instead, with the occasional firefly buzzing around.

We were surrounded by people so foreign to me that they seemed like they were from another planet. Frankie D, the single black female living across the street, had four kids: Zandar, Zebadee, Adrina, and Janice from four different daddies. She had a very thick, Southern-Jamaican accent, and I could barely understand her most of the time. However, we always had a good laugh when at mid-conversation, I would look over at Jenna to ask her to translate for me. In the morning, when I left for my workday, Frankie would be outside hanging her laundry. She would yell across the street: *Irishman! Have a good day!* She knew I was Canadian, but sadly, I don't think she knew the difference.

Then there was Joe, his wife Lana and their two children. He was the stereotypical redneck, out in his carport, blasting tunes with Dale Earnhardt posters hanging in all their glory on the back wall. He had a jealous streak, and their abusive relationship was obvious as soon as we were introduced. One night, in the dead of winter, Jenna and I woke up to something outside. We looked out the window to see him chopping wood at two in the morning. It was well below freezing, and because they had not paid their bill, the power was cut off. Out of desperation, he was trying to build a fire in their fireplace, with his family sleeping on the living room floor, all huddled together to keep warm. My kind heart got the best of me, so I went over to offer them a place to stay until they could get the bill paid. We both couldn't stand the thought of those kids suffering, and they accepted, saying they could pay it within a few days.

The kids slept in our living room while Joe and Lana used the spare room. It didn't take long before we woke up to them arguing back and forth in our house! Lana went to the bathroom, and when Joe thought she had taken too long, his twisted mind concluded that she made a detour to our bedroom to have a threesome. I burst out of the bedroom with guns firing and told them to get out and go back where they came from. I had no issue with the kids staying, but they had to go. I had to get up the next morning for work, and I was stunned by the audacity they had, acting the way they did, especially since we were helping them out. Lana wouldn't even open the door to her own house, afraid he would abuse her, and sadly, her fear was warranted.

This was a far cry from the environment I had lived in most of my life. We even had out-of-control little thug wannabes stirring up shit further down the street on more than one occasion. One day, a neighbour down the street was having a yard sale, and when we drove by, we saw a spectacular print of a black panther walking over the earth, and we both agreed it would be a perfect fit for our living room. The print was an attention-getter, especially when we would have people over, and in a way, it mirrored a new beginning for us. Little did I know at the time, what it truly signified, but I found out years later at the most unexpected time.

There were times I worked up to 18-hour days, trying to

finish projects all on my own. The price I paid damaging my body was higher than the reward on my paychecks, but it was still better than what I had experienced previously.

I was good at my trade, and the value I provided my customers was well above average, but the value I had for myself was well below.

Then, one of the twins, Kyle, was desperate to get out of Panama City based on the dysfunction at home. He and his brother were like family to us, so we offered to rescue him by inviting him to stay in our spare room. He lived with us for a few months, and we had some fantastic get-togethers in that old house. We set the scene by hanging sheets with crazy faces on them to create a small, comfortable seating area with black lights and fans blowing the sheets back and forth. We dropped ecstasy, trying to recreate what it was like back in Florida, and it worked very well. Even though it wasn't the best of places to live, we made the best of it, and we trusted the people in our house, even if our neighbours were all borderline crazy in the head.

Life was interrupted on the day that is etched into most Americans' minds forever—9/11. As a Canadian, I can honestly say that it was one of my most disturbing days. I was loading up my work truck in the early morning and heard the announcement on the warehouse radio that the World Trade Center had been hit. I ran into the office just in time to watch the second plane hit live, and like so many, I was in a state of absolute shock and horror at what I was watching. Warner Robins Air Force Base was right across the street, and it went into immediate lockdown. I could see a black cloud over the base, and for a moment, I believed that the U.S. was under a full-scale attack. A level of fear I had never experienced hit like a wave over my body. Unfortunately, it's a fear that many people in the world have daily, but I personally had never dealt with anything like it.

I had no idea, but my old friend, Ron, had been thrown in jail while 9/11 was happening. His insane ex-wife with multiple personalities had smashed the T.V. remote over her own head, reporting to the police he had beaten her. He told me about this incident years later. He also stated that if the government started drafting young men like he had been, they would find him standing at the door with his gun, protecting his boys, and he wasn't kidding. He eventually expressed that if the Iraq War had required a draft, it would never have happened. He may have been wrong, but he may have been right. No one will ever know, but I respected his perception due to his experience in a war that ended so tragically for his generation.

I immediately went home that day to be with the most important people in my life because I had a wake-up call that tomorrow is not guaranteed. As Kyle, Jenna, and I stood there horrified, I almost instantly appreciated what I had in my life. Although money would have solved many of our problems, I knew it was only part of the solution. I had been living in a comfort zone, taking my partner for granted long past the honeymoon stage, living a reality leagues away from our life in Florida. We had multiple moments of financial struggle and animosity when my frustration boiled over. The wisdom I have today could have resolved so many of those conflicts simply with me taking the time to understand my partner, and more importantly, understand myself. Instead, the control I had over Jenna held her back from her true potential and dissuaded her from becoming a better version of herself. Our sexual and chemical addictions held us together like glue, but by not allowing her to grow, the ties that bound us gradually began to unravel, strand by strand, without me even realizing it.

The history of my past so skewed my perception of my partner. As a Canadian, I was born and raised in a multi-cultural society that was more socially and racially tolerant through my lens. Canada is far from perfect, but there is an acceptance of mixed-race couples that is far more tolerant than what I stereotypically witnessed living in Middle Georgia. One night, Jenna broke down emotionally and revealed something she held back throughout our two years of marriage. She was deathly afraid of how I would react when I heard that the first boyfriend who meant everything to her at the time was black. She sincerely believed that if she told me, I would end it. My reaction was far from what she expected, and I was disturbed that she would even think such a thing. It turned out that most of her family members had turned their backs on her over this taboo relationship. Her adopted father even explained to her that no white man would ever touch her if they knew. As sad as it was watching her explain this to me with tears streaming down her face, it was a breakthrough moment for us. She realized that she could open up to me about her biggest fears, and I would still be there without batting an eyelash. Initially, it angered me that she looked at me through that lens, but the words of the people she loved dramatically impacted her perception of what others might think of her. I couldn't blame her because Middle Georgia is a different world from the one I grew up in, never being ridiculed, teased, or abused, and with this realization, my anger turned to sadness. I believe that she didn't want anyone to pity her; she just wanted acceptance for the person she was.

When I had conversations with some of her relatives, I tried my best to understand their perceptions based on their past and how mine affected me. I had religious and political differences with many of them, but I still did my best to respect their perspectives even though I disagreed. Getting into an argument about these subjects was wasted energy. Just because I believed the sky was blue didn't necessarily mean someone else's perception that it was green was wrong. The lens they looked through could have had a filter or two different from mine, and that was ok as long as they didn't try to convince me to wear their glasses.

After 9/11 and multiple conversations with a man who had walked the walk and lived to talk about it, I became obsessed with political issues. When I think back, I realize that I wasted energy obsessing over things I had no control over. If I had been more focused on being the president of my own household instead of who was running the country I was living in at the time, I would have had a far more blissful life. However, I found it hard to ignore. Jenna also had her opinions, but she kept them to herself most of the time. She found discussing politics annoying and blew me off when I went on an unexpected rant, preferring not to get into it.

I even had a political argument with Jenna's cousin, Ethan, spurred on by his sharing of ideological opinions while he was drinking. Drug addictions were detrimental to our marriage, and common ground was getting harder to find with my added death sentence of a political addiction. The lens of innocence that I looked through changed around 9/11, and even though we made some great and not-so-great memories in Georgia, we agreed it was time to go to the Sunshine State to get back to what we knew and loved.

The Naked Truth

We just about fell off that tightrope the night I almost lost Jenna. I often wondered: *What if we had fallen? What if she didn't make it?* These questions haunted us both, but especially me. Thinking of how this day may have turned out made me realize that life can never be taken for granted, even though I had done exactly that in the past. The worst-case scenario was averted that day, but it could have been a matter of minutes or even seconds for the outcome to have been completely different.

At the time, I did not think with a clear head as I do now. I had someone who would have done everything in her power to save me if I was in her shoes. But even though I did what I could, I should have done far more. If I wasn't there, she might not have made it, but looking back, I should have never waited so long. It was beyond irresponsible and a shot across the bow, letting me know that, although Candy was close to us, she was a bad apple with bad intent.

It was a horrible experience for both of us, but Jenna thought I was afraid of calling the ambulance due to the possibility of being deported. She may have been right, but keeping it real, being deported was minimal compared to losing her. I wasn't thinking straight. I was scared to death at that moment, with a massively blurred perception of reality due to the drugs in my system, viced into trying to handle everything myself due to my illegal immigration status.

When I quit the revue out of justified frustration, I started dying inside, sacrificing my creativity to do a job that provided a minimal amount of it. The excitement that fed me from my past experiences on stage was gone, which deteriorated me personally and professionally. Unfortunately, animosity was developed because I was in The Land of the Free, but we were far from free. Jenna and I were stuck in our own cages with different realities, and neither of them was good, continuing to walk the path of codependency, struggling through every day of it.

The end result of this might have been far different if we had taken the time to understand our values and the emotions attached to them, living authentically. Although I was never 100 percent harmonious in living within my values, when my creativity was taken away, so was my excitement. Days turned into weeks, then months with no common goals between us. The monotony of working long hours day after day was depressing. I realized I had settled, being forced to work a career that was completely unnecessary. If only I had been responsible enough to get legal while leaving my wife at home depressed in her reality of what our life had become.

Codependence, Desperation & Humility

X

The Con Artist, The Hulk,
and The Bad Apples of Good Intent

Making the transition back to Florida was long overdue. It was the light at the end of a long tunnel that we both embraced and appreciated more than ever before, noticing the little things neglected and taken for granted. We were living in the now, even if it was only for a short time, and it was glorious finding a little yellow beach house all for ourselves in an area secluded from the insanity of spring break and summer travellers. We took the time to enjoy the unmistakable smell of the ocean breeze coming off the Gulf of Mexico and palm trees swaying in the wind in our front yard. This was a new beginning, getting back to being ourselves with no distractions of negative outside influence.

Our time in Georgia had taken its toll on me, sacrificing my creativity and experiencing the deterioration of the excitement that came hand-in-hand with it. Although I was proud of my work as a tile setter, my pride took a beating in other ways due to financial struggle and my general lack of enthusiasm.

Regardless of how much I attempted to be *man enough* to show up as the stereotypical man of the household, I allowed the struggle to continue by *protecting* my partner from the outside world by encouraging her role of the traditional housewife.

My father worked in the construction industry for as long as I remembered, but I did not paint that picture for my life. Although I always respected a hard day's work, it was hard to accept the mediocrity and minimal ingenuity that being a tile setter provided. Holding onto this *hunter-gatherer* mindset and unrealized codependence, there was no one to blame but myself for this. However, I continued to cling to this struggle while desperately attempting to create a stable life within our new environment. I had minimal tools at my disposal due to my illegal immigration status, but fortunately, I was able to subcontract my services through a small local flooring store that provided some stability. However, the codependency continued.

We didn't have children, but our four-legged family expanded with two dogs and three cats in that little beach house. We produced a home environment, even though my real home seemed like a million miles away in Canada. I continued making the sacrifice of working long hours on the construction site, leaving Jenna at home alone on the other side of the city with little to no communication. She did boring daily chores such as folding laundry, and although I never knew it, she was folding clothes with tears in her eyes on more than one occasion. Our young friends lived too far away to visit as often as they had in the past, and she was in an understandable state of depression. We had one another but minimal socialization, and due to this, we separately started seeking external sources of happiness without focusing on what we could accomplish as a team. We were married for three years, and experienced so much struggle as a young couple, holding our relationship together through mistakes and failures. It was a battle for both of us in different ways because, in our hearts, we truly wanted to make one another happy, but we were not willing to face our happiness within. Each of us accepted codependence as normalcy without even realizing it. Our ability to grow was being hindered, and as a result, we attracted some people who were simply there to use us for what they could with their twisted intentions.

One of these people was someone named Jeff, who I crossed paths with at a local corner store I often visited on the beach. When I stopped by, he always greeted me with a smile, and through our brief conversations, we found commonality that eventually opened the door to a degree of trust that should never have been opened. He mentioned that his girlfriend, Linda, had epilepsy, and when I met her, the look on her face indicated a long, hard daily battle with it. I empathized with their situation because they mentioned that her random seizures forced them to avoid exposing themselves to certain situations. My heart went out to both, and although they had their own set of issues, we believed we had formed a genuine friendship with this nice young couple who only lived a few short blocks away.

Installing tile for a living paid the bills, but we still struggled to get ahead, living paycheque to paycheque. Instead of getting my social security number to provide more options for myself, I decided to take the easy route when one of my DJ friends, Kris, gave me another option. Unfortunately, it could have had me thrown in jail, and it brought unnecessary drama and stress into our life. He had been touring all across North America at the time, and after doing shows in Canada, he brought pounds of high-quality marijuana back across the border, stashing it inside the tires of his vehicle. He offered to front me as much as I needed to sell to the people in my circle, and as insane as it was, I took him up on his offer while, simultaneously, living in a no-tolerance drug state. Through my lens at the time, I was doing what I needed to do, but I could have gone to jail for years, and I didn't even consider that threat.

Jeff was one of my best customers because he liked to smoke it, but it also helped his girlfriend deal with the pain she experienced after a bad seizure day. She preferred this alternative in comparison to taking prescriptions with dramatic and obvious side effects. He was always good for the money, and although selling weed wasn't exactly living the dream, I was doing a good thing in my eyes by helping them out. However, it didn't take very long for Jenna and I to witness a very dark and scary side of this new relationship we had formed. Jeff asked me if he could buy some weed, and while trying to fill his order, my scales broke. Without thinking, I sent him a text to see if I could borrow some scales from him, but he didn't reply. So, after going out to buy a new set of scales, I decided to stop by their place to drop off his order.

He opened the door without looking at me and walked to the other side of his living room without saying hello. He grabbed something off the counter, then turned and warned me never to text him about anything related to illegal activity again. He put his gun down on the table in front of him with a look in his eyes I had never seen before; I stood there with my heart beating out of my chest. Through all our past conversations, he had only revealed so much of his past, and I was not about to make any assumptions, especially with his gun laying there on the table.

It was the first indication that something wasn't right, but shortly afterward, the situation became far worse.

He became friends with Lee, the owner of the convenience store he worked at, and that was when everything moved in a very dark direction. They had high hopes for some shady business they were planning, intending to drag Jenna and I into it with them. Lee was a massive hulk of a man with some untrustworthy connections. Between the two of them, they invited us over to give us their sales pitch and introduce Jenna to Lee's girlfriend. They wanted Jenna to be her personal assistant while dressing in provocative attire to attract a certain type of customer to their business. However, from the start, they were not clear about what the business was. They continuously focused on how much money we would all make while being extremely cagey in the process. The vibe said it all when we walked into that room, but we were trapped in a house with two dangerous, unstable people who had their own intention, which was a mystery to us both.

Nothing was good about this situation, and I knew it was trouble right from the get-go. As soon as I sat down, they started mocking me for the pain I was experiencing resulting from working all day on the construction site. The degradation continued as they pointed out the ten-year difference between us. They continued by saying that if I kept complaining about my back pain, someone who had a younger and less broken body would come along to take my place. The situation went from bad to worse when they assigned Jenna her first duty as the *personal assistant* when the two girls left the room. She was to assist by holding a mirror up to this girl's nose so she could snort cocaine. As soon as Jenna held that mirror up, she became sick to her stomach. At that moment, she realized she would rather be broke and living under a bridge than work with these people, supporting whatever their plan was. She was beyond disgusted, and I couldn't blame her. She was trying to be something she was not, and she recognized it immediately. Being in that house was like being caught in a spider's web, trying to figure out an escape plan.

In conversation that night, Jeff expressed frustration with his girlfriend's brother, who seemed never able to do anything right in his eyes. He mentioned he would like to wipe him off the face of the earth, and at first, I figured he was just talking out of his ass, but I truly believe he meant it. Eventually, Jenna and I thought that he had either already disposed of him, or he was tied up somewhere in that house. I can't prove it, but we both had the same impression when we left that night. We never saw her brother again, so I will never truly know, but the looks on their faces said it all. Eventually, we fearfully broke free from the web and made our way home, trying to forget everything we had just experienced.

We did everything we could to avoid them from that day forward, but I had previously lent Jeff 300 dollars because he was always good about paying his bills. I needed my money, and weeks went by with no contact, so I dropped by his house to see what was going on. I heard his girlfriend say: *Come in* with a very weak voice from behind the door. I opened the door, seeing Linda lying on the couch in obvious pain, and she mentioned that Jeff was in the back room and to knock on the door before I walked in. When I entered the room, he was sitting in front of his computer, downloading illegal files and watching twisted pornography. He told me to sit down, and I noticed a look of pure evil in his eyes while looking at the screen with a huge smile on his face, getting off on watching some poor woman being sexually abused. It was so disturbing that I had to leave, mentioning I would see him another time. After witnessing this, I should have counted my losses and moved on, but he still owed me money, and I was not about to let it go. I made one last effort to get my money back from this insane person I had considered a friend just a few short months before. When I stopped by his house, he was desperately packing up his stuff, and when I asked him about the money, he said that everything was fine, and he would get it back to me. But the next day, he was gone, never to be seen again.

I got off lucky compared to his *partner*, Lee, who was scammed for thousands. Lee went out looking for Jeff's head, but he was nowhere to be found. I truly believe that Jeff and Linda were grifters, using her epilepsy as a cover for their scam. It was a way to draw vulnerable people in to empathize with them, and when the timing was right, they took them for everything they could. He was the only con artist I ever stumbled upon, and the whole experience was strange and scary at the same time. I had no idea at the time because he was good at what he did, finding common ground with his victims and working his game from there.

At this point, my desire to get back on stage had grown, and although I left the dance review behind based on my Colorado experience, I made an effort to contact AJ, who had formed a partnership with my old roommate, Jason. Time had passed, and the conditions had changed, so I wanted to give it another shot. However, I quickly realized it would never be the same as when I first went to Florida. Everyone's egos had grown dramatically, and when I eventually got back on stage, it didn't feel like a team anymore. They were more into degrading one another than collaboratively working together, and although Christian had obvious issues, he was one of the only remaining dancers who still treated me with respect. The shows were a far cry from what I experienced in the late 90s, and although I tried to fit in the best I could, I was never truly accepted.

My attempt to rejoin the revue was short-lived, and the night that ended it all was when Jenna stood side-stage with Christian's girlfriend, Catherine, while I performed. There was so much negativity in the air that even Catherine, who we considered a friend, joined in, trying her best to put me down right in front of my wife. She asked Jenna if I was straight or if I might be bisexual based on the way I danced. If she had said this to my face, I would have laughed it off because I had already achieved so much in a career that spanned almost 15 years at that point. But Jenna wasn't having any of it. She took it to heart and defended me with everything inside of her, telling Catherine how disrespectful the comment was to both of us and to never speak to her again. After everything we had been through, she should have known better than to open her mouth the way she did, especially since I was just coming back to the revue. Of course, my sexuality was none of their business to start with, but Jenna said it wasn't so much about what she said as how she said it. Shortly after that night, I left the group for good, and it was the right decision because it would never be the same.

I wasn't getting any younger, working with a bunch of cocky, new dancers who thought they were far better than they actually were.

The little beach house we initially happily moved into was now a source of uncomfortable memories, including the insanity of the people we surrounded ourselves with. This drove us to move once again, this time, to a house on the outskirts of town closer to the tile store I worked at. It was small and needed work, but we fixed this new little place up to the best of our ability. Once again, we started over.

Ron, Kyle, and Jeffery were like a second family to us, but now we lived on the opposite end of town, so they introduced us to some good friends in our area. We held some of the best get-togethers in that little house with a bunch of kids who others would consider stoners, going nowhere with their lives. To us, they were solid as rocks, and despite of their ages, we made good memories never to be forgotten. To them, we were friends at times and mentors at others. They were there to help when we asked with no expectation for anything in return. I rarely hear from them anymore, but I will always fondly look back on those times. Unfortunately, Ron's battle with alcoholism continued, falling off the wagon from time to time. It was difficult to watch this in a man who had so much to offer. He loved his two boys with all his heart, but Jenna and I witnessed the many conflicts he had with them. In general, brothers tend to argue with one another, but they also tend to have each other's backs when it counts the most, and Kyle and Jeffery were no different. We tried to gently guide them as much as possible while still respecting that they were family and had to figure things out for themselves.

There was one night when Ron fell off the wagon in a big way, and as Jenna and I pulled into his driveway, we saw him through the window, standing in his kitchen slamming back a bottle of hard alcohol—straight, no chaser. We looked at each other, wondering if we should go up to the door, but before we had the chance to make a decision, Ron came out. He got in the vehicle with us, and through the alcohol, his emotions spilled out like never before. He thanked us for being there for his twin boys when he wasn't. It must have been hard for him to admit that he was not present for them when he should have been for so many years. He said that their story might have turned out completely different if we had not been there, and his gratitude was obvious. Even though he was drinking, I knew he meant every word. He knew he had a major struggle with alcoholism, but he didn't know how to win the battle.

Shortly after that, his sons decided to take matters into their own hands, having their father committed by using the Baker Act that enabled them to acquire emergency health services on his behalf due to his inability to make decisions based on his treatment needs. He spent two weeks in a facility with people he referred to as crazy, but it awakened him to the brutal reality of his situation and forced him to drop the bottle. The boys both loved their father and couldn't take another day watching his struggle no matter how much it hurt to make the decision. Ron sacrificed so much for his country, but one of his biggest sacrifices was for his two boys. He would do anything for them, regardless of the dysfunction, and it was sad to see a man who taught me so much about life's realities be degraded to this extent. However, it was the best thing that could have happened to him at the time. He always told me that if a person finds five true friends in their life, they are doing better than most. He held his hand up with his five fingers spread apart like a fan when he said it and looked me straight in the eye—I understood the message every time. I was blessed to have more than a handful over the years, but if I could only choose five, he would most definitely be one of those fingers. Our friendship was unique, and we had each other's back, regardless of the circumstances.

I admit that some of the relationships I formed were not motivating me to move to the next level in my life. However, each had the best intentions within having been dealt a crappy deck of cards. One of those relationships included Madelaine, Keith, and Karly. They were a family left behind by a broken system. I was referred to them because I had great weed, and Madelaine was dealing with Fibromyalgia. She used it as medicine more than entertainment and appreciated me dropping by to see them. She had been dealing with several diseases for many years, and it all started with the death of her 11-year-old son. She explained that he had been put on a horse, and before anyone had a chance to stop it, the horse ran off with the little boy on its back. It ran under a tree, and her son was killed instantly from a branch that happened to be at the perfect height to do the most damage. This poor woman witnessed her son's death right in front of her, which in turn, caused trauma in her body from that day forward. Unfortunately, Madelaine didn't help things by living an unhealthy lifestyle, eating southern cooking, and smoking like a chimney. What started as one disease in her body escalated to multiple conditions that she could not control. That one event on that fateful day altered her life forever, and I could never truly understand the pain she went through. However, Jenna and I were always there as an ear when she needed us the most. Prior to managing ill-health, she owned a restaurant with great potential for success, but the tragic loss of her son that day changed everything. Sadly, she had no coverage in place to help when everything went sideways.

To make matters worse, her husband Keith, who had been a machinist for most of his adult life, was not provided support from his employer when he was injured and needed it the most. He devoted the majority of his life to a company that valued his abilities while he had them but was then hung out to dry for quite some time after being injured. With no benefits or way to make money, he fought for years to get some sort of relief, but they didn't listen. Eventually, he got coverage, but his family struggled to get through most months.

They lived with their niece, Karly, a very kind-hearted,

sweet young lady, struggling with her own unhealthy battles while living in the same environment. She was an amazing person in so many ways, keeping the household going as best she could and working hard to keep a roof over their heads. It is difficult to paint an accurate picture of this family because their struggle was hard for me to comprehend. As much as Karly was the glue in the family, they still needed help. Fortunately, someone came along who was able to do so. His name was William, and although he was worth over 43 million dollars, owning multiple companies all over the U.S., he was one of the saddest men I ever met—not in a degrading way, but he was genuinely sad inside his soul. William was someone who had everything most desire right in front of him, but he sacrificed his closest relationships as a result.

Although I was doing well as an installer, William filled the gaps when I didn't have work. He invited me to come out to his beautiful estate overlooking the ocean and had me do everything from designing ceramic tile patio tables for his pool deck to landscaping his yard. Occasionally, he gave me the keys to his Porsche 911 Carrera to take out for a spin instead of leaving it to collect dust in his carport. He had two Mercedes that he drove most of the time, and he needed the Porsche driven, so I made the sacrifice. He lived alone in this beautiful mansion and welcomed me, Jenna, Madelaine, Keith, and Karly over on many occasions, covering the costs simply to enjoy spending time with us. He also covered their bills without demanding anything in return, simply out of the goodness of his heart. He enjoyed having friends around, and it wasn't about money for him anymore. Like most people, he was seeking happiness, but he was far from happy.

When we first met, he was hiring call girls for their company, but I never looked down upon him for it. Although I was happily married, I understood what he had gone through to acquire the material objects around him. It was just the two of us one Friday night when he opened up while drinking a bottle of wine. He knew my financial situation but never looked down on me because of it. In fact, he envied me as he spoke his truth. He was not born with a silver spoon in his mouth, starting off with 500 dollars in his pocket. He had been married with two children, who their father neglected due to his hunger for success. Years later, 18-hour days caught up with him, and he ended up divorced and alone. He was lucky enough to take advantage of contracts he arranged with the U.S. government to build hanger doors for the military that propelled him to a financial position most never achieve. He envied me because I had something he didn't—a partner I loved and loved me back. William provided the awareness that money can solve some problems, but it doesn't bring happiness.

The call girls he hired were being paid to give the illusion he was loved. He bought them high-end clothing, purses, along with anything it took for them to express some form of love, regardless of whether it was real or not. He was at the point where a marriage would cost him just as much or more, so why not hire someone to service his needs without the headache of a contract? As much as that may seem wrong to many, I understood where he was coming from. He was in his sixties with a very introverted personality and was at a point in his life where people just used him anyway, so he decided to use them as well. It may be a sad story, but I respected the man for revealing his truth while simultaneously not wanting to be in his shoes.

The fall of 2004 arrived, and once again, we chose to move into a place closer to town. We were beyond happy about it because it was an upgrade from the little house we had.

Although it was a trailer, it was a perfect spot, well taken care of with a beautiful yard and nice front porch shaded by an awning. However, due to uncontrollable circumstances, our stay there was very short-lived. Hurricane Frances ripped apart much of Florida on a path of destruction, which carried over to the middle of the state and continued its wrath into the Panhandle. We saw the track of the storm and the devastation it left behind, so we decided to evacuate to Georgia and stay with Jenna's family. We loaded up our animals, and it was fortunate that we did.

While having dinner with her family one evening, I got a call from our landlord, telling us that our new place was hit by one of the multiple tornados spinning off the hurricane. It was the only house in the neighbourhood that took a direct hit, and when we arrived back home to inspect the damage, we were in a state of shock as we drove up the driveway. The awning that covered the front porch was gone, and the roof had been peeled off the trailer in the process. It was left hanging over the back fence that divided our yard from the neighbours. We looked inside the house and realized it was a freak accident. Everything else was left fully intact, but the house no longer had a roof. Once again, we were stuck with our animals with nowhere to live. Desperation set in as we walked around the remains of our new home. Fortunately, the Red Cross stepped in and found us a brand-new house for roughly the same monthly rent. Ironically, my good friend, Cole, had a house in the same neighbourhood with his girlfriend, Sandy, who was a doctor in town. Cole had been going to school to become a paramedic, and I had no idea how valuable they would be to Jenna and I over and above our friendship. Although we seemed to be moving more often than not, having a brand-new house with tons of space was a blessing in disguise. More importantly, our lives were still intact, but we were starting over once again.

I was determined to do whatever it took to maintain control through these rough times, and I became damaged through the process.

Time passed by, and my work took more and more of a toll on my body. I had been a tile installer for a few years, and for most of it, I worked alone due to my immigration status. I knew deep inside that the entire house of cards was at risk of falling. However, I didn't file for a social security number because I had been in the country illegally for so long that I feared I would be rejected and deported. At one point, I had to go to the Department of Motor Vehicles to exchange my almost expired Canadian driver's license, which was taking a risk in its own right. Surprisingly enough, they exchanged it for a Florida license with no questions asked, but I still had no health insurance, and I used a joint bank account that Jenna opened just to cash my cheques. We were living a life with no established credit, along with a bleak future because of it.

I believe that most people have a bad apple or two in their family and friends' tree. They appear to have the best intentions but unknowingly change an environment by no fault of their own. In some ways, my father, who I loved with all my heart, was one of those bad apples with good intentions because he had a heart of gold and gave everything he could. However, the result of his emotional disconnection cascaded down my family tree. Jenna and I tried to keep our heads above water throughout our ongoing financial struggle that put us in a state of dis-ease. We could use all the help we could get. Jenna's sister, Amanda, was going through some hard times after getting divorced from a very short-term marriage that simply didn't work out. Jenna and I discussed the possibility of having her and her young son, Jayden, stay in our spare room until she got back on her feet. I always liked Amanda because, even though some may consider her a bitch, she is authentic in what she communicates, and she always listened to me when I attempted to give her advice. I knew she would have helped us if the tables were turned. However, little did I know how the decision to support her would change everything.

As soon as she arrived in Panama City Beach, she got to work immediately, applying for multiple jobs and successfully landing a position with a local telecom company. She did her part, chipping in to cover the bills and her portion of the rent. We were beyond proud of her, and although she had newfound light, Amanda was still in a dark place, and to manage that darkness, she spent many weekend nights drunk and passing out on the couch. Being her sister, Jenna accepted this and even joined her from time to time. Although her little boy was nothing but a pleasure to have around most of the time, for a married couple with no children, the change of having him in our daily lives was dramatic. I was not the biggest fan of having kids in the first place, and this change of dynamics created a slippery slope. I know in my heart that Amanda never meant to do any damage, but it was a slow bleed that couldn't heal during a time when our marriage already had disconnection issues. However, we both decided to support Amanda and her son, and we were committed to doing so.

I was working long hours on a project with a deadline, and I simply could not do it all on my own, so I hired a helper to get the job done on schedule. We worked in the sweltering hot summer temperatures of Northern Florida on a new construction site with no air conditioning, so I wore shorts to deal with the heat and humidity. We broke for lunch, and as always, my helper, Deano, and I placed our kneepads on a box of tile. I didn't realize it at the time, but we both had the exact same colour and brand of kneepads. When we came back, I made the grave error of putting on the wrong set. As the day went on, the discomfort of being on my knees for hours on end turned quickly to pain in my right knee. I stood up and peeled the kneepad off to see an infection so extreme that it looked like I had two kneecaps. Little did I know that my helper had an untreated staph infection that spread rapidly through the kneepad rubbing under the sweaty conditions we were working in. With my deadline looming in the back of my brain, I tried to carry on, blocking the pain as I continuously put more pressure on the area while kneeling to install. Finally, when the pain became too extreme to bare, I packed it in and went home, attempting to treat it with peroxide—I needed medical attention, but we had no health insurance. This wasn't the first time we struggled with this issue; when we lived in Georgia, Jenna ended up in the hospital for two days, and we were presented with a bill for over 3000 dollars. Having previously walked that road, I tried to do whatever it took to avoid going there again.

Thankfully, I had an option that included someone who had stood by me from the beginning. I contacted my buddy, Cole, to see if he could do anything to help, and since he lived in the neighbourhood, he came over to assess the situation immediately. He opened the door, and when he saw my knee, he told me to get off the leg and wait for him to get back with crutches. While waiting on the couch, he got on the phone with his girlfriend, Sandy, but she was already almost home from her shift at the hospital—she had her medical bag with her, but no anesthetic. So, they gave me two options: she could go back to the hospital to get some, which would take at least another hour or perform surgery without it. After a brief discussion, we chose to move ahead without the anesthetic. Cole brought me back to their house, and although they put their careers at risk, they helped me when I needed them the most. If the infection spread, it could have killed me. There was no other choice—it had to be done.

Jenna stood there, watching with a look of concern as Sandy opened her bag and filled a large needle with peroxide. Cole told me to squeeze his hand as hard as I could, and he looked straight into my eyes as she injected the peroxide into the massive boil on the side of my knee. It caught on fire as Sandy took out a razor and lanced it to relieve the pressure. Taking out a pair of Hemostats, she then pulled out the mass of infection while flushing more peroxide in the process. While she pushed the remaining infection out of my leg, Jenna watched me turn every colour of the rainbow as I approached the borderline of losing consciousness. Then a wave of relief came over my body, and I burst into a laughing fit, being overcome with exhaustion and disgusted by the visual I was experiencing. At that moment, I truly realized how much I had taken Canada's health-care system for granted. This would not happen back home, and although I put myself in this position, I was beyond grateful to have two angels rescue me that day. The pain was beyond extreme, but I made it through, and I hope I never have to deal with anything like that again. That day I was reminded that nothing else matters if my health is compromised, yet so many people experience this demise at a very young age.

During this time, the health of my marriage also started deteriorating. Living the life of a construction worker was a far cry from the life I previously had as a performer. This slow-moving deterioration was spurred on by working long hours, thus neglecting the one person I should never have—my own wife, who already walked a similar path in her previous life. I settled into a *comfort zone* by choosing to come home to turn on the T.V. and play video games. Jenna tried to get me to pay attention, making an effort by putting on lingerie while standing right in front of me. But I was too concerned with getting to the next level on some stupid game I was playing. Her perception of me started to change because my perception of myself had changed. I wasn't happy with the situation, and although she made every effort to get through to me, it was like trying to break through a brick wall. I didn't notice the person I was married to anymore, even as she constantly took the time to express her love for me. I found it annoying and obvious in my mind, so I let her know that our sharing of love for each other shouldn't be an everyday thing because that took away from the power of that very expression. She was starving for attention, and my egotistical mind looked down at her with the false belief that she owed me for giving her this *amazing* life we had.

**My creativity was completely diminished,
and my excitement for life went with it.**

I was done with the party lifestyle, but Jenna was just getting started at her age. I was at that point where I was not only physically exhausted due to my job, but the club lifestyle was unappealing. Following my father's footsteps, I worked extremely hard to provide a nice place to live and food on the table, but it wasn't enough. I pushed her away, wanting to be alone, and justifiably, she felt like more of a burden than a benefit. Our intimacy was more of a chore than an experience, and the connection we had in the beginning dissolved, leaving her there, with me, but I wasn't present. The door to my house was wide open, but my ego assumed it was locked.

Jenna started working at a video store within walking distance of our house and made new friends in the process. She began seeing things from a different perspective while still trying to make our marriage work in her way. However, some of the people she associated with started to push her in a new direction. I am sure she vented her frustration to them on more than one occasion, which was understandable being as disconnected from her as I was. In addition, they took advantage of the convenience of living just a few doors down by frequently dropping over for a few drinks. I had very rarely seen Jenna drink in the six years I was married to her, and these new entities acted like a virus slowly spreading into a relationship that already had a weakened immune system. I was losing control as I desperately tightened my grip and slowly watched her slip through my fingers.

With all this happening in the background, I was forced to hire a full-time helper due to getting more work than I could handle. Chad was a likable enough kid referred to me by another installer, and I chose to give him a shot. He was a hard worker, and after a few months, we built trust while working together. As a result, I invited him over to the house, and within a short time, he was one of the crew. Over a short period, we brought many new elements into our lives, and the change I was starting to see became a concern. Jenna started getting the attention from Chad that I wasn't giving her, and I watched it develop right in front of me while still not making any effort to connect with her. We still slept in the same bed but became more and more distanced. In a way, it was borderline self-sabotage because, as much as I loved her, we were both unhappy in different ways and for individual reasons.

Then Jenna's 15-year-old sister, Susanna, asked if she could stay with us for the summer that year. She was a good kid who was also a casualty of the environment where she was raised, and she had a limited education. Unfortunately, her timing couldn't have been worse regarding what was going on with us, but I reluctantly agreed to add one more person into our already packed household. As time went on, the virus started to really take hold, with Chad hanging around more and more. Looking back, all the signs were there, but I was wearing rose-coloured glasses and blinded from reality. My parents were married for over 50 years, and although they were from a completely different era, I subconsciously used them as a model, having faith that Jenna would never break our agreement. It's hard to admit the ignorance and egotism that I carried within this situation. Although I was no longer an entertainer, I never dreamed that the girl I met while performing on stage so many years before would consider someone else.

My suspicions magnified when she chose to go out one night with her friends, knowing I had to be up for work very early the next morning. When I woke up, I looked over, and she wasn't next to me. Shaking the cobwebs out while walking out into the living room, I saw her passed out on the couch, and at that moment, it was evident that our disconnection had turned into something far worse and very real. I went off to work with suspicion coursing through my veins all day long, and when I came home, I saw it but didn't want to admit it, and I went into a complete state of denial.

A few more days went by, and then all hell broke loose. After work one day, Jenna flew into a rage, telling me that Chad had snuck in through Susanna's bedroom window in the middle of the night and had sex with her. My first reaction was to confront him about it since not only had he broken into our house while we were sleeping in the next room, but he had sex with a minor. But Jenna was adamant that she take it into her own hands. I had never seen her so upset and angry as when we drove up to his house to confront him. This was about her little sister, and she wanted to handle it on her own, so she burst through his door, leaving me standing outside, listening to their conversation. There was something not quite right, and I suddenly realized that it didn't have to do with *what* she was saying, but instead *how* she was saying it, while asking him how he could do such a thing. I heard a lot more in her words than just anger—I heard jealousy. She told him that as upset as she was, there would be hell to pay if Corey found out, and what came out of his mouth next made me fly into a violent rage: *What the fuck is he going to do about it?*

Breaking through that door, I answered his question by flying over her shoulder and beating the hell out of him. I ended up holding him in a headlock, and just as I was about to plant his head into the wall, I heard Jenna scream for me to stop. So, just as my anger peaked, I grabbed him by the back of his shirt and backhanded him into his bathroom mirror and watched him slide down the wall into a pathetic heap on the floor. With my heart beating from the adrenaline of jealousy, I told him never to cross our paths again, and if he did, he wouldn't survive to see the next day. I had never experienced that kind of rage before and hopefully never will again. It came hand-in-hand with realizing that she had slept with Chad only a few short nights before when landing on the couch. After the shit he pulled, it didn't take long before Chad decided to leave town, but the virus had already done irreparable damage with a 15-year-old kid getting caught in the crossfire. The signs were all there, but I refused to see them, sticking it out through thick and thin—till death do us part.

Every one of these new entities brought unnecessary drama into our lives. Some were bad apples with good intent, and some were not. When things went sideways, we didn't experience the beautiful connection we had in the past due to my inadequacies, but we also allowed this deficiency into our relationship. We brought that avoidable drama into our lives, and we were both to blame for not putting our marriage first while simultaneously masking our truth. For Jenna, it was alcohol that eased the pain, and I even tried joining her friend base, but alcohol wasn't my thing, and I wasn't moving in the same direction. Jenna enjoyed this new normal, being liberated from her cage, which made us drift even further apart and allowed her to grow in good and bad ways.

As my personal life spun out of control like a tornado, William appreciated the work I did for him. Although he didn't have to, he extended his hand, offering me a once-in-a-lifetime opportunity. He wanted to support my career and take it to the next level by fronting me the money to start my own tile store. We planned on finding the right location, and he let me know I would never be in the red. He was willing to invest in me, and regardless the outcome, I owed him nothing. I supported his friends when they needed it, and he wanted to support me. I would no longer just be valued by the number of hours I put in or the amount of tile I laid on a customer's floor. I was excited to have the opportunity to run my own show, and I was beyond confident in my ability to do it. I only had one thing standing in my way—a social security number.

You only know what you know, and I didn't know enough to do all of this on my own. However, I foolishly tried to. I had been illegally in the U.S. for many years, and although I should have gone to my friend for help, I went to the social security office and asked for advice about handling my situation. The lady I spoke with had no idea what she was talking about and advised me to return to Canada to get my Canadian passport and driver's license reinstated before they could do anything. This advice ended up haunting me for years to come. I had this massive opportunity staring me in the face that would finally provide stability after so much struggle, but in the meantime, my home life was in shambles. The situation turned ugly when Jenna and I finally had it out, and in her drunken state, she got up the will to end it with me. She told me that it was over, and my heart fell out of my chest. I walked out of our house, broken down in tears as she stayed there. I should have kicked her and her family members out of the house I was paying for but instead chose to pack up my belongings to stay with my friends, Madelaine, Keith, and Karly to let the dust settle. Within a combination of confusion, sadness, and anger, I desperately packed up everything I could into the back of my pickup and realized I was not going to leave behind the print I bought back in Georgia at that yard sale. It was one of my most valued possessions, and if I was leaving, it was going with me.

I drove through our neighbourhood with a full truckload of my belongings when I hit a bump, causing the print to fall over and smash. It was completely destroyed, and when I walked back to access the damage, I saw something written on the back of it that was hidden all those years it hung on our wall. *Master of his Domain* was the sign that had been staring me in the face for quite some time without me even realizing it. I was no longer the master of my domain, and the damage was obvious. With my heart torn out, I didn't know what I would do because I had failed to protect my house as my whole world fell apart right in front of me.

I stayed with my friends the next day, but later in the evening, I couldn't take it anymore. I had to go back to try my best to communicate with Jenna. It was late, but I needed to talk to her. Desperately trying to hold on, I walked into the bedroom to see her lying in bed sleeping. I woke her up and tried to say anything to revive our relationship, but she wasn't interested in listening to me. She flicked the switch on her emotions based on both of our actions and she had already started to move on. I had been paying for the roof over her head, and I thought she was taking my hard work for granted. My feelings were all over the place, so I chose to leave and go back to stay with the people who supported me at a time when I needed them most. While I was gone, Jenna stayed with a mutual friend to get away from the negativity she was living in. Austin had been the *fill-in* best man at our wedding, and she confided in him that we had broken up. As soon as he found out, he systematically attempted to catch her on the rebound like a vulture by making his move on her and telling her he loved her. I can only imagine what went through her mind at this point. It was like the men who were our so-called friends stood in line, waiting for their chance. Knowing this now, it disgusts me that he was the person standing next to us while we said our vows.

He was a wolf in sheep's clothing,
and I was reminded that we allowed someone
into our lives with their own agenda.

I finally went back home again to let Jenna know I was flying back to Canada. Regardless of how things worked out between us, I planned on getting my social security number to start my business with William. We agreed to put everything on pause to see how things shook out when I got back. Grasping, I took this as a sign that we were not yet over, and there might still be a remote possibility we could save our marriage. Without thinking, I decided to send flowers to her at work. I had never done something like this before, and her response was far from positive. It was an act of desperation, along with an assumption that we were getting back on track. However, this was not the case, and understandably, she did not take it well. I finally showed up when our relationship was threatened, and it appeared to be too late. Where were those flowers before? At this point, they were received as a slap in the face, and if I had been on the other side of the equation, admittedly, I would have felt the same way. Why didn't I do the little things before instead of taking us for granted for so long?

I left for Canada, and the loving look I saw in her eyes so many times before had faded away. However, I had a massive opportunity in front of me, and I had not seen my family in almost eight years. Leaving Florida was bittersweet because a fear of the unknown was directly in front of me with another fear of the unknown that I had no control over left behind. My passport had expired, so I arranged to fly into Washington State, meeting my biological mom on the U.S. side of the border and driving across instead. I needed my family in a big way, and as always, they were there to help. My folks had no idea I had come back, and when we went around the corner to the familiar house I had grown up in, my father was out in the backyard, puttering around finding things to do.

The look on his face said it all when I got out of that car. He came up, shook my hand and said: *Welcome home.* I walked in the backdoor as my mother came around the corner to see me standing in the entrance, and she almost fainted. She grabbed the side of the counter, looked at me and said: *Oh my God, Corey.* She sat down in the living room, and I walked over and gave her a huge hug. I let my parents know what happened, and they supported me in my decision to try to make my business and my marriage work. My parents were far from perfect, but they stayed together because, in their eyes, marriage was permanent, and although divorce was a reality for many, it wasn't for them. I gave Jenna the benefit of the doubt even when it was apparent there was much more going on because I saw my parents stand together through thick and thin, even if it didn't seem like the right thing to do sometimes.

While I was there, my dad did everything he could to help me through my situation. He drove me to apply for my passport, which would take three months to be assigned after application, and I needed to be present to pick it up. Also, to get my driver's license reinstated, I had to retake a driver's test, and my folks supported me by letting me use their home address. It was good to be back home, far away from the addictions that haunted me from my past. I wanted to get it right, and I was not about to give up on my marriage, which my father respected. But both my mother and father only knew what they knew; they may have had a different perspective if they had been there with Jenna and me. However, we put together a game plan whereby I would be back in three months to get my passport. In the meantime, they wanted me to do whatever I could to save my marriage, giving me money to take Jenna on a trip when I got back to Florida. Their intention was for us to have the ability to get away from all distractions and try to work everything out the best we could. The generosity of my family was astounding, especially because I needed their support more than ever.

I left to go back to Florida with an expired passport, and I was nervous as we drove across the border into Washington

State. Surprisingly, we made it through, and I was relieved to head back to attempt to rebuild my marriage, even though it was against all odds. The break had done us both a lot of good, and the woman who wanted to end it all had a renewed will to try again. She agreed that our marriage was worth saving after everything we had been through, even if I buried what I knew into my state of denial. We were both excited to have a chance to get away from the drama that constantly surrounded us, so we chose to go on a spontaneous road trip through northern Florida to explore areas we had never experienced. The main destination was St. Augustine, the oldest city in the U.S., and we took full advantage of the restaurants and the nightlife, including a ghost tour in a horse-drawn carriage. It was magical at that moment. All the negativity and drama back in Panama City Beach no longer existed, and our emotions were stronger than ever as we both blocked out the reality of our recent past. On our way home, we stopped south of Tallahassee at Wakulla Springs to tour the area where the original Tarzan and The Creature from the Black Lagoon were filmed. We took it all in, enjoying every second because it had been so long since we experienced anything as a couple without the distractions of everyday life. We were falling in love again, and I was open to letting it happen, bending my morality in a desperate attempt to hold on because if my suspicions were correct, I would have forgiven her.

The closer we got to Panama City, the more my heart sank, knowing the reality we faced in front of us. When we arrived home, the bad apples with good intent gave us more distance to work things out, and we made every effort to do so. The next couple of months seemed to fly by, and everything was going so well that I chose to take Jenna with me, flying directly into Canada. It was exciting because she had never been out of the southern U.S., and she had never met my family. It was important to me that she have a taste of what my family represented. Regardless of what our future held, I wanted her to know where I came from, and I also wanted my parents to meet the woman I committed almost eight years of my life to and understand why she meant so much to me.

When we arrived in Vancouver and introductions were made, all the drama we had been experiencing faded away in the background. Unsurprisingly, my parents welcomed her with open arms, and although they could tell she was from a place they had never explored, they showed love and accepted her. I was hopeful that after she met my parents, she would have better respect for our marriage. We stayed at my folks' place for a few days, but they were elderly, and it had become an added pressure having us there, which was unnecessary. My biological mom offered to have us stay at her place for the remainder of our trip, and I was happy for her and Jenna to get to know each other. Everything was falling into place perfectly. I had my new driver's license with my passport, and my parents unexpectedly gave us some money to go home with, which was beyond appreciated.

It was five a.m. when we arrived at the airport to take the long flight back to Florida. With our documents ready, we stepped up to the booth to speak with the customs officer for our entry back into the U.S. He went through the typical questions with Jenna, but when he got to me, he started asking questions I could not answer. My stomach started to sink when he asked me why both of my ID's were brand new. Then he asked why, as a Canadian, I only had a flight to Florida with no return ticket. Asking where I worked, I lied to him, randomly mentioning a tile store I saw on the way to the airport. However, it was early on a Sunday morning, so he had no way to make a call to verify.

I watched him scribble something across my paperwork, and my nerves escalated drastically when he told me to go to the back for fingerprinting.

We were utterly helpless with nowhere to go and only the cash in my pocket that my parents had so graciously provided. My irresponsibility and procrastination had finally caught up with me. We were both in tears, sitting outside of that office with the world crashing down on us. She could have gone back but was too scared to leave me there. Finally, we had no other choice but to stick it out and do what we could to get through the ordeal. We listened to the last call for everyone to board our flight, and I realized that I might never see my faithful dog, my house, or my business opportunity again.

The combination of humiliation and fear
I experienced was indescribable.

I instantly heard the stress in Gayle's voice when I called to give her the news about our uncertain situation and how we were trying to figure out how to handle it. Her main priority was taking care of her parents, the people who had raised me, and this was sure to add stress to their lives in a big way. We awkwardly stayed with her for the next few days, trying to figure out our next move. The pressure finally came to a head when she broke down with me, expressing her frustration with Jenna, who was an earshot away, standing downstairs. She loudly demanded that I put her on a fucking plane and send her ass back down to Florida. In my opinion, it was the worst thing that could have been said at that moment because she wasn't some girl I had picked up on the weekend; she was my wife. Jenna was destroyed and told me that even after everything she had been through with her past trauma and abuse, that was one of the hardest things she had ever heard someone say about her. It was beyond a slap in the face, mainly based on who said it, and those words made her realize that we were definitely at the beginning of the end. However, Gayle intended to do whatever it took to protect her parents at all costs, and the burden we presented was massive.

Packing up our belongings, we used the money my parents gave us to stay in a hotel within walking distance. It was barely enough to get us through as we scrambled to figure out our next move. The cold November rain poured as we remained trapped in our little room after attempting at one point to speak with a government official in Vancouver, but she had no solution. My sadness turned into depression as the situation became more dire by the minute. Our only choice was to have Jenna fly back while I stayed in Canada for as long as it took. Her anxiety was at a maximum, and she was too scared to fly back to Florida alone, but thankfully, there was one saving grace within that horrible time. My old buddy, Ron, was visiting family in Ohio, and although he was far from Vancouver, he made an effort to fly to the west coast and accompany Jenna on her flight home.

We met him at the local Denny's for a very short visit before they were scheduled to fly out, and Ron assured me everything would be ok. Then, concerned that I didn't have enough money to make it through, he unexpectedly slid 500 dollars across the table and told me not to stress about paying him back. He needed us in the past, and when we needed him in our most desperate moment, he came through with flying colours.

As I walked through the airport, fear and uncertainty hit me like a bomb: *When would I see either one of them again? What would happen to my business opportunity with William? Where was I even going to live?* Arriving at the gate to board the plane clarified the reality in front of us when Jenna said that this would be the biggest test of our relationship. Her words proved to be accurate, but at the time, I had no idea how big this test would be. I stood there, watching them walk down the boarding ramp, and in my heart, I knew it was the last time I would see her, and there was nothing I could do about it. Humiliation, pain, and guilt overcame me as I walked through the airport. Stopping in front of a massive jade statue, I broke down with loneliness, fear, and sadness coursing through my veins.

Little did I know that as Ron and Jenna boarded the plane, she was also in tears. Ron was there to comfort her in one of her most challenging moments. However, she also told Ron that she was excited to get back to Florida to see her friends and family. He said that she had a sense of relief on her face to a certain extent, which all things considered was understandable. The decision was made for both of us, and although I thought things were back on track, I was now considered dead weight, and maybe I truly was. I made the mistake of taking her for granted and procrastinated on getting legal when I easily could have for years, being married to an American. Maybe the financial and emotional struggles were just too much for her, but neither of us were the same people we married. Now that I was out of the picture, she had an open ticket to live her own life instead of living life through me, and as scary as it was, she was liberated. I was reduced from the top of my game to the bottom of the barrel. Nothing was as horrible as the emotions I experienced in that airport through all my ups and downs. I came to realize that I, too, was a bad apple with good intent.

The Naked Truth

Without intent, I had borderline misogynistic control over Jenna, not permitting her to grow as a person. Looking back, the similarities I had with my father are striking yet understandable. I mirrored his image, being the provider, still trying to live in a foregone era that does not exist in most cases. Admitting this is not easy but recognizing my truth has been a massive part of my growth.

My life was created by the path I chose and the people I associated with while seeking happiness. The use of ecstasy provided a gateway to tapping into emotions I didn't know existed, which made the addiction to access them far stronger than I ever realized. I had every reason to be happy with what I had right in front of me but living in the now was not something I understood how to do until later in life after my addictions were far behind me.

Admittedly, I didn't protect my *house*. I use my house as an analogy referring to many things: in a physical sense, the sidewalk in front of my house may be open to the public, which of course, cannot be controlled. People always came and went, but now I monitor who I let through the front gate and interact with. When I sense negativity or drama, they don't get as far as the front porch. Trust comes in layers, and when I trust someone enough to let them in the front door, they have earned their entry. Even the people I trust don't have access to certain areas of my house. If the kitchen is the place for gathering, my true friends occupy that space. My bedroom remains my sanctuary due to the personal belongings and energy that exists within its four walls. However, I also refer to my house as my headspace, and I only allow certain people into certain areas of my mind. Jenna and I did not protect our house from people who should have remained on the sidewalk. We assumed our relationship was like an impenetrable wall based on our history, but it's never good to assume.

However, humility was a component within my mindset change, helping me to address the ego I didn't realize I had in the first place. It knocked me off my perch of perfection and made me realize that my *dream life* was only a dream. It wasn't reality, and I could not rely solely on my exterior self anymore. As painful as it was, I was humbled by the experience, and it quickly made me realize that taking what I had for granted created a catastrophic result. I had to start from bare naked and put my clothes back on to begin my journey of self-discovery. It was another lesson learned the hard way, and it was almost impossible to avoid.

I still remember the lesson taught to me by my grade six teacher, Mr. Cousins, but I wish I had implemented it far earlier in life. He asked me to speak with him after class one day, and I immediately knew I had done something wrong. Reluctantly, I showed up for our *appointment*, concerned about what he had to say to me. He let me know that, along with my many opinions, I had massive potential. However, I needed to take the time to truly listen and be humble.

Looking through my lens, first and foremost, humility is one of the most important keys to success. It blocked the arrogant, self-indulging lifestyle I had created and forced me to start listening more instead of constantly talking. I stopped dominating conversations and avoided talking over others, becoming curious about what they knew—being humble inspired my obsession with learning. On the other side, when I take my time to speak my mind, I speak without fear of being wrong while doing my best to be grateful. I prefer to learn about others while openly accepting feedback when sharing my perspectives. I now take responsibility by speaking up and owning my authentic point of view. I am no longer afraid to ask for help from others because I fully realize that I am not perfect, and I do not have all the answers.

When I'm in conversation with someone, I take the time to fully absorb what they are saying without thinking about how I'm going to reply. This opens a window to learning and growth based on another individual's successes and failures. In addition, understanding that it's not all about me drastically improves my ability to manage my self-worth.

Egotism & Authenticity

XI

The Casualties of Divorce

Holding on to someone who does not reciprocate was like having them hand me the scissors to cut the cord. And regardless of how hard it was to sever, I knew I should take the initiative to make a clean cut and move on.

My relationship with my biological mother was strained to a point it had never been, and my grandparents were far too old to deal with the drama happening in my life. Fortunately, out of the goodness in her heart, my Aunt Carol offered me a place to stay, helping me get back on my feet. It was not ideal, but I am forever grateful for her stepping in at this time of my life. If not for her and considering my fragile state of mind at the time, I may have given up.

Jenna was flying in one direction as I flew in a completely different one. I didn't know where I was going and had no clue what I would do with my life. The pit in my stomach lasted far longer than the short flight to Kelowna, and although it was a new beginning, I fought it every step of the way. I was determined not to stay in Canada, even if my marriage was falling apart, because I still had high hopes of starting my business and reuniting with my friends in the states. My main motivation was to get back there, and I made every effort to do so.

My wife and I put together a game plan to help me get back home, doing whatever she could on her end while I did the same in Canada. I had a friend who was an advisor for a U.S. senator, and he also tried to help me, but nothing ever came of it. However, I was living in a pipe dream, still hoping my marriage would survive, even though I knew in my heart it would never be the same.

Aunt Carol and I had some long conversations, whereby she supported me to realize that this was a new opportunity— having the ability to move forward without being forced to work construction while further damaging my body. Taking her advice, I applied for an entry-level sales job, upgrading cell phone plans. It was far from perfect, but it took me out of my comfort zone and distracted me from what was happening back in Florida. I knew I was holding on to my marriage far too long, still sending money home to Jenna to cover the bills in my absence. My intention never strayed because I was steadfast in my decision to do whatever it took to get back to my wife. I felt an obligation to her, and I didn't want to leave her hanging high and dry due to what happened. It was a time in my life when I was alone once again. But this time, I had a victim mindset and tried to figure out what I had done wrong and how I could fix something that seemed beyond repair. Time went on, and we each dealt with the increased stress in our unique ways. My focus was on doing whatever it took to get back to her while she focused on partying with her new friends instead of addressing what needed to be done.

Eventually, we realized I would not be coming back to

Florida for quite some time, so I offered to fly her back to Canada to start a new life. I told her we could work on our dreams here, but she refused, and in hindsight, that came as no surprise. She gave the lame excuse that it was too cold in Canada, and she could never live that far away from her family. However, in the back of my mind, I knew she was saying things I needed to hear to avoid confrontation. Then reality hit me square in the face and knocked my rose-coloured glasses off forever. I made a call to someone I knew in our circle of Florida friends to reconnect. I am keeping this person's name anonymous because I promised I would, and I stand by our agreement to this day.

Our conversation moved toward my hope of getting back there, but I was not sure when. I mentioned that Jenna was on board to help in any way she could from her side of the border. The conversation immediately stopped when this person asked me to sit down if I wasn't already. They said it was the last thing they wanted to tell me, but it was necessary because, in their opinion, I was too good of a person to be taken advantage of by someone who no longer cared about me—my wife.

I never experienced the pain of someone cheating on me the way I did that day. It was one of the hardest things I have ever gone through—worse than death because death is uncontrollable in most cases. But in this situation, there was a conscious choice in the matter, and she made it. The slow bleed we had been experiencing for quite some time instantly became a life-threatening wound that could never heal.

This person I spoke to had the guts to tell me the truth when others who knew what was happening chose to help cover her tracks. They told me never to send another dollar back to Florida because not one dime was being used for the right reason. I instantly saw red, and my stress level went through the roof when I received the news that Jenna had moved her new boyfriend in straight away. Her new man had been living with her for a month and had the luxury of walking straight into the void I left while sleeping with her in the bed I paid for. It was a slap that could have been heard halfway across the world. I only knew my confidant for a very short time, and they had no idea what they did for me that day, even though their words pierced my heart.

As soon as we ended the call, I tried to contact Jenna, but the phone rang until it went to voicemail. I tried again, but it went to voicemail again. So, this time, I left a message in my rage, demanding she get back to me as soon as possible. I ended my message, stating I could make her new boyfriend's life hell, and I had no issue doing that from Canada. It didn't take long for her to become available.

She did not deny or have any remorse for her adultery but was concerned with who told me about her indiscretion. I deflected her question by telling her that providing my source was irrelevant and out of the equation. I had been married to this woman for almost eight years, and the only concern she had was who let the cat out of the bag! She kept pressing, and I was beyond disgusted and broken, repeating that my source didn't matter. Finally, and out of spite, I dropped a bomb back on her by telling her that I had only suspected, and she, herself, confirmed it.

Evidently, she couldn't be alone and had to depend on someone else when I was no longer in the picture. I understood this reality when the smoke cleared, and strangely, it felt like a weight being lifted off my shoulders. I was beyond angry, but now he bared the burden of responsibility while I was free to live my life. However, I still didn't for quite some time because of the long-dead emotions I held on to—such wasted energy because she had moved on. I wondered why I couldn't.

My self-worth was so low that my only choices were to drown myself in self-pity or move on with my life and build back better. Fortunately, I chose the latter. Jenna was only 18 years old when we got married, and even though we had many amazing experiences, the ties were not strong enough to bind, and she was finally freed from the cage she was in. Of course, this in no way justifies her behaviour, but I forgave her in the end because I could acknowledge how I contributed to her actions. I could not carry the negative weight on my shoulders anymore because that tore me apart mentally for years; I could not admit that I was at least 50 percent of the problem.

It was a cold night in December when it finally ended, and although it was snowing and the weather was nasty, I needed to get out of my aunt's condo. I had to do anything I could to protect my peace of mind that was in overdrive. So, I walked to a little park with a covered area and sat down on one of the benches. It was around one in the morning, and as I sat there alone, watching the snow fall in silence, I thought about my Florida life a million miles away. I held a bag of weed that my biological mom had given me and listened to some music, and a multitude of memories started running through my head. Sitting there in a pile of tears, I became lost inside a rollercoaster of emotions. And at that moment, I made a decision that became a turning point in my life—I was going to do whatever it took to rebuild myself again by getting back to what I knew. I wanted to bring back the person who had the self-discipline to get in the gym every day. Finally, I had clarity that if I did it before, I could do it again at the age of 38. To this day, I stop at that little park from time to time to reflect on how it changed my life. It began as a space of indecisiveness and negativity but shifted to a place where I discovered clarity and positivity.

I chose to see a therapist to get an unbiased opinion, and one thing she said stuck with me: regardless of whether I was able to figure things out with my wife or even start a new relationship, the only way it could ever work was if I built myself up first. I could not rely on anyone else to do it for me, and I had to take action personally because the world would keep on spinning, with or without me. She was right, and I was determined to get back to the person I was before entering this beyond co-dependent relationship. My sadness turned to anger as I drove every ounce of rage into the weights I lifted. I stayed beyond dedicated to this practice of rebuilding my exterior. With no vehicle, I was forced to walk down the mountain every day to my job and then to the gym. As the sun set, I climbed back up that mountain, getting home well after dark.

I could only take one step at a time,
and although I needed to work on my inner self,
I stayed the course, laser-focused on my outer image...for now.

Jenna was in the rear-view mirror, but I still had faith she would help me with something she promised before we even got married. No matter what happened, she said she would help me be legal to work in the U.S. I still hoped to start my business with William, and I needed Jenna's help to make that happen. Although she and I had not spoken in quite some time, I tried contacting her to see if she would stay married until my paperwork was processed. In conversation, I mentioned that we needed to have our story straight based on the possibility the government could question us. Looking through my lens, I believed it was a small sacrifice for her to state that she was still my wife. But she had a different perspective. She didn't want to take the risk. However, she made the excuse that she wanted to start a family with her new boyfriend. Admittedly, those words hurt and angered me with one last kick in the teeth in the middle of my attempted rebuild. However, in hindsight, I understand; we were not together, and this request put her at risk because I had been suspended for re-entry into the United States for three years. Looking back, if the roles were reversed, I would have had the same perspective. However, frustration consumed me in my state of mind, and I texted her a message that put her into shock: *The torch has been lit; let the games begin.* Being in pain and out of control, I threw a punch out at her without considering anything else. This ended any chance of going into business in Florida, which closed yet another door to my past.

Without being too cliché, I believe this whole experience happened for a reason. Seeing as my business plan with William was to open a flooring store, the stock market crash of 2008 would have guaranteed a challenging mountain to climb, and although it seemed like I was the victim again, I was far from it. This blessing in disguise proved that, although moving toward resistance is a good self-discipline practice, when the resistance comes from multiple directions, it may be a sign. No matter how hard I tried to get back to Florida, roadblocks appeared around every corner. But, being forced into a change of environment and mindset, I was blessed with the space that provided the ability to grow, and I took many long walks while trying to figure out my path.

Nothing would stop me from my rebuild, but every so often, sad memories crept in. It was tough, accepting Jenna had betrayed me. I had entertained thousands of women over the years, with only one minor hiccup with Kaitlen way back in

Little Rock, Arkansas. The road I took back then was blocked, and regret started to consume me, thinking about the other route that could have been. The last time we connected, Kaitlen spoke through tears of pain, and now, I was experiencing the same, just in a different way. I had the urge to contact her, foolishly grasping onto a memory from almost nine years prior. I remembered that her grandmother lived just south of the border in Washington State, so I looked up her name and contacted her. She mentioned that Kaitlen was living with her husband in the south of Seattle, but she would give her the message that I called. I should have asked her grandmother not to bother, but I awkwardly said thank you and left it at that.

When Kaitlen called me back a few hours later, she sounded surprised to hear from me, but we had a good conversation. I was happy for her through my sadness, and I recognized I needed to close that door. She figured we were just stupid kids, flying by the seat of our pants, and she was probably right. However, one more door from the past closed while another one opened once again. I was in Vancouver, visiting my family when Jessica contacted me unexpectedly. Whether she was prompted through social media or heard through the grapevine, it didn't matter because I was happy to hear from her. It had been over a decade since I had seen her. And even after everything that had happened, it was evident that time can heal, especially when two people grow. So, within no time, she was at my parents' place, picking me up to go on a random adventure. Driving into Vancouver, we started laughing at some of the insane shit we had done and shared our ecstasy stories. Interestingly, we had never done it together, so when she asked me if I wanted to, I had a hard time refusing.

A good number of Jessica's friends were gay, and neither one of us was the least bit homophobic. Back in the day, we occasionally went to a gay bar without judgement to avoid the distraction of having anyone hit on us while we cut loose. Sticking with tradition, we decided to relive that memory all over again, bumping and grinding on the dance floor. The attraction had not gone away, and we ended the night back at her place. Sex is one thing, but what happened the next day is what sticks in my memory. The image of Jessica sitting on my lap while we ate ice cream cones together on a Sunday morning with the sun coming up over English Bay was surreal and near perfection. It was a beautiful experience, even if it was only for that vision in my mind's perspective. A sense of ease from the struggle I was dealing with came over me as I sat with the woman I adored in so many ways. However, as sweet an experience as this was, this was a just sex moment for both of us. I lost so much and wanted to feel again, so this was a rebound to a certain extent. However, I had no regrets, and neither did she. We both lived in different areas with different lives, and I returned to mine, only to manage another casualty of my divorce—my dog.

Back in Florida, my old buddy Ron had been doing his best to take care of her since I left well over a year ago. She was a 12-year-old Labrador who saved my soul when I originally ended it with Jessica years before. She was just a puppy back then and had given me so much and expected little in return. I admit I had faults as an owner at times, but she ended up being a casualty of divorce. She was the closest thing to a kid I ever had, and she had great instincts. I look back on some of the things she did and laugh. Being the only female in my life, she never accepted Jenna the way I did when I met her, and she made that clear right from the beginning. With us going to the club for long hours, she developed separation anxiety, so even though we didn't have a pen for her, we dog-proofed the house to ensure she couldn't destroy anything. I made sure all our boots and shoes were safely stored away behind the bi-fold doors of our closet with the added precaution of sliding a heavy coffee table in front of it. I have no idea how she did it, but that dog moved the table, opened the closet door, and chewed up every one of Jenna's shoes, leaving all of mine standing straight up and undamaged. It was quite the sight to behold, and I believe she was trying to tell me something in her own way.

Ron suffered another heart attack and had no choice but to move into a place where he could receive closer attention, but they didn't allow pets. I did everything in my power to save her, calling as many people as I could for help, but nobody jumped in. My next step was calling the airlines to arrange to have her flown to Canada, but it was not allowed without an owner onboard the same flight. To make matters worse, Ron mentioned that she might not survive the flight based on her age. Jenna and I were not communicating, and even if she could take her, I had already shared enough of my life with her as it was. Eventually, it came down to two choices: Ron offered to take her to the vet to be put to sleep, or he could have the boys set her free in a good neighbourhood, hoping that someone would find her and take her in. Neither option was ideal, but if I had to choose, I should have had her put down. However, I was still dealing with trauma, and as a result, my old dog was abandoned due to the mindset of her irresponsible owner.

I wasn't even responsible enough to do the right thing for my dog. I was definitely not the master of my domain, and my poor pup suffered the consequences through no fault of her own. Ron's two boys dropped her off somewhere I will never know, which is the saddest decision I ever made to that point in my life. I will regret it forever, and I will never know what happened to her, and I deserve that. I know it killed Kyle and

Jeffery because they loved her as well, and I'm sure we all shed more than a few tears over it. I swore I would never get another animal should there be the possibility it might suffer the same consequences at my hand. I would ensure that I would be stable enough to be a responsible pet owner before I made that commitment again, and I held true to that statement.

The next time I crossed paths with Jessica was late 2009, but the vibe was not the same, and it was kind of like trying to push a square through a circle. There was distance between us and an unusual lack of communication when everything came to a head over the dinner table at a restaurant in downtown Vancouver. She suddenly realized why she was being borderline bitchy to me, not able to let go of the fact that she had to sue me to get the money I borrowed from her, regardless that it was all paid back years earlier. In her next breath, looking down from the pedestal I had put her on, she said that she had lost all respect for me. She neglected to remember her part in our original breakup, and although it was a bitter pill to swallow, I wondered where this suddenly came from. I wished she had just picked up her water glass and thrown it in my face, but instead, she carried on, making it clear that she was going to find the right person and get married again. It was beyond obvious that I was not going to be that person, and at that moment, I didn't want to be, so I left without looking back. She felt that she deserved better, and maybe she did, but I definitely knew that I did too. So, I continued to focus on independently moving forward while detaching from her completely.

Then, I found myself in a different place where not only did I have my body back, but my mind was also moving in the right direction. I was older now but not too old to give dancing another go. I received inquiries from the ladies at work, and there was no competition in the area where I lived. Even though

I realized it would never be the same, it still wasn't about money as much as my addiction to capturing emotion from my audience. The twilight of my dance career was now based on private parties, but as long as I wasn't *that guy*, I was grateful to be back out there. Fighting so hard for my perception of what was the best thing for me was simply holding on to an already dissipated dream. The roadblocks I faced in these dark times appeared for a reason, but they also brought me to where I had no choice but to take uncomfortable action, forcing me to move in a new direction. I was in a rut and willing to do whatever it took to avoid the discomfort of my reality. Even through all the exterior work I recently did, I still let my past control my present by staying in the comfort zone of misery I had created.

The best analogy I have heard on comfort versus discomfort is the story about the farmer and the rut. A farmer can take the exact same path every day to plow his field. However, the ruts are so deep that they can literally take their hands off the wheel, and the tractor will drive itself down that same path on autopilot. That farmer can settle for staying in that rut forever if it is producing what they want, or they can choose to make a slight adjustment to their path to get what they need. Getting out of that rut requires going over a bump, and depending on how deep the rut is, determines how big of a bump must be overcome. The question I needed to ask myself was:

*Am I willing to go over the bump to get to
a different destination?
Is the comfort of the rut I'm in providing enough pain or
discomfort that I'm willing to do what it takes to put my
hands on the wheel and make the shift?*

I was jaded, looking at the world around me as it was still turning. I had new people in my life who saw my pain and made an effort to help, but I was too consumed with my personal struggle. One night, they attempted to drag me out the door by taking me to a local nightclub, and although most of the people around me were having a good time, I stood there in disgust. My perception of everyone surrounding me was negative because I had been screwed over, so I saw nothing but people putting themselves in a position of heartache. I predetermined that everyone would suffer the same pain I had, and due to my insecurities, I was judgmental and not willing to let anyone in. I went home that night, sad and lonely, not providing myself with a way out of the rut. Every waking minute, my mind remained in the past, focusing on my failures without understanding their purpose was to encourage me to grow. I walked by people on the street, thinking to myself: *If that person only had a clue what was going on in my head right now, they would think I was insane.* I even had a moment in the middle of the day on a busy street when our wedding popped into my head, and I suddenly broke down in tears. Being alone through this struggle made me realize that waiting for something to come to me would never amount to anything, and the negative energy that consumed me would keep me in this rut for the rest of my life if I let it—I would die if I stayed in the rut. Maybe not necessarily in a literal sense, but I have had many people in my life still living on the outside, yet they are dead on the inside. Quite frankly, I understand that they may not have any other choice due to circumstance, but I decided that would not be me.

So, I willingly took that uncomfortable bump, moving in a new direction because I was unfulfilled within the reality I was living. I was in a dark and lonely place, and although I could barely see the light at the end of the tunnel, there was a glimmer in the distance. The end of my marriage forced me to detach from everything toxic. However, truly detaching from my Florida life took far too long. I made a mistake regardless of how things ended because detachment was my nemesis and staying attached wasn't serving me. Instead of taking the time to heal my wound, I put a band-aid on it and pretended it wasn't there. Detachment helped me rebuild without having others' opinions blur my vision. In my situation, detachment was forced upon me, and I am now grateful it was. Having the stresses and drama a million miles away permitted me to clarify my next steps. I avoided social media while keeping a very tight circle of friends focused on my progression. The reality was still there, but by detaching, I could take control of my actions instead of letting my past control me. The only way I could attract new quality relationships into my life was to detach from the old damaging ones, even if it was just temporarily.

Surrounding myself with the right people who motivated me instead of hindering me was key through my journey of finding my *true self.* I sought those who inspired me to reach the next level and who were unwilling to settle for mediocrity. I used this philosophy many years before when I first entered the gym, and I used it again at 38 years old, finding the most driven and determined people in the gym to train with. Seven years of codependency had weakened me physically and mentally, and although the bump to get out of that rut was huge, I was willing to drive right over it to do whatever it took to find the part of myself I had lost.

I trained like an animal, doing everything I knew how to come back bigger and better than ever before. It didn't take long before I achieved my physical goal through straight-up determination. I chose to guide my life in the right direction by starting in the gym as a base, but if I ever wanted a life-partner who wanted to learn and grow with me, I had to represent who I was on the inside as well. I had to finally take accountability for my actions because it wasn't about Jenna anymore. This was about diving deep to discover why I had such low self-worth in the first place, always seeking acceptance from those I put on a pedestal. I often got an ego boost, seeing a stranger's reactions when I walked by them with my shirt off, which gave me short-lived confidence and acceptance for all the work I put in. But that was far from gratifying and definitely not fulfilling.

I used my body to feed my addiction through entertainment;
to pull emotions out of others,
even though I could barely pull them out of myself.

My alter-ego, Dalton Strong, showed his face again, and although I experienced stability through my day job, I could still work a side hustle while feeding my sex addiction. After living in my aunt's basement for months, I found a higher-paying sales position in one of Canada's leading telecom companies with a team of roughly 200 people. I was older than the majority of them, but it didn't take long until word got out about my dancing career, and suddenly I was being booked regularly. I moved in with one of my work colleagues, making yet another shift in a different direction.

My new job required training for roughly two to three weeks, and I was fortunate to be trained by a woman named Kylie, who was very outspoken, independent, and an expert in her field. Getting to know her, I realized very quickly that she was a straight shooter. She was a Portuguese firecracker who was the exact opposite of most women I had gravitated toward in my past. She related to what I had gone through, and in her way, she was pivotal in helping me understand that some people in this world are simply ruthless. We formed an instant friendship, and she was part of my new friend circle. Kylie was a hard worker and an even harder partier who had fought abuse and addiction. She had two young children through a former marriage, and my mindset was not to change her but instead accept the situation in front of me.

Our company had a very strict rule about employees dating one another, especially between supervisors and sales staff. Still, it didn't take long before our attraction for one another took over. She was a little rough around the edges at times, but I saw the sweetheart she was, and her *boss* status attracted me in a naughty way. It was risky dating her, and our undercover relationship made it even more of a turn-on. We fed off it, passing one another in the hallway at work while giving each other that *fuck me* look without saying a word. Her physically attractive, confident, bad girl image escalated my attraction towards her even more. However, she still had luggage sitting outside her door from a recent breakup, but the chemicals between us took over, and I was happy to let it happen.

I knew from the beginning she was far from an angel, and I was attracted to her fun, cute tendencies in public. However, I was even more attracted to her when it was just the two of us, free to be our authentic selves, laughing about all the crazy shit we'd been through. Lying in my bed fast asleep one night, I awakened to something hitting my bedroom window. Next, my phone started buzzing, and when I answered, Kylie was on the other end telling me that my drunk girlfriend was standing in the backyard throwing rocks at my window. It was two in the morning, and when I looked outside, I saw her standing in the snow in fuzzy slippers—she looked intentional. Being careful not to wake my roommate, I met her at the front door to get her out of the cold.

There was no question about what she was looking for, and I had no issue warming her up. Smiling, I picked her up, carried her into my bedroom, and our clothes came off, fuzzy slippers and all. She had massive sex appeal, and even my roommate was a little envious I was dating her. I'm sure he heard every move we made through the thin walls of our side-by-side bedrooms, but we didn't care. She showed up unexpectedly, we had spectacular sex together, and then she went home. It felt like I had been in a dream when I woke the next day, but the reality was that we fed what we each needed at that moment. Maintaining our relationship for the next few months, we knew in our hearts that it was not going to last because she had still not gotten rid of her most recent baggage, and I was too nice for her. She wanted someone who would *put her in her place*, but I was respectful and reserved, and I desired stability. Whereas she was a wild child, and although I have no regrets having been with her, she had addictions I could not permit in my life. We have remained friends to this day, and just because her journey was different than mine does not mean hers was wrong. She was there for me multiple times when I needed her, and regardless of her faults, I will be forever grateful to her. We all have shit to overcome, and I am proud of her for doing exactly that.

After Kylie, my slut side came out, thinking that sexually satisfying women would achieve happiness. I danced at private parties, found beautiful girls interested in Dalton and had one-night stands with the skewed hope that some sort of relationship would develop. I even asked one of these women to be my girlfriend, but she explained that she could never date a stripper—it was only about the sex. When I showed back up at her door unexpectedly, she was embarrassed and explained that she had someone up in her room, and it wasn't a good time.

My struggle with unworthiness continued. On more than one occasion, I hooked up with some girl with bigger expectations than they were willing to fulfill. Eventually, I resorted to getting sexual satisfaction without emotional attachment and dropping them off with no remorse. I became hardened by the skewed reality that I was only worth as much as a male dancer in his early 40s who had failed at almost every relationship he'd been in. I used these women for what they were worth and vice versa, and my frustration was a weak attempt at emotional expression barely reciprocated. I was lost, looking for stability where there was none to be found. However, even during these dark times with my best shows behind me, I achieved some memorable moments.

Some ladies from work booked me for a show, renting one side of a local nightclub with a DJ to emcee a private party for one of their friends who was getting married. Waiting outside in my car, I saw them walking up the street excited to get inside to begin the festivities, all dressed up in their Hooters outfits. The bride-to-be was placed on a chair at centre stage as I made my entrance. Her enthusiastic friends cheered her on through what appeared to be embarrassment, but she was far from reserved. She willfully participated when I passed her my baby oil bottle, and to the delight of the audience, she rubbed it on my bare chest. However, she was excited and squeezed the bottle so hard that she drenched me with it, and more ended up on the floor than anywhere else. The dance floor turned into a slip and slide, leaving both of us in a mess of baby oil combined with sweat. Slipping and falling multiple times while trying to maintain some sort of sex appeal had everyone in hysterics—I was just grateful I came out of there with no broken bones. Even if it wasn't exactly what they paid me for, they received a show, which created an unforgettable memory. I'm sure they still reminisce about it to this day.

My next booking was a group of ladies who rented a houseboat on Lake Okanagan in the middle of the summer for one of their friends who was getting married. They wanted to surprise her with a stripper, so I played the role of the *first mate* until we arrived at our destination in the middle of the lake. The captain gave me the cue when we got close, and the rest of the ladies were up on the top deck. It was then that I made my way into a very small change room to get into costume. After putting my cowboy outfit on, I made my way up the stairs to the top deck to the sound of screaming women overtaking my intro music. The sound of Kid Rock's *Cowboy* blasted out over the lake, and as I made my entrance, I stepped up the ladder to the outdoor deck, and a gust of wind blew my brand-new cowboy hat straight into the lake. It didn't ruin the show by any means, but the hat was gone, and soon after, my costume was as well. The tips made up for the loss of my hat, and the ladies ended up really drunk. When we arrived back on shore, I left the scene and waited for a friend to come to pick me up. I saw them walk off the boat one by one across a plank connecting them to dry land and immediately noticed a disaster waiting to happen. I watched in amazement as one of them lost her balance and fell straight into the lake.

Fortunately, she rose out of the lake laughing, and after they recovered her from the water, the party continued when they stumbled over to a nightclub by the lakeshore. I stood there chuckling to myself, reflecting on similar situations from my past while adding yet another memory to my present. As much as these shows provided unique memories, they dulled in comparison to the creativity I experienced throughout the majority of my career. It soon became evident that I was trying to keep a candle burning whose lifespan had already ended. It was never going to be the same again—similar to trying to recreate the feeling of using ecstasy for the first time.

The last show of my career came at an unexpected time and from the most unexpected clients. Ironically, an old friend from high school contacted me on social media, inquiring about doing a show for a friend's wife who was turning 40. I explained that I wasn't in prime shape and gave her an overinflated show price, hoping I wouldn't be forced into a position of being *that guy* However, they immediately accepted my offer, and at 43 years old, I chose to get back out on that stage one last time.

The stage was set in a wide-open space separated into two sections at a local community hall. The men watched sports on a big screen on one side while the ladies anxiously waited for the show to start on the other. I walked in nervously, looking at the crowd who had a striking resemblance to the type of crowd I grew up around back in my hometown of Surrey. As I stood there, the husband who was paying for the show approached and introduced himself to me. My chin hit the floor because, even though I had never spoken to him before, I instantly knew who he was based on the picture Jessica had painted for me multiple times in the past.

My entire career came full circle to the beginning, sitting in homeroom class admiring the girl from afar with the older boyfriend who eventually damaged her almost beyond repair. I stared him straight in the face and awkwardly carried on with small talk, intently watching him as he explained that he was also raised in Surrey. We knew many of the same people, and he said that Jessica was his first love—I told him we had that in common. He suddenly realized who I was, and the look on his face said it all. I knew the truth, but I wasn't about to bring it up. Business was business, and I had to move ahead with the show.

If someone is only as good as their last performance,
I quickly realized that this was the end.

I was *that guy* I never wanted to be who didn't cut it like he used to in his prime, and I hung up my G-String for good. In an industry that was slowly fading away, I was not as valuable as I had been in the past, but I also recognized that I had been devaluing myself from the first time I stepped out on stage at the age of 17. All those years, I could never get rid of the belief of lack, sitting in the back of my mind while having money literally thrown at me the entire time. It was never about lack of money, but instead about me choosing to listen to people I had put on a pedestal. I absorbed their words that embedded their beliefs, which drove an emotional block in me that was unintentionally harmful. Without introspection or understanding, I chose to carry this with me, and the vice they inflicted upon me was damaging through no fault of their own. I put myself in the position of looking up to them on that pedestal, and one of them was Jessica, who I adored from the first time I laid eyes on her.

With my dance career fading behind me, I received an unexpected call from Ron, who had shockingly fallen off the wagon. It was Christmas Eve, he was alone, and I could hear the sorrow in his voice. He reached out during a time when he needed to talk to someone who cared, even if I was on the other side of the continent. If I had no money, he was always the first to offer some, and if my heart was broken, he was the first to share the reality of the situation without judging me.

He ended every conversation with: *Hang in there* because he knew I could make it through. As hard as it was to hear him in the state he was in, I quickly realized how much he valued me by choosing to reach out instead of doing something drastic. He was the one person who truly accepted me for my friendship and nothing else, contacting me in desperation. Through my tears, I let him know how much he had to live for and supported him to hang in. And although it was Christmas Eve, it was the best present I could have asked for because I was able to talk him off the ledge. That conversation clarified the value I was able to provide someone who was living on borrowed time, using alcohol as his outlet when times were tough.

Ron was now an empty nester because those 15-year-old skater kids of his grew into young men with careers. Kyle had become an electrician, and Jeffery was climbing the ladder of success in the food and beverage industry. Their father was incredibly proud of each of them. After years of being restricted from the U.S, I received an invite in the mail for Kyle's wedding in Florida with an offer to pay for my flight to get there. I refused his generous offer and covered the flight myself. As strange as it was being back, not much had changed when it came to our old crew because they were still like family to me—that group of five fingers Ron had held up, representing my true friends. Even though Jenna was far away in my distant past, she was the missing piece of the puzzle, and it was weird not having her with me. However, the wedding was spectacular regardless. It was so great to see us all together and happy again. Kyle showed up as a proud father of his firstborn, and Ron was ecstatic to be a grandfather. The time I spent over those few days was priceless. However, I knew it might be the last time I would see my old friend face-to-face again. With no idea if I would ever return, we said goodbye in our own way. Tragically, it ended up being the last time.

We spoke many times over the phone to check up on one another, but in the end, his health finally caught up with him. With an untreated wound that spread to gangrene, his leg was amputated from the knee down, and although he hung in there the best he could, he called me one last time, knowing he wouldn't make it. Through my tears, I told him that he was my hero, but he humbly laughed and told me that he was no hero. However, in my eyes, he truly was because he had repeatedly battled adversity through his life that most can't relate to. I was blessed knowing what many others never did, and although he was held back from life in many ways, he was too stubborn to quit doing the things he wanted in the process. He may not have taken the same type of path I did, but we respected one another for our decisions, and I am grateful I was able to say goodbye in that last call and tell him how much I loved him. Since his passing, I often envision Ron holding up those five fingers, and even though I only see four fingers now, I still feel the fifth. The last one is irreplaceable, and I promised him I would hang in there, and I intend to keep that promise.

Putting people on a pedestal was a problem for a good portion of my life because, in some cases, they had unintentional control over me. Likewise, Jenna put me on a pedestal, and I looked down at her, which resulted in controlling and equally unintentional consequences. I never connected with her, and although we had a relationship with a very powerful sexual connection, I was so oblivious to her truth that, up until a few years ago, I didn't recognize her bisexuality until she revealed it. This revelation clarified just how out of touch I was within my marriage, and it was just one more reason for its disintegration. I had a habit of seeing something in my partners that they didn't see in themselves, and in some cases, they very likely had the same impression of me. I am sure that if I had taken the time to better myself internally, I would have attracted someone I didn't feel the desire to *fix*. But how could I even hope for this unless I was willing to lead by example by *fixing* myself first? Instead, I created a vicious cycle and continued to attract all the wrong exterior elements into my life.

I started relationships with women who had issues because I had my own that I refused to acknowledge. I gave them short-lived sexual satisfaction to block the pain they were dealing with, leaving them wanting more for all the wrong reasons. I even had a couple of stalkers, forcing me to cut the cord for my safety. My inner value depleted to the point that I simply didn't care anymore, and I was done with the emotional pain of rejection. It wasn't about self-care at that time—I was simply being selfish. I believed the whole world was out to get me, and I was going to take what I could and throw the rest away.

However, through this season of life, I was able to form some priceless friendships. My neighbours watched me grow from low self-worth to understanding the definition of value. They followed my journey and always supported me no matter what direction I was moving in—forwards or backwards. Through my journey of self-discovery, they witnessed Dalton Strong become Corey again, and at this point, with much of my family becoming more and more distant, I am grateful to have them. Reflecting back, I wish I had taken the time to check in with my partners to get their honest perspective on where our relationships were heading, whether in a positive or negative direction. I never took the time to ask Jenna, being consumed in my perspective and assuming that everything was fine. Even when things were moving in a good direction, I could have taken the time to ask her how to make it even better. And when things were not going so well, I wish I had been more supportive and accountable for my actions. If I even took a minute to ask these things in the late stages of our marriage, the outcome might have been different...or maybe not. Unfortunately, I will never know the answer because I never asked their perspectives.

Eventually, I discovered that behind my biggest fear, my greatest purpose waited for me. Not in a trepidatious way, but in a way that opened me up to being vulnerable and facing my truth to live as my authentic self. I am grateful that this book brought Jenna and me back together 15 years after we ended it all in that airport. Not in a physical sense, but in a way that served each of us well. Since that day, we only spoke a few times, and most of the conversations were far from pleasant. However, long after the dust settled, I asked her some questions to get her honest perspective, and she was open to sharing everything she could. Even after all that time, it was not easy for us to open a door that had been closed so long ago. However, finally sharing the emotions we experienced was well worth it because it proved that the introspective work I had done was successful no matter how much damage had been done.

It wouldn't have been the same without her perspective. We made a lot of mistakes and did horrible things to each other, but I am finally at peace because we did the best we could, given the many cards stacked against us. Our relationship was a tough act to follow. Obviously, we had our issues, but the love we had for one another was unique and special. We never wanted to hurt each other, but we did because of how we devalued ourselves. To this day, I still have a sense of unworthiness in the back of my mind. However, I now manage it because I know it's just a saboteur trying to creep in from my past. I have a deep understanding that, if by chance, everything is taken away from me again, I will not be destitute because I focus on my inner self-worth instead of my external status. I acknowledge that my destination is not to destitution and that in turn protects my peace. I am no longer that kid, scared at the top of the massive Ferris wheel because it's not about my blurred perspective anymore. It's about my truth.

The Naked Truth

When I approached middle age, I was so blessed that I could take a year off from the distractions of life to focus solely on introspection; to truly discover the root cause of my emotional blocks. I needed to understand why I could not provide value to the world—something I had but was blind to. It took asking others what gifts they saw in me because it was too hard to see them through my perspective.

My life was not moving in a forward direction, and a change of environment made the difference. The people I was associating with the most were not allowing me to grow. It took me a while, but I discovered that if a flower isn't growing in the sun, it needs to be moved to the shade. And it is never too late to start. I understand what it takes to support people to take it off because without removing my layers, the cycle was sure to continue. I had to detach from negativity to make space for positivity, including inviting others into my life who experienced success in what I was passionate about.

Through introspection, I understood that my ego, along with unhealthy codependency, not only affected my marriage but also damaged almost every relationship I ever had. Even my work relationships suffered because of my perfectionistic tendencies, complaining about problems without making honest attempts to provide solutions. I needed a real hard look in the mirror and shifted to using my thumb instead of pointing my finger at everyone else.

Codependency motivated me to reject my needs, desires, wants, and inner self by focusing on someone else. I tried to do whatever it took to maintain my marriage in a quest for safety and security, but in the end, I became my own saboteur, trying to do everything else but focus on my wants and needs. It was a survival instinct, and yet, what I needed to do was understand my trauma to support me to leave behind what was not serving me well. Unfortunately, my super-ego led me to view the world through my lens, and everyone else's through a different one.

Following my ego to this degree provided a false sense that I was separate from those around me, but I eventually realized that not everyone thinks like me. Living guided by my authentic self ensured that I could not be offended anymore because I was finally presenting as real and worthy.

Before reaching these revelations, I constantly judged and compared myself to others—another reflection of my inadequacies. When someone didn't do something I expected them to do, I became frustrated and detrimentally expressed myself every time; I was the bad apple with good intent. I needed to get out of my head and realize that not everyone has the same strengths or weaknesses. I would have been far better off to have tried to understand what motivated my partner and find out what challenged her to help her face her fears and expose her greatness. I needed to be more compassionate and put myself in her shoes by connecting and genuinely communicating with her instead of simply talking to her.

When I began accepting these truths, I realized I had nothing to protect. Instead of dwelling on how badly I messed up, I now accept my failures and work on being better next time. Just because it's the end of one dream doesn't mean another can't begin. I learned how to stop repeating my lifetime patterns of irresponsibility by following the breadcrumbs of my past—loving and accepting my imperfections. I changed how I went about the world by communicating with people I normally wouldn't communicate with. As a result, I realized that I was programmed by what I learned growing up, and I had to re-aligned with my authenticity. I started to understand the pitfalls I was dealt, and in turn, created space to understand better who I truly am. Initially, I was fearful of what would be uncovered, so I resisted for years, knowing I had a block but not knowing what it was or where it came from. It was the elephant in the room that I wasn't willing to address, but it was too hard to admit the things I wasn't paying attention to.

To a certain extent, I had inherited trauma, but I used that as an excuse to keep repeating the same patterns over and over again. Letting unworthiness control me resembled a turtle hiding in its shell unwilling to break down my past walls and create proper boundaries. I knew I had my voice but never allowed it to come alive, always hiding behind my alter ego. Then, the humiliation of my past awakened me, allowing me to open to my shame instead of sweeping it under the rug.

This is not about perfection; it's about progression, changing and stepping into a new space to repair myself with clarity about how I can be a better person while attracting the same type of people into my life in the process. I now know that perfectionism is a pipe dream. I'm being authentic and honest, saying that life can be hard while simultaneously realizing that not everything that occurred in the past is my fault. It is my responsibility to determine what I want to do about it, but I chose to shift from the victim mindset of wondering why all this happened to me to how it happened for me? This changed my perception from victim to victor, and I recognized this transformation through the wisdom that lives in between the spaces of my experiences. As a result, I took action to break the cycle.

I also take full responsibility for my part in the failure of our marriage because it was a two-way street. However, when I first started my journey of self-discovery, I did not—being accountable dissolved the negativity of my past and inspired the acceptance of my part, which was liberating and educational. It freed me from the chains of not being *man enough*, believing I did everything perfectly and was screwed over.

I experienced circumstances that were out of my control and brought me to a very dark place, but it didn't serve me to hold onto the negative emotions associated with them. There may have been an element of responsibility that was overlooked or ignored to prove I was right, and I know this because I did it for years, but it didn't get me anywhere. There were times when I felt completely screwed over by an employer, family member, or a partner without taking the time to see through the anger and focus on what I was responsible for. If the result was not what I was hoping for, performing an accountability autopsy helped determine why it didn't work out in the first place.

Final Revelations

XII

Forgiveness is a Funny Thing;
It Warms the Heart and Cools the Sting

I may not know you, but now you know me. My former career concealed what ate away at me inside and covered up the person I was destined to be. Externally, I shed my clothes, but internally, I covered everything up to protect myself. That was bullshit because it wasn't until I put on my clothes that I became the man I really am. I got out of my head and reconnected with my ex-wife, who I blamed for my biggest heartbreak. Writing this book clarified imperfections in me and others, and I was finally able to put skeletons to bed that had been rattling around in my closet for decades.

Over the course of a year, I put all distractions to the side to work on myself, detaching from relationships and, literally, quitting everything I was doing to finally invest into the most important work I have ever done—to improve my self-worth through a journey of not only addressing my faults but also exploring and understanding my family background to determine why I experienced an ongoing string of failures. I wanted to determine why I was never satisfied with the life I was given, even though it was filled with more abundance than many receive. To achieve this clarity, I had to ask myself and honestly answer: *Why?* But, more importantly, I knew that I needed to go beyond one level of why to eight:

Level 1: *Why was I obsessed with perfection and acceptance? Because I felt mediocre from an early age, unworthy of receiving recognition from those I looked up to.*

Level 2: *Why did I feel mediocre? Because from my perspective, I was never the popular kid in school but also never the loser—I was right in the middle.*

Level 3: *Why was that an issue? Because I desired more than mediocrity but didn't believe my authentic self was worthy of greatness.*

Level 4: *Why did I feel unworthy? Because I looked up to my father and rarely heard emotional expression from him.*

Level 5: *Why did I put my father on such a high pedestal? Because I viewed him as the perfect father I so very badly wanted to be proud of me.*

Level 6: *Why was his expression of pride so important to me? Because I understood he was my birth father until the age of 12 when my biological mother informed me that I was adopted and she was my real mother.*

Level 7: *Why was that such a pivotal moment? Because I was supposed to meet my biological father at that time in my life, but he never showed up.*

Level 8: Why was I obsessed with perfection and acceptance? Because my real father turned his back on me, which subconsciously created an overwhelming desire for acceptance from the only father I knew. Since I only saw him express his acceptance of me a few times, I looked for it through perfectionism and never addressed why I felt like this. For most of my life, this blocked me from true emotional expression when it counted. I found it on stage as my alter ego, and I became mentally addicted to ecstasy because it opened a door I was not willing to open on my own.

I never understood the power of forgiveness. In a strange way, my perception of forgiveness was accepting the wrongs that someone had done to me. This was conflicting for me because how could I forgive my biological father, a man I never met, for not showing up in my life? How could I forgive my ex-wife for cheating on me? How could I forgive myself for my irresponsibility? How could I forgive the father who raised me for not expressing how he felt?

I needed to understand that forgiveness was not for them; it was for me. Just because you forgive someone doesn't mean you have to associate with them or even like them. By forgiving myself and others, I was able to move on. I was able to open my mind to new possibilities without feeling like I had a ball and chain around my leg. I was able to forgive by simply voicing it. I told people in my life that I had forgiven Jenna for what happened. I also told people that I forgave myself for the bad decisions I made in the past. I also forgave the father who raised me for his lack of emotion, which affected me most of my life until I understood where the pain came from in the first place. I even forgave my biological father for not showing up. The more I voiced my forgiveness to others, the more it became real, warming my heart and cooling the sting.

That ripple effect was like an affirmation that improved my self-worth because it allowed me to cut that cord I had held onto for so long. Forgiveness allowed me to turn a negative into a positive. It didn't erase the past, but it improved the future. Being a dancer from the time I was 17 gave me the ability to do things that many never do, but it also hindered me. When I used to hear the word egotistical, I always pointed my finger at others instead of pointing at myself. Ego was part of the character I portrayed on stage, and I never wanted to be categorized as egotistical. I was too busy worrying about what others thought of me than addressing the fact that I was.

When I explain this to people from my past, they initially disagree because they don't see me as egotistical, but I was. It took many, many years to be man enough to open my eyes up to this fact. Admittedly, I have always been obsessed with self-image, but when I look in the mirror now, I see someone different; someone who has surrendered to his own misgivings and taken the time to understand why he constantly passed blame on others.

My perfectionist side brought me to the top of the world in my former industry but also made me critical of others with high expectations for them to be perfect in my mind. I have never been perfect, and I never will be. How could I possibly have expected anyone to live up to the standards I was expecting of them? The bar I set was extremely high for them, with my ego assuming I was so amazing that my partners would somehow be inspired to set a higher bar for themselves. I had high expectations without offering support for them to get to the next level. When I look back now, it's no surprise that things worked out the way they did.

I intend to build a bridge for you because I don't want anyone to fall into the same pits and valleys of life that I went through. Being fully transparent, you may not be ready to ask yourself all eight levels of *Why?* But maybe you can start with a few, or perhaps you can support someone else to begin asking themselves *Why?*

Have you ever sat back and considered that, even though your heart may have been broken, you may be partially responsible? Be honest and consider that we create our scenario in most cases, and it usually takes two to tango.

Are you finding yourself consistently in the same situations with failed relationships or turning your back on opportunities life puts in front of you?

I admit it completely. I screwed up, blaming my family background, my failed marriage, my lack of financial stability, and my emotional detachment on everyone else but myself... until now. I had to learn to fall in love with my imperfections and laugh at myself when I fucked things up because being kind to myself is part of my progression.

I didn't work with my ex-wife as a team player. I was going to be the man and take control of everything. I never took the time to understand that she was part of the team. Long after my dance career, I had other business opportunities that required working as a team, but I always heard my dad telling me that the only way to get the job done right was to do it myself. There was one major problem with that theory—when things got difficult, I gave up and blamed others for things going sideways. It was never me; it was always the other person who screwed up. I was perfect, right?

There came a time when I had to finally address that superego that I didn't think I had. My ex-wife adored me, but our connection wasn't strong enough. My employers thought I was the model employee until things got tough, and I started creating an exit strategy. I was always so worried about the clean image I sold to everyone while avoiding my truth.

My life changed when I started to own my shit by living authentically, understanding my core values and the emotional connection I had with each of them.

I had a desire for Jenna, which was indescribable. The sexual emotion we shared was so deeply tied that in many ways it ended up being too much of a basis for our relationship. We neglected the side of setting goals together and supporting one another, making our fair share of mistakes in the process. I was devastated by her cheating on me because it fractured the foundation of our emotional connection with one another. When that foundation broke, I would not take anything else into consideration. I wouldn't address why it happened—it was all her fault.

I can look back and wish that things would have worked out differently, but I am grateful for a learning experience that is sure to last a lifetime. My perspective changed on how to sustain balance within a relationship. I was living completely off-balance, suppressing my wife while trying to be a version of the man who raised me, simply continuing the cycle that was never addressed until now. I tried to live in an old-school reality that no longer exists in this generation, and I wouldn't want it to. Jenna needed to have her unique life and make decisions without being bound to me. Unfortunately, based on my own insecurities, I held those ties so tight in fear of losing her to the unknown. The hard truth is that I looked at our separation as a one-sided thing for many years. She may have been the one to make the first move in the sexual department, but I had already made a move long before that.

She did everything in her power to wake me up, but I refused. I assumed that I deserved to be in control of that situation based on the environment I brought her out of. I assumed that she would be forever grateful for the new life I gave her. But the truth is, I didn't deserve to have this person in my life anymore because I assisted in creating a toxic environment. I neglected someone who was neglected most of her life. She couldn't end it through words, so she used action to end it with no way of going back. I now know that the decision she made was just as hard as the heartbreak I felt when it was confirmed. By continuing to pass the blame, I continued the cycle. Again, I thought I was perfect and unforgiving.

By considering others as the unforgiven, I kept myself locked in a prison. I would NEVER be free. People have different definitions of freedom, and mine is based on the liberation of being accountable and standing firm on my authenticity. Regardless of how great the present moment was, I was in a state of constant stagnation long after my marriage ended. It didn't matter how much money I had in my bank account; I was still in prison. It didn't matter how many shiny objects I had; I was still in prison. It didn't matter if I flew halfway across the world for the vacation of a lifetime; I was still in prison.

The first step to growth was facing my fear of failure head-on, getting back up after I fell. After that, it didn't matter what anyone else thought; it only mattered what I did. I was sick and tired of my life being a constant rollercoaster of ups and downs without true fulfillment. It was time to steer my tractor in a different direction to provide fulfillment in my world.

I asked the people closest to me what my gifts were and wrote them down. I then asked those same people what I needed to work on, looking for consistencies in the answers I received. It provided a new perspective on my skills as well as my inadequacies. I am not saying that everyone's perception is correct, but if there is a common thread, you might want to dig deeper to understand why they have similar perceptions. Remember, you could be your own worst judge and enemy.

Consistency is the key, and if others are consistently giving you similar answers, there may be some truth to what they are telling you. Get addicted to your own growth by understanding what may be hindering you subconsciously. It may be your environment. Are you finding that you are the smartest person in the room most of the time? If so, you may be in the wrong room.

Is this easy? No. It's hard to admit to the things that are wrong in your life. Most of us don't take the time to face our truth, being distracted by trying to be the best husband, wife, partner, parent, or employee by selling our perfections without being vulnerable enough to address our imperfections. This, my friend, is a road to stagnation, pooling like water into the easiest, least resistant place for it to go.

My skin was so thin that I could never admit to what I did wrong, trying my best to be perfect in an imperfect world, and I felt weak.

It was time to stop blaming the world for my shit. I'm not here to say that I understand what you may be going through, but I played the blame game for far too long, both personally and professionally. Everyone gets dealt a different deck of cards in this life, but we all have the choice to address our truth, no matter how hard it may be to face. Maybe it's ego, trauma, or abuse that you had no control over. I can only provide my perspective, which may resonate with you or not. Either way, think about this...

Most people I've crossed paths with have their own perception of who they see standing before them. Many think

312

I lived a rock-star life, and in many ways, I did. They assume that being married to a male dancer was incredibly hard for my wife because of the lifestyle that went along with it. How could any man work in a career like that and still be faithful to his partner? I was blessed to have a partner who did her best to love me, but my ego got the best of me. As someone who entertained women for 25 years with more opportunities than most, I'm not sure that most would come out in the end with a different result. Not many people can sustain emotional detachment and neglect. Being married to a male dancer wasn't hard but being married to a partner who neglected her was.

I blew so many opportunities that I started to believe there may never be another one to come my way. You don't want to end up like I did, looking back asking yourself: *What if?* I look back on many of the relationships I have written about in this book with the realization that it was me; it wasn't them. I was trying to be the man, but I was not man enough to address my inconsistencies. Once again, I was perfect, right?

You can keep trying to manipulate reality in your favour to prove you are perfect, but eventually, you are going to run out of chances to accept your imperfections. Avoid being like me, whereby I couldn't fix my marriage because it became so broken. Instead of trying to be Mr. Fixit for everyone else, I became curious about working on myself because it is the most important work I can do. People in your life are relying on you, so lead by example because you may eventually run out of those opportunities.

I was sick and tired of self-sabotaging myself and showing up within mediocrity. I was done selling perfection because I was never perfect. That wasn't reality, but then again, I didn't live in reality for most of my adult life. I never faced my emotional blocks and chose to take a pill to make everything better. I searched for something that was always there in the first place—love and acceptance.

I was loved and accepted,
but I didn't love or accept myself for the person I always was.

Instead of selling myself as something I am not, I find it far more gratifying to serve others while living within my authenticity, enjoying the positive result it brings. Through this process, I lost people in my life, and gained others while appreciating the fact that I am still breathing. You may not think you have value or that you can make an impact, but that couldn't be further from the truth. It may be as simple as telling someone they are beautiful and seeing the look they give you when you say it.

I know I don't have all the answers. However, regardless of the perception others may have, what is important is the one you have of yourself. My life being an entertainer is long over, but my self-perception is better than ever because I took the time to detach and truly explore why I experienced so much love and loss. It doesn't matter how old you are because it is never too late to commit to your journey of self-discovery.

There was a time when I chose to continuously beat myself up over the past with little to no regard for my future potential. This is a rut that some of the most talented people in the world never get out of. Unfortunately, some of those people are no longer with us, but you are. I was stripped naked more than once, and I am not referring to my former career. It took losing everything I loved and cherished to finally figure it out, but you can choose _a far less detrimental path._

Lead by example because _faking it till you make it_ is bullshit and inauthentic. Instead of just talking about what you want out of this life, start taking the steps regardless of how big or small to get where you want to go. Human beings naturally like to complete a job from start to finish, and when they don't, their self-worth naturally depletes. Every time you settle, you take away a portion of your self-worth. How many times have you given up on something because you didn't think you were good enough?

The mind always plays tricks on you, being the defence mechanism that it is. It takes a strong-willed person to stay focused when your courage kicks in to protect you from the things in life that make you fearful. It may depend on how you were raised, but I can tell you that I feared success, which was all in my head, but not now. I stopped blaming the world for my lack of understanding and effort. Everything in life is temporary, no matter how good or bad things may seem at this moment. Once you take off the limiting layers of bullshit, the better life becomes.

We all come into this world naked, and we all leave naked. The question is, are you willing to expose yourself while you are still alive? Are you *man enough* to address what *man enough* means to you? Are you the type of person who refuses to cry because it is a sign of weakness? Do you need to be the hunter-gatherer to solidify your *man enough* status? Crying is not a sign of weakness but rather a sign of power. Bottling up your emotions never ends well but releasing them shows that you are human.

Let the dam break, before you damn break!

Being *man enough* is about understanding that your perspective may not be your truth. It's about accepting the person you see when you look in the mirror and being disciplined to make changes if necessary. It's about staying strong when being exposed to people or environments that may bend your morality, but not break it. It's about being clear about your intent without the perception of limiting beliefs altering your journey. It's about admitting your naivety of the past and being grateful that you made it through. It's about having true emotional connection in your relationships instead of settling for simple communication. It's about walking the unstable path of discomfort and failure to achieve personal growth. It's about understanding the addictions you may or may not have and controlling your own life instead of trying to control others. It's about empathy for the struggle others may be going through while keeping your integrity to protect your peace. It's about addressing a codependent relationship and allowing the humility that came with the territory to be a learning experience instead of a detriment. It also may be about dropping the ego and living guided by your authentic self. Lastly, it's about becoming the best version of yourself for you and others around you. You have people who depend on you. You are unique, you have value, and you are worthy.

The question I leave you with is...

Are you Man Enough to Take It Off?